MW00773691

CEREMONIES EXPLAINED FOR SERVERS

PETER J. ELLIOTT

Ceremonies Explained
for Servers

A Manual for Servers, Acolytes, Sacristans,
and Masters of Ceremonies

Illustrations by Clara Fisher

IGNATIUS PRESS   SAN FRANCISCO

Nihil Obstat: Rev. Gerard Diamond MA (Oxon), LSS, D. Theol
                 Diocesan Censor
                 Archdiocese of Melbourne

Imprimatur: Very Rev. Joseph Caddy, AM, Lic Soc, E.V., P.P.
                 Vicar General
                 Archdiocese of Melbourne

                 August 16, 2019

The Nihil Obstat and Imprimatur are official declarations that a book or pamphlet is free of doctrinal or moral error. No implication is contained therein that those who have granted the Nihil Obstat and Imprimatur agree with the contents, opinions or statements expressed. They do not necessarily signify that the work is approved as a basic text for catechetical instruction.

Cover design by Roxanne Mei Lum

ISBN 978-1-62164-299-2 (PB)
ISBN 978-1-64229-102-5 (eBook)
Library of Congress catalogue number 2019931423
Printed in the United States of America ∞

Mariae Matri Filii Sui Servorum

Contents

CONTENTS

CONTENTS

CONTENTS

Foreword

"Good serving is more than following rules or being correct or learning to adapt. It is a sacred duty."

With these words in the preface to his *Ceremonies Explained for Servers*, Bishop Peter Elliott succinctly states the great value and need of the book you are holding in your hand. As the West continues to drift farther away from a sensitivity to the divine, it is more urgent than ever that the Church do all in her power to recover a sense of the sacred. In this effort, the old adage is true: "Little things mean a lot."

In explaining ceremonies for servers, Bishop Elliott does, indeed, offer very clear and detailed explanations of all the varied actions servers perform in a way that is easy to understand and to follow. But this volume offers far more than instructions. His Excellency delves deeply into the theology of the Mass as well as such subjects as the meaning of liturgical symbols, from material objects to time. The practical advice he offers in what might seem mundane matters (such as cleanliness and good grooming) underscores the reality that in the worship of God—and all the more so for one who has a leadership role in it—no detail is unimportant, for we owe our best to God in everything. Recognizing that any role in liturgical leadership cannot achieve its goal of lifting the minds and hearts of God's people to an encounter with the divine without it flowing from a deep spirituality, he also weaves throughout his explanations of the rites of the Church exhortations to altar servers to develop the proper spiritual disposition toward the sacred liturgy, even including an appendix of recommended prayers specifically suited to servers.

We can say, then, that the approach Bishop Elliott takes in his explanation of serving at the liturgy is one of *formation*, not simply training. Indeed, his approach reflects the four dimensions of priestly formation: human formation in the practical advice that he gives in regard to more mundane, but nonetheless important, matters; intellectual formation through his teaching about the theology of the Mass and the meaning of liturgical symbols; spiritual formation through the prayers he suggests and by highlighting the spiritual disposition a server must have; and "pastoral" formation in the sense of the detailed instructions he gives for all of the actions a server must perform. Formation is, ultimately, exactly what is needed for the whole people of God to be renewed in a sensitivity to the sacred, and a sensitivity that must first and foremost be modeled by the ministers at the altar.

This latest work of the renowned Australian liturgist and prelate is timely, needed, and comprehensive, including explanations on serving all forms of liturgical services far beyond the Mass, such as weddings, funerals, and Exposition of the Blessed Sacrament. Bishop Peter Elliott has done a great service for the Church, and I pray that this book will be widely read and implemented in parishes all throughout the world so that it may become a catalyst for authentic liturgical renewal in the Church. Serving God well in the liturgy is, indeed, not simply a matter of following rules correctly but, above all, a sacred duty.

—Salvatore Cordileone
Archbishop of San Francisco

Preface

A large portion of this book first appeared as *Ministry at the Altar* (Sydney: E.J. Dwyer, 1980). In the intervening years, there have been many requests for a new edition and not a few developments in the liturgy. Therefore this new book, *Ceremonies Explained for Servers*, not only incorporates these changes but can be used in conjunction with my other works, *Ceremonies of the Modern Roman Rite* (San Francisco: Ignatius Press, 1995, 2005) and *Ceremonies of the Liturgical Year* (San Francisco: Ignatius Press, 2002). In the light of the provisions of Pope Benedict XVI in *Summorum Pontificum* (2007), directions are included for serving Mass according to the Extraordinary Form, described in this book as the "traditional Latin Mass".

In this detailed and comprehensive guide for servers, careful attention has been paid to the directives of the Church. These have been interpreted with a blend of practical common sense and pastoral reality. In light of the *continuity of our tradition*, sound customs have been maintained and high standards and ideals are promoted to enrich our worship. Good serving is more than following rules or being correct or learning to adapt. It is a sacred duty, the worship of God, acted out in the ways the Lord has inspired within his Church. It is a noble Christian art.

I hope that this book will encourage servers to value and enjoy serving. To make this possible, explanations of sacraments, ceremonies, and customs have been included. If we know what something *means* and *why* we do it, we assist with greater understanding and reverence and we can carry out our duties easily and well.

This book incorporates the work of a group of dedicated people who were inspired by the ideals of the Australian Guild of Saint Stephen. They proposed the details, points, and procedures included in *Ministry at the Altar*. In preparing this new book, *Ceremonies Explained for Servers*, I thank Thom Ryng, not only for his technical assistance but for sharing ideas from his own *Altar Servers Training Manual*. I also thank Rev. Msgr. Gerard Diamond for scholarly guidance on the role of the Levites.

In offering this guide to servers, acolytes, M.C.s, sacristans, and clergy, I would ask for a little patience! To describe a ceremony accurately may take ten times as long as actually carrying it out.

—Most Rev. Peter J. Elliott
Titular Bishop of Manaccenser
Auxiliary Bishop Emeritus, Melbourne

1.

The Server

1. You are a server. As you assist the priest, who leads the worship of the Church, so you make Catholic worship more reverent, efficient, and beautiful. Your work for God is very important, and this manual is designed to help you.

2. At the altar, your service is directed firstly to God, secondly as help to the clergy, and thirdly as assistance to the people who have been gathered by God for worship. Your actions are visible. You appear in public, but you are never a performer. By your faithful duty, you remain always a servant of Jesus Christ in the community of his Church.

3. A good server is not only skilled in a "craft" or duty at the altar but a humble and sincere person. The good server is a member of a team, working together in harmony with others, serving for the glory of God, learning that work at the altar is prayer in action. The good server is careful and reverent, even if there is only some small duty to perform.

The Tradition of Serving

4. Special assistants in public worship can be traced back to Israel, to God's Chosen People, because we find "servers" in the pages of the Old Testament. Before the great Temple of Jerusalem was built by King Solomon, boys were dedicated to the service of God in certain holy places. In

1 Samuel 2–3, we read of the boy Samuel, who served God in the sanctuary of Shiloh. God called this boy to be a great prophet.

5. The men of the tribe of Levi were chosen to serve in those holy places. Their sacred role developed when God's People wandered in the desert but took a more precise form in the permanent Temple. Within that tribe, the descendants of Aaron, the *cohens*, provided priests and a high priest, with specific duties of offering sacrifices and prayers of praise and blessing. Levites who were not priests acted like "servers" at the altars of sacrifice. They assisted in the complex ceremonial and music of the Temple "cult", the worship of God, and they provided a security service to protect worshippers in the holy place.

6. It is not surprising to find the early Church continuing this Jewish tradition of men and boys assisting in public worship. From the underground Church, persecuted in Rome, we have the story of Saint Tarcisius, a young Christian given the dangerous mission of secretly taking the Blessed Eucharist to those in prison. He was caught and martyred, but he did not reveal the sacred Gift he was carrying.

7. The Church gave official status to those assisting the bishops, priests, and deacons in worship. They were called "acolytes", from the Greek word for "followers" or "attendants". Acolytes were ordained to this office, a "minor order" as distinct from the major orders of bishop, priest, and deacon. Gradually the order of acolyte lost its distinct role and became only one of the steps toward the priesthood. In recent years, the ministry of acolyte has been restored. It is seen no longer as a step toward priestly ordination but as a lay service (ministry) within the Church community.

8. Servers developed from this order of acolyte. When there were not enough deacons to assist the bishop or priest in the ceremonies of the Mass, their role was largely deputed to acolytes. As the Church expanded, there were many places where the only ordained man was the local priest, so the assistant role of acolyte was deputed to men and boys. As the ceremonies of the Church developed, so various forms of ritual required many assistants, especially for the solemn celebrations in the distinct Rites: in Western Europe (Roman), in Eastern Europe (Byzantine), and in the Middle East (Eastern Churches).

9. However, in Western Europe, emphasis on daily Mass celebrated by each priest—for example, in monasteries—led to the simpler form of "Low Mass". One server assisted. Later, an unfortunate trend developed of using only small boys to serve in parishes, incorrectly but inevitably called "altar boys". In major centers of worship, cathedrals and basilicas, the original tradition continued and only men or youths served. In 1994, the ministry of serving was opened to permit the inclusion of women. This is another reason to use the inclusive term "servers" rather than trivial language, "altar boys" or "altar girls".

10. You can see that you are part of a noble tradition that has developed in the Church. You are to carry out sacred duties that once were entrusted only to ordained clergy. The Church is giving you a serious responsibility—to take on the sacred role of ones called and chosen to serve. This is an honor. In a real sense, you reflect the sacred role of one of the major orders of ministry, the deacon. That word "server" has the same meaning as "deacon", one who is ordained to serve God and his People.

Serving Today

11. The *Second Vatican Council* (1962–1965) authorized a great reform and renewal of the Sacred Liturgy, the public worship of the Catholic Church according to the Roman Rite that developed in Western Europe. As we are part of the Roman Rite, we have to work out the best ways we can all play the various roles given us by the Church in celebrating her liturgy, for example, those who sing in the choir. But servers in particular have an important place in the celebration of Mass and the sacraments. Their efficient and devout assistance is second only to the action of the priest and deacon in its power to enhance, enrich, and strengthen the liturgy in our churches.

12. What does the Church expect of you? Obviously the Church expects you to *know* what you are doing. Servers should not wander around the altar, uncertain, clumsy, and confused. This manual has been written to promote efficient serving, which can only occur when servers know what they are doing. Great care has been taken in this manual to bring together the official directions of the liturgy and the best practices of style and technique. Serving is a craft, which the Church expects us to carry out well.

13. The Church also expects something deeper than knowing how to serve. An altar server is a Christian lay person who plays a key role in the celebration of the liturgy by carrying out a true liturgical ministry. That word "ministry" means "service". By assisting the priest, the Church sees your service as a ministry to God, a ministry to God's People.

4

The Ideal

14. We all have ideals. Sometimes they become rather weak, and we may lose them. This is unfortunate. It means we are no longer striving toward some fine goal.

15. Servers have ideals. It should be harder for them to lose these ideals, because they can easily put them into practice within the beautiful structure of the liturgy. One of the simplest ideals would be to be as helpful to the clergy and sacristan as possible. In serving, there are higher ideals, because you are not only someone who has been called in to help the priest.

16. By Baptism and Confirmation, you are empowered to share in the priestly Sacrifice of Jesus Christ, the Eucharistic Sacrifice, summit and source of the life of God's People. By these sacraments of initiation, we are given access to God in the celebration of Christian worship. The third permanent way God raises some men into this great action of eternal worship is by Sacred Orders: bishops, priests, and deacons, who are empowered to preside over and direct the Church's worship.

17. You can see your place in this action of worship. Whenever you serve at Mass, you are using the priestly consecration of your Baptism and Confirmation. You are assisting those ordained by a further priestly consecration. You are carrying out your lay duty in a special way, part of the active participation of all the other lay people gathered by God at the altar. You are carrying out sacred duties, delegated to you by the ordained men. You are a special link in the combined action of adoration and praise that the whole Church celebrates every day in her liturgy.

18. You have been "consecrated" by Baptism and Confirmation. This word "consecrated" means to be set apart, made holy, given a special share in God's grace. But it also means that Christians are expected to be men and women of faith, sincere believers who really live out this gift of God. Other ideals come from our "consecrated" life.

Reverence

19. By consecration, you are holy, which does not mean you are a saint! But it does mean that you belong to God, soul and body. You should show this by the way you serve. Reverence for God and for sacred objects is most important when you serve. Reverent actions, peaceful and dignified behavior, should be seen by the people when you stand at the altar.

20. It is said that justice must not only be done, it must be *seen to be done*. It is the same with reverence. A server may feel reverent, feel prayerful, but this is of little use if accompanied by casual or careless behavior. By distracting and disturbing people, that server is not *seen to be reverent*.

21. One key to this ideal of reverence is the *memory*. Always remember who you are, what you are doing; then you will not become careless. Remember how close you are to the sacred mystery of the Eucharist. Remember that you are allowed to handle and use sacred objects. Remember that even holding a book or carrying a candle is a small part of the great and holy action of the liturgy. True reverence is helped by our understanding the liturgy. In the Constitution on the Sacred Liturgy, *Sacrosanctum Concilium* (*SC*), the Fathers of the Second Vatican Council taught:

> *Servers, lectors, commentators, and members of the choir also exercise a genuine liturgical function. They ought, therefore, to discharge their*

THE SERVER

office with the sincere piety and decorum demanded by so exalted a ministry and rightly expected of them by God's people.

Consequently they must all be deeply imbued with the spirit of the liturgy, each in his own measure, and they must be trained to perform their functions in a correct and orderly manner. (SC 29)

22. This servers' manual is written to help you become "imbued with *the spirit of the liturgy*". This spirit is most important because servers "must be trained to perform their functions in a *correct and orderly manner*". Moreover, from this important statement of the Second Vatican Council, we can take three ideals that make serving reverent and sincere. These ideals are *discipline*, *decorum*, and *piety*.

1. Discipline

23. You must be *trained* to serve. Imagine trying to serve a funeral without being trained! What chaos would take over during the final rite over the casket. How hurtful it would be to the people assisting at the funeral of someone they loved. But with training, this particular ceremony can be carried out in an orderly and smooth fashion; then the people are consoled and helped because reverent respect was given to someone they loved.

24. Training involves discipline. In each parish, some capable person should take charge of the training of servers and the planning of teams and rosters. People who serve well should be encouraged, and those who do not cooperate should be asked to leave the team. Part of the discipline of serving is teamwork. Even when you have to serve Mass on your own, you are part of a team, priest and people. It is more obvious in a Solemn Mass, when precise teamwork helps makes a great act of worship more beautiful, peaceful, and prayerful.

25. Discipline involves obedience. For the server, there are two kinds of obedience: (1) to the clergy, the master of ceremonies (M.C.), sacristan, and servers' team leader, that is, obedience to responsible people; (2) to the liturgical law of the Church, obedience to correct procedures. The server always behaves with sense and cooperation and quickly carries out practical duties, such as setting up the sanctuary before Mass, cleaning up the sacristy after Mass. Good servers always keep to the correct rules of liturgy. They never "do their own thing", because this disrupts good liturgy. Faith always involves obedience. A strong life of faith always involves self-discipline.

2. Decorum

26. Have you ever been to a church where the servers came out wearing robes that were too small for them? How silly it all looked. They lacked *decorum*, a word that means "what is proper". Their costumes may have been proper for a clown show but not for the Holy Sacrifice of the Mass.

27. Different forms of dress and behavior are fitting for different occasions. The Second Vatican Council requires not only training for servers, but that servers have a sense of this decorum. Fooling about in the sacristy, untidy or grubby appearance, talking during Mass: these are examples of a lack of decorum, a failure to see what is fitting for this occasion.

28. Decorum requires a sense of dignity. This does not mean looking pompous, marching around the sanctuary like a proud pigeon. It means behaving with a quiet reverence, not pushing yourself forward, but moving around confidently and carrying out each action without fuss or speed. It also includes having the sense to cover up any small mistake, remembering that most of the people at Mass may not

be aware that you have made a mistake. Decorum is the way we help reverence to be "seen to be done". It shows how you respect the presence of our Lord, in his sacrifice, in his sacraments, and in his People.

3. Piety

29. The Second Vatican Council also mentioned "piety"; a word that seems old-fashioned until we understand it correctly. It does not mean looking "pious", walking around with your eyes raised to heaven like a saint in an old holy picture. Someone can be sincerely pious without looking odd.

30. Piety is the soul or spirit of all our worship of God. It is an attitude. It is an attitude that directs your whole life toward God. In serving, piety helps us to say silently, "I'm doing this for you, my God."

31. Piety is not some kind of force we turn on and turn off, just to cover the time spent in the sanctuary. Piety runs right through life, which is why it is one of the gifts of the Holy Spirit in Confirmation. With sincere piety, I recognize the fact that God caused me, that I came from God, that I am going back to God. This keeps me humble before my Creator. In prayer, I can adore God, express sorrow for my sins, thanksgiving for the good life, petition for the needs of others and for myself.

32. This interior motive of piety is shown in visible acts. When I share in the liturgy, whether I am serving or not, I make an act of living worship that springs from a heart afire with the love of God. Altar servers who accept this ideal play their role in the liturgy worthily and well. They will set out to practice a regular personal spiritual life, including daily prayer, Bible reading, visits to the Blessed Sacrament,

frequent reception of the Sacrament of Penance and Reconciliation, and devotion to our Blessed Mother, Mary. These
practices nourish sound spirituality and help you to take
part in public worship "penetrated with *the spirit of the liturgy*", not allowing it to become merely an empty ritual or
routine.

Together at the Altar

33. Teamwork was mentioned as part of good serving. In understanding how the Church calls you to a special role in
worship, you also understand that you are part of a larger
group, a member of a worshipping community. You do not
serve on your own, as an individual. You must always be
aware of other people when you serve.

34. You will always be helpful when the priest requires some
small task of you. You will be considerate in such small matters as holding the book so that he can easily read from it
or not keeping him waiting when you are meant to hand
him the cruets. As you serve with various priests, you come
to know them as men of God. You will find that they are
your friends and that they are grateful for your work. Always, you will treat your priests with respect and cheerful
cooperation.

35. As you serve, you make many friends among others called
to this ministry. It is most important that servers help one
another, that they are friendly and kind to one another,
that there is never a spirit of competition or pride. If a new
server comes to your team, you will be helpful, explaining
procedures and making the newcomer welcome. A group
of servers who are friends can carry out their duties in the
sanctuary with a greater sense of unity, purpose, and effi-
ciency.

36. In his new commandment, our Lord told us to "love one another as I have loved you." We put this Christian love into practice by an ideal of true service and friendship. We are united in the service of God, a service of unity, which brings together one people at the altar, which makes us one through the eternal Sacrifice of Jesus Christ our Lord.

2.

The Liturgy

37. The word "liturgy" comes from *leitourgia*, a Greek word for a public duty, a service, a public obligation. Its original meaning was some public action performed by a leading citizen to benefit other citizens. When the word was adopted by the Church to describe her public "services" of worship, the meaning changed. In Christian liturgy, we are not talking only about what we do; rather, we are talking about what God does.

38. As the Second Vatican Council points out so clearly, the liturgy of the Church is the action of Jesus Christ, an action of eternal worship in which he involves us, the members of his Mystical Body, the living Church. In the *Constitution on the Sacred Liturgy*, the Second Vatican Council developed this teaching, emphasizing Christ's priestly work in and through his Church (*SC* 7), proclaiming the good news and carrying out Christ's work of salvation (*SC* 6), the earthly liturgy as a taste of the heavenly worship that is to come (*SC* 8), and the supreme activity of the Church and summit and source or font of her strength and holiness (*SC* 10).

39. The council teaching always places the first emphasis on Jesus Christ, the eternal High Priest. He is present and active in his people, for he is the risen Lord whose perfect sacrifice is accepted by the Father in the Holy Spirit. This is why the priest, offering the Body and Blood of the Lord, sings or says: *"Through him and with him and in him, O God almighty Father, in the unity of the Holy Spirit, all glory and* *honor is yours, for ever and ever . . .",* and the priestly people respond, *"Amen!"*

40. Christ died once and for all on the Cross, his one perfect sacrifice. The Mass is that same sacrifice but in a sacramental form, with a visible priest, an altar, and the basic matter of bread and wine to be changed into his offered Body and Blood. This Eucharistic Sacrifice is offered for four purposes: (1) to adore God (worship); (2) to offer God praise and thanksgiving (Eucharist); (3) to pray for the world and all people (intercession); and (4) to atone for the sins of the living and the dead (propitiation). This is exactly what Jesus Christ, the eternal High Priest, accomplished on the Cross. Now he is active for us and with us when his Cross and Resurrection are made present in the liturgy of the Mass.

Christ Is Really Present

41. The Second Vatican Council indicated the ways in which our Lord and Savior is present and active in our liturgy (*SC* 7).

42. *1. In the Assembly of the Faithful:* "He is present when the Church prays and sings, for He promised: 'Where two or three are gathered together in my name, there am I in the midst of them' (Mt 18:20)." Gathered by God to worship, we are Christ's Body, offering praise and thanksgiving to the Father.

43. *2. In the Sacred Minister:* "He is present in the sacrifice of the Mass . . . in the person of His minister, 'the same now offering, through the ministry of priests, who formerly offered himself on the cross'." The priests are the true representatives of Jesus Christ as he uses them to renew his Sacrifice for us.

44. *3. In the Word*: "He is present in His word since it is He Himself who speaks when the holy scriptures are read in the Church" further explained in no. 33, ". . . in the liturgy God speaks to His people and Christ is still proclaiming His gospel." At Mass we hear and receive this living Word.

45. *4. In the Sacraments*: "By his power He is present in the sacraments so that when a man baptizes it is really Christ Himself who baptizes." Saint Augustine set out this truth in his comments on the Gospel according to Saint John. Christ our Lord is present and at work for us in every sacrament.

46. *5. In the Sacrifice of the Mass*: "He is present in the sacrifice of the Mass . . . especially under the Eucharistic species." This is the supreme and unique Real Presence of Jesus Christ, under the appearances of bread and wine, once these have been changed by Consecration into his Body and Blood, offered up *for us*, given *to us* as our food.

47. The first four ways in which our Lord is present and active all lead to the fifth way: (1) The people are gathered together by God, (2) led by their priest, the personal representative of Christ the Priest, (3) and they hear and receive the Word of the Lord, which reminds them that, (4) by Baptism, Confirmation, and Orders, they are empowered to offer Christ's saving Sacrifice, (5) which happens when the Last Supper is reenacted in the Consecration and Communion of the Liturgy of the Eucharist.

48. In these moments of the liturgy on earth, Christ the Priest involves the whole Church with himself in glorifying his heavenly Father and making the members of his Body holy. His presence in our worship is dynamic, living, active. But he involves us in his great action of worship. He chooses us and gives us special roles in liturgy.

God's People in Worship

49. Catholic worship is "hierarchical", meaning it involves people on different levels with different powers, duties, and roles. By Baptism and Confirmation, you have the power and right to take part in public celebrations of worship. By Penance, you renew the grace of Baptism to share better in the Eucharist. But all these sacraments make us a priestly people, gathered to offer perfect worship, in Christ, for the whole human race.

50. We not only offer worship in the Lord's Sacrifice. We also celebrate the great events of Jesus Christ: his life, death, Resurrection, and his future coming. We celebrate all God has done for us in these events as a great Memorial. As we celebrate, the events become real and present again, so we are also celebrating the way God comes to us now. At the same time, we can look to the future, celebrating what God will do to us if we are faithful to him, the future glory of living in the light of heaven for ever.

51. God calls us to be his People. That is what "the Church" means, "the called and assembled people", *ecclesia*. Within our community, God calls men to special service, the sacred ministry. By the Sacrament of Orders, these men are permanently empowered by the Holy Spirit, consecrated to serve their brothers and sisters, already consecrated by Baptism and Confirmation.

52. In the liturgy, this sacramental ministry can be seen in the roles and duties of the ordained men.

53. *1. The bishop*, as successor to the apostles, always leads and directs worship. Early in the second century, Saint Ignatius

15

of Antioch wrote: "Let no one perform any church duties without the bishop. Let that be considered a valid Eucharist over which the bishop presides, or one to whom he commits it" (*Letter to the Smyrnaeans*, 8). To show the "shape" of the Church in her most typical and supreme action, the bishop often has priests concelebrating with him, his deacons assisting him. If he does not celebrate the Mass, delegating this to another, he may preside during the Liturgy of the Word and the Dismissal Rite.

54. Every bishop uses the rites and ceremonies authorized by the pope, the Roman Rite, or one of the Eastern Rites. Therefore he is in communion with the Bishop of Rome, Supreme Pastor of the Church, head of the college of all Catholic bishops.

55. 2. *The priest*, as "presbyter" or elder, shares in the Priesthood of Christ with his bishop. He is also a true representative of Christ the Priest, but delegated to celebrate public worship in a particular place or community, usually the parish. As celebrant, he presides over the assembly: acting in the person of Christ, leading his people in prayer, proclaiming the good news of salvation, and joining the people with himself in offering the Holy Sacrifice. From the altar of sacrifice, he gives his people the Bread of eternal life and the Chalice of everlasting salvation, sharing with them in the heavenly banquet.

56. Every priest uses the rites and ceremonies for Mass and the sacraments that are authorized by his bishop. By following these rites of the Church, he shows he is "in communion" with his bishop and, through him, with the pope. We can see how the worship of every parish is directly associated with the worship of the cathedral of the diocese, the center of the local Church. The worship of all Catholic dioceses

is regulated by Rome and thus expresses the visible unity of the whole Church on earth.

57. *3. The deacon* does not have the specific priestly powers, but he ranks first in ministry, the service of God and his People. His order was held in high honor in the early Church, and he is directly associated with the bishop in public worship. He proclaims the Gospel, preaches, reads the General Intercessions, assists the bishop or priest, gives Communion, in particular ministering the Chalice, and gives direction to the congregation.

58. The ordained ministers carry out the central roles in worship. But the Second Vatican Council restored a strong emphasis on the roles of service, ministries, among the people at Mass. The liturgical directives make it clear that everyone has a particular role at Mass and should not take over the role of another person. A priest or deacon should never take over the readings if there is a lector present. A priest should never read the Gospel if there is a deacon present. A lector should never read the responsorial psalm if there is a cantor present to sing it, the people responding. Servers should not read or take up the collection or act as cantor unless this is unavoidable.

59. We show how we depend on one another and serve members of the community by our distinctive roles. The *people* have the ministry of being the praying and praising Church, united in words and actions. The *choir* (schola) sings parts of the Mass with skill and beauty and leads the people, helping them to sing their parts better. The *choirmaster* leads the choir, and there should be a *cantor* to lead choir and people, but not from the ambo where the Word of God is proclaimed. The *lector* uses the ambo to proclaim this living Word and should be trained to read clearly.

Your Role in Liturgy

60. The *General Instruction of the Roman Missal* describes servers as "lay ministers" (*GIRM* 100). Paragraphs of the *Instruction* make it clear that there should be at least one server to assist the priest (*GIRM* 115). Mass is not to be celebrated without a server except for a just and reasonable cause (*GIRM* 254). One server may carry out all the various ministries required (*GIRM* 110), but the emphasis on roles makes it clear that this is not desirable. There should be several servers at least, performing such roles as carrying the missal, cross, bread, wine, water, and thurible (*GIRM* 100). To signify their role as ministers, servers are to wear robes, either the alb or other vesture approved by the Conference of Bishops (*GIRM* 339), such as the soutane and surplice.

61. The leading role of serving is the ministry of the *acolyte*, a layman instituted into this ministry by the bishop in some dioceses. As an assistant to the priest and deacon, his ministry destines him in a special way for the service of the altar, and he may act as an Extraordinary Minister of Holy Communion (*GIRM* 98, 191, 192). He could act as *master of ceremonies* at a more solemn Mass, directing the servers in their duties. As will be explained in chapter 4, a server takes over much of the work of the acolyte when he is not present or in dioceses where there are no acolytes—for example, spreading the corporal and bringing the vessels to the altar.

62. Servers and acolytes are a kind of direct link between the people and the priest. On behalf of the people, they assist the priest, representing the people in the sanctuary area. We see this clearly when the servers assist at the Procession of the Gifts.

63. In each parish, there should be an agreed plan and procedure. Servers should be organized along team lines, under the direction of a head server or a deacon or parish acolyte. This may also be the role of the *Master of Ceremonies* (M.C.) who must be skilled in liturgical matters, with access to the texts and directives and familiar with manuals such as *Ceremonies of the Modern Roman Rite* and *Ceremonies of the Liturgical Year*. The M.C. should work well with the clergy, servers, and sacristans in coordinating ritual and planning more complex celebrations of the liturgy.

64. Serving at Mass is not the work of little children. Adults should be encouraged to serve, and teenagers should realize that you do not drop out of serving because you start to grow up. The directives of the Church assume that adults or young people are carrying out the serious duties and responsibilities of this particular ministry.

The Server Is a Sign

65. Signs and symbols are very important in the liturgy. The server is a visible sign, an instrument through whom God acts. We may even say that the priest and server are God's "actors". Through words and actions (such as a procession), through the objects we use (incense, candles, etc.), through ritual actions (genuflecting, bowing, etc.), God gives the message of his love. He causes it to become real in the people present at Mass. A server may be part of a sacred sign —for example, when walking in a procession—or helping the people to see and understand other sacred signs, by assisting the priest at the altar.

66. If you understand what you are doing and do it well, the people are helped to understand what God is doing in the saving action of the liturgy. They find it easier to worship God. If you do not understand the meaning of a ceremony, or if you carry it out carelessly, you irritate and distract people. You hinder the message of Christ and make it harder for other people to worship God. As a server, you are part of the signs and symbols of the liturgy, able to help or hinder the meaning and power of worship.

Symbolism in Liturgy

67. We use visible symbols and signs in Catholic worship. The basic reason is that God became visible, in our flesh, in the Person of his Son, Jesus Christ. The *Incarnation*, coming-into-flesh, of the Son of God means that the religion of the Incarnation, Catholic Christianity, places much importance and value on what we can see, hear, and touch (1 Jn 1:1–4).

68. In the liturgy, Jesus Christ is really present and active. In the liturgy, many spiritual realities are happening: self-giving, love, sorrow, trust, forgiveness, new life, grace, faith, etc. These are *real*, but we cannot see them. Because we are only human, made up of body and soul, we want to see these realities. Just as the reality of our own person, the soul, is clothed with and made visible through our body, so in the liturgy we clothe the unseen realities with something we can see—the symbols and signs.

69. To express sorrow, we strike the breast. Incense is a sign of prayer and holiness. In the greeting of peace, we have a visible sign of love and unity. The supreme signs of the liturgy bring Jesus Christ to us, his Body and Blood, under the outward appearances of bread and wine. In the Sacrament of Baptism, the water is a sign of life and cleansing. As with the Body and Blood of the Lord, it is more than symbolic, for it really brings cleansing from sin, rebirth, grace, divine life, and membership in the Church.

70. Liturgical symbols, therefore, range from those we have invented or inherited, such as candles, incense, kneeling, etc., to those special signs given to us by Jesus Christ himself. We can guess the meaning of these signs, but for an accurate understanding, we need to learn what they really mean— for example, that smoke rising from a thurible is a symbol of prayer going up to heaven. We also need to distinguish between the signs of the liturgy. Some are merely symbolic. Others really cause a supernatural event to happen. Some help us to think of God. Other signs are the chosen instruments of God's work for us—the *sacraments*.

71. Some people see Catholic worship and ask, "Why all this fuss?" Unfortunately, they may have lost the ability to appreciate signs, symbols, ritual, and custom, a rich human heritage. Other people raise moral objections, claiming that we waste money on liturgy that could be spent on the poor. This may be compared to Judas complaining because a repentant sinner poured out her best perfume on our Lord (Jn 12:1–8). The liturgical Church always goes from the altar to serve Christ in his poor and returns to the altar to be strengthened for practical charity. This Eucharistic service of the poor marked the life of Saint Teresa of Kolkata. So we come to learn that the liturgy forms the character and mentality of Christians who have to face and meet the problems of living in our changing world.

Authority for Liturgy

72. As we have noted already, the way in which signs and symbols are used is directed by the supreme authority of

the Church. The pope himself authorizes official liturgical books, and he has entrusted the great task of guiding Catholic worship to the Congregation for Divine Worship and the Discipline of the Sacraments. From Rome comes our authority for public worship, the directives, texts, and guidelines.

73. The server should know that the official books of the Roman Rite lay down the principles for ceremonial and provide the texts for public prayer.

74. *1. The Roman Missal*, translated from the standard Latin *Missale Romanum*, contains all the texts used by the celebrant at Mass. It contains the *General Instruction of the Roman Missal*, describing the ceremonies of the Mass. Part of the missal is published separately as the *Book of the Chair* (or *Excerpts from the Roman Missal*) held before the priest by a server for those parts of Mass that are celebrated at the chair. Part of the missal with texts for Holy Week ceremonies is published separately in a *Holy Week Book*. The *Missale Romanum*, 1962 edition, contains the texts of the traditional Latin Mass.

75. *2. The Book of the Gospels*, used in the ceremonies of the Liturgy of the Word, is the most sacred liturgical book and may be richly decorated with fine metalwork, jewels, and enamels. The Gospels are taken from the *Lectionary*, which contains all the readings from Scripture and intervening chants for Masses throughout the year. The lectionary is the companion volume that accompanies the missal. The *Missale Romanum*, 1962 edition, includes all the readings for the traditional Latin Mass, but a Book of the Gospels is used at Solemn High Mass.

76. *3. The Roman Ritual* provides the texts used in the celebration of the sacraments. It includes texts for Communion

outside the time of Mass, public adoration of the Eucharist, blessings, and processions. The ritual may be published as a collection of rites or in separate books for marriage, funerals, baptism, etc. Blessing rites are set out in the *Book of Blessings*.

77. *4. The Roman Pontifical* contains the sacraments and other sacred functions performed only by bishops—for example, Confirmation, ordination, the dedication of a church.

78. *5. The Ceremonial of Bishops* describes in detail the rules for the regalia and ceremonial of bishops, with clarifications for the clergy and servers.

79. *6. The Roman Calendar* gives details of the arrangement of feasts and celebrations during the year. It is published with the missal and books used for the Divine Office. It forms the basis for the *Ordo*, a booklet that is kept in the sacristy, published every year by the bishops' conference of a particular country or by the superiors of a religious order. It adapts the calendar to local needs and moveable feasts.

80. *7. The Liturgy of the Hours* or *Divine Office* is the official "Prayer of the Church" published in a book commonly known as the *breviary*, which provides the texts for the various "hours" of the day, centered around Morning Prayer (Lauds) and Evening Prayer (Vespers). The Breviary is published in various editions for public or private use by clergy and laity or by certain religious orders and congregations.

81. These major books of the Roman Rite have all been translated from original Latin editions. The Church also provides other books such as the *Graduale* for musical chants, the *Martyrology*, providing biographies for the martyrs and other saints, the *Handbook of Indulgences*, official teaching on indulgences and prayers and devotions to which they are attached.

82. The Second Vatican Council taught that the liturgy can be adapted to meet local culture and local needs. A bishops' conference may seek adaptations of official texts to enrich the worship of the people of their nation or region. Religious orders also obtain approval for customs in their own parishes and religious houses. But the authority of the Holy See is required for these adaptations. This is laid down clearly by the Second Vatican Council, in no. 22 of the *Constitution on the Sacred Liturgy*, which includes the directive, *"Therefore no other person, even if he be a priest, may add, remove, or change anything in the liturgy on his own authority."*

Liturgical Time

83. In the *Roman Calendar* we have the great plan of the Christian year. The Church recalls and celebrates the whole Mystery of Christ, his coming and birth, his ministry, his saving death and Resurrection, his Ascension, and the sending of the Holy Spirit and our lives in him, as we await the Second Coming.

84. Each day of the year is made holy by the celebration of Mass and the Liturgy of the Hours. *A liturgical day* runs from midnight to midnight, but *Sundays and solemnities* begin with the evening of the preceding day, with First Vespers. Easter is the greatest Solemnity, the climax and the original feast of the liturgical year. Every Sunday is a "little Easter", when the Church celebrates the day of Resurrection, the "Lord's Day". Also, in the course of the year, days are set aside to honor Mary, the Mother of God, and the martyrs and other saints.

85. There are four kinds of liturgical observance: (1) *Solemnities*, including all Sundays, the days of greatest importance, which begin with Evening Prayer I (First Vespers), with a

special vigil Mass for some solemnities; (2) *Feasts*, which are celebrated within the limits of a calendar day; (3) *Memorials*, which are either obligatory or optional, with only one memorial celebrated when more than one optional memorial falls on the same day; (4) *Ferias*, on which there may be an optional memorial and when the priest may select a Mass of his own choice, unless otherwise directed by the calendar.

86. The server should be aware of the seasons of the year, the ceremonies and customs to be observed, and the liturgical colors.

87. *Advent* celebrates the twofold coming of Christ—as Man, born at Bethlehem, and in judgment at the end of this world. In Christian hope we await his coming. The color is violet. Advent begins with Evening Prayer I of the Sunday that falls on or closest to November 30th. It ends before Evening Prayer I (First Vespers) of Christmas. The Sundays of Advent take precedence over all solemnities and feasts of the Lord. The weekdays between December 17th and 24th take precedence over obligatory memorials. During Advent, on December 8th, we celebrate the Solemnity of the Immaculate Conception of the Blessed Virgin Mary.

88. *The Christmas season* celebrates the Son of God becoming Man, the Incarnation. The Church regards the Christmas season as second only to the annual celebration of the Paschal Mystery, Easter. There are two focal points: (1) Christmas Day with its octave (eight days), including several feasts and concluding with January 1st, the Solemnity of Mary, the Mother of God. (2) Solemnity of the Epiphany, celebrated on January 6th, where it is a holy day of obligation, or on the Sunday between January 2nd and January 8th. The color is white.

89. *Lent* is the season when we give ourselves to prayer and penance, to hearing the Word of God, and to acts of charity. We prepare for Easter, and we recall the grace of our Baptism. The color is violet. Lent lasts from Ash Wednesday to the Mass of the Lord's Supper on Holy Thursday. The Sundays of Lent take precedence over all solemnities and feasts of the Lord. All weekdays of Lent take precedence over obligatory memorials. The Sixth Sunday of Lent, marking the beginning of Holy Week, is known as Passion Sunday, or, in popular language, Palm Sunday. Holy Week recalls the sufferings of our Lord.

90. *The Easter Triduum*, the *three days* of the Passion and Resurrection of Jesus Christ, is the culmination of the whole year. What Sunday is to each week, the Solemnity of Easter is to the whole liturgical year. The Triduum begins on Holy Thursday (Maundy Thursday) with the evening Mass of the Lord's Supper, continues through Good Friday with the solemn commemoration of the Lord's Passion and death, and reaches its high point in the Easter Vigil in the Holy Night. The Triduum closes with Evening Prayer II on Easter Sunday. The color is white, but red for Good Friday.

91. *The Easter season* covers the fifty days between Easter Sunday and Pentecost. These days are celebrated as feast days, but the first eight days of the season make up the Easter Octave and are Solemnities of the Lord. The color is white. The Sunday after Easter is also Divine Mercy Sunday. On the fortieth day after Easter on a Thursday or the following Sunday, the Church celebrates the Ascension of our Lord to heaven, his glory, and the beginning of our glory. In the days after the Ascension to the Saturday before Pentecost, we prepare for the coming of the Holy Spirit. The color is white. On Pentecost Sunday we celebrate the fulfillment of Christ's work in sending the Holy Spirit to form and energize the Church. The color is red.

92. *Sundays throughout the year* fall into two groups (1) Sundays between the Epiphany and Ash Wednesday, (2) Sundays between Pentecost and Advent. The color is green. Major solemnities are: the Holy Trinity, the Sacred Heart, Corpus Christi, and Saints Peter and Paul (June 29th). On August 15th, we celebrate the Assumption of the Blessed Virgin Mary. We honor the saints in the Solemnity of All Saints (November 1st), and we pray for the dead on All Souls Day (November 2nd). The last Sunday of the liturgical year is the Solemnity of Christ the King.

The Liturgical Setting

93. Liturgy is normally celebrated in a dedicated church. The *General Instruction of the Roman Missal* emphasizes that our churches should be beautiful and artistic (*GIRM* 288, 289), that they should be dedicated buildings so that we may hold them in high esteem as symbols of that spiritual Church which we are committed to build up and extend by our own vocation as Christians. The planning of a church reflects the hierarchical form of our worship, that is, different people playing different roles in the life and worship of the Church (*GIRM* 294). The shape of the building shows that we are all one, but a separate area, *the sanctuary*, is marked out by steps or some other distinction (*GIRM* 295). The people, the choir, servers, and clergy each have their convenient place. Servers are meant to have places *in the sanctuary* with the clergy (*GIRM* 295).

94. *The altar* is the most important object in the church. It is the great sign of Jesus Christ among us because he is the true altar, temple, priest, and victim. As a server, it is your

privilege to assist in the "holy place", the *sanctuary*, and to serve at the place of sacrifice, which is what "altar" means. At the same time, the altar is the table of the Eucharistic Lord, where he nourishes us with his Body and Blood. This center of our celebration, thanksgiving, intercession, and offering is made of stone, marble, or wood or some other durable material. It is arranged so that the priest may celebrate Mass facing the people and to be the focus of attention in the church. If it is a permanent fixed altar, it is dedicated and anointed by a bishop and holy relics of martyrs or other saints are set beneath it or sealed within it (*GIRM* 296–308). The step around or in front of an altar, where the celebrant stands, is called the *footpace* or *predella*.

95. The altar is covered with at least one *white cloth*. It may also be adorned with an antependium or frontal, which changes color according to the feast or season. Representing the light of Christ and the presence of angels, *candles* are lit for liturgical celebrations, two, four, or six, on or near the altar. *A cross* with the figure of Christ crucified on it is placed on or near the altar, or above or behind it. This may be the processional cross. The altar and sanctuary may be adorned with extra candles, flowers, banners, etc., to mark special days or seasons or for a more "solemn" (i.e., important) occasion.

96. *The ambo* is the place reserved for the readings of the Word of God in Scripture and usually for the homily (*GIRM* 309). Like the altar, it may be adorned with an antependium appropriate to the occasion, known as the "fall". There should be only one ambo in the sanctuary, and, like the altar, it should be fixed and prominent. The ambo should not be used by a commentator or choirmaster. They should use a portable reading stand in some other place. In some churches, the lectionary is set up in front of the ambo to remind us that this is the focus for the Liturgy of the Word.

97. *The chair* is a sign of the celebrant's role as presider over the assembly during the Liturgy of the Word and in the concluding rite of the Mass (*GIRM* 310). Because a server holds the book at the chair, it is not correct to use a small lectern in front of the chair unless no server is available. The chair should not look like a throne, because that form of chair is reserved for the bishop in his cathedral. The word "cathedral" comes from the name of the bishop's throne, "cathedra". Servers sit in convenient places in the sanctuary. But it is not correct for them to sit facing the people, because this is a position of presiding. In the solemn form of the traditional Latin Mass, the priest, deacon, and subdeacon sit to the right of the altar on three seats or a bench known as the sedilia.

98. *The credence table* is usually placed to the left of the altar viewed from the congregation. This should be a convenient table of reasonable size and normal height, not a small stand or wall bracket. In the liturgy, the credence table plays an important role. It should be covered with a cloth during Mass. A second credence table is useful for certain occasions, placed to the right of the altar, viewed from the congregation. This is a good location for books used at the chair and ambo. In the traditional Latin Mass, the credence table is to the right of the altar.

99. *The tabernacle* is used for reservation of the Blessed Sacrament. It is to be firmly attached to an altar, niche, or stand and securely locked. It may be located in the sanctuary of the church, normally at the center, or it may be in a Blessed Sacrament chapel or some similar sacred place (*GIRM* 314–17). The sign that the Blessed Sacrament is reserved in the tabernacle is the *lamp*, which burns day and night near the tabernacle. A *veil* over the tabernacle reminds us that "tabernacle" means the tent of the Lord, his dwelling place among us on earth.

100. *The baptistery* is the sacred place where Christian Initiation is celebrated in the Baptism of adults and children. It may be a kind of chapel or a separate area or, less preferably, a designated part of the sanctuary. The *font* where Baptism is administrated is the focus of the baptistery. It may be designed so that candidates can be immersed in the water of new birth. During the year, the Paschal candle is kept near the font to be used during initiation rites and to remind us that we have been baptized into the death and Resurrection of the Lord Jesus.

Liturgical Colors

101. One of the main signs in the liturgical setting is color. The Roman Rite follows a "color code" that gradually became standardized. We can recognize a season or the mood of an occasion from the liturgical color used for the vestments as well as for the frontals on the altar and ambo, the tabernacle veil, and seasonal banners.

102. *White* is used for Masses of Christmastide and Eastertide, for the feasts and memorials of our Lord, other than those that concern his Passion, for feasts and memorials of the Blessed Virgin Mary, the angels, and saints who were not martyrs, and on certain solemn days, as well as for festive occasions such as marriages and Baptisms, times of joy and glory. Cloth of gold or silver may replace white.

103. *Red* is used for Passion Sunday (Palm Sunday), Good Friday, Pentecost, and commemorations of our Lord's Passion and on days celebrating martyrs. Red stands for blood or for the fire of the Holy Spirit.

104. *Green* is used during the Ordinary Time of the year because it is the color of growth.

105. *Violet* is used during Advent and Lent, a sign of sorrow for sin and waiting for the Lord. It may also be used for Masses for the dead and funerals.

106. *Black* may be used for Masses for the dead and funerals, as a sign of mourning. As noted, violet may also be chosen for such occasions, or white when appropriate.

107. *Rose*, a soft pink, may be used for the Third Sunday in Advent and the Fourth Sunday in Lent, as a sign of rejoicing as the great feasts of Christmas and Easter draw near.

The House of God

108. The server treats the church with respect. This begins in *the sacristy*, which is part of the church, a place for the preparation for worship. It may even be a chapel with its own altar. The *sacristan* is in charge here, and he or she should be treated with respect. Servers should be ready to assist whenever the sacristan asks for something or needs help, particularly in putting things away after Mass. In the sacristy, the *sacrarium* or *piscina* is a sink where old holy water, blessed ashes, etc., can be poured because this sink goes directly into the natural earth and not into the drains. However, servers should have their own separate *vesting room*. Only servers and those authorized to supervise them should have access to the vesting room.

109. The Church is the house of God, the house of God's People, the center for prayer and worship. Our churches are not only used during the time of Mass or the sacraments. They usually remain open during the day so that people may make a visit to our Lord in the Blessed Sacrament or spend time in prayer or meditation or in particular

devotions—for example, the Stations of the Cross or prayer to our Lady.

110. The server should be careful not to become casual about behavior in church. It is said that "familiarity breeds contempt." As we become familiar with sacred places and sacred objects, so we may become careless or even irreverent. We may even imagine that we only need to come to the church when serving duties require our presence there. But the good server "drops in" to the church for a quiet prayer when passing by, especially to visit Jesus Christ really present in the Blessed Sacrament. Other signs and symbols in the church are helpful—for example, the sacred images, statues, icons, and pictures of our Lord and the saints— because shrines and side altars are part of our liturgical heritage (*GIRM* 318). In particular, a server ought to visit that special place in every church, the shrine of our Lady. She is the Mother of the Church, our Mother, and she has a special care for those who assist in the liturgy of her divine Son.

3.

Ceremonial Actions

111. The practical server must know the customary ceremonial actions of the liturgy. If these actions are carried out efficiently and well, the server is giving the best in the service of God. Before the actions are described and explained, it is also necessary to know and understand the various objects used in the liturgy.

Sacred Objects

112. Because you may handle the sacred vessels, you must know their names and their purposes.

113. *The chalice* is a cup supported by a "node" (the central part of the vessel, usually including a knob) and set firmly on a base. This vessel holds the Precious Blood of our Lord at Mass. It is usually made of gold or silver or some other nonabsorbent metal that does not break easily. The bishops of a local region interpret what may or may not be used to make a worthy chalice. The chalice is blessed by a bishop or a priest before it is used at Mass.

114. *The paten* is the plate on which the bread is consecrated and from which the Hosts are distributed in Holy Communion. As with the chalice, it is usually made of a precious metal or some other valuable material. A large paten may be used at Mass when appropriate. It is also blessed before use.

115. *The ciborium* is really a paten in the form of a chalice with a lid. It is used in addition to the paten when many people receive the Eucharist. It is also used to contain the Hosts reserved in the tabernacle. It is blessed before use.

116. *The monstrance* is a noble vessel designed to display the Sacred Host at exposition of the Blessed Sacrament, so that we can see the Host and adore our Lord. The priest uses the monstrance to give the Eucharistic blessing at Benediction and to carry the Host in a Eucharistic procession. There are many imaginative designs for the monstrance, but a typical design is circular, with rays coming from the center point. The *lunette* is the gilt clip that holds the Host in the monstrance.

117. *The pyx* is the round container that holds the Host and lunette in the tabernacle. A smaller pyx, like an old-fashioned watch case, is used to take the Eucharist to the sick.

118. *The chrismatory* contains the Sacred Chrism used by the bishop for Confirmation and ordinations. The *oil stocks* usually take the form of a metal cylinder, with three compartments for the sacramental oils, marked with a sign to indicate which oil is contained therein. (1) I = "oleum infirmorum", the Oil of the Sick; (2) B or Ca = "oleum catechumenorum", Oil of Catechumens or Oil of Baptism; (3) C or Ch = the Sacred Chrism for Baptism, Confirmation, ordination of priests and bishops.

119. The vessels listed above are the most important objects used in the liturgy. If you handle any of them, treat them with care and reverence. Other objects are used mainly by servers.

120. *The cruets* are small pitchers or jugs that hold the wine and water. They should be of clear glass, so that the wine can be recognized at a glance and so that the cruets may be cleaned easily. Other material, such as metal or pottery, may be used for cruets, but there must be clear indication of which cruet contains the wine. For concelebrated Masses, and especially when Communion is given in "both kinds", a larger cruet is needed for the wine and for the water for cleansing the chalices. The cruets usually stand on a dish or tray.

121. *Ewer and basin* means a pitcher to hold the water for the washing of hands (*Lavabo*) and a dish to catch water as it flows over the celebrant's hands. The bishop uses a ewer and basin of precious metal. The priest uses a simpler ewer and basin. Small pitchers and bowls should not be used because the priest or bishop washes his hands, not merely the tips of his fingers.

122. *The holy water vessel* is also known as the "bucket" and the sprinkler as an "aspergil". The sprinkler may take the form of a brush or of a hollow bulb, perhaps containing a sponge, with openings so that drops of water may be sprinkled on people or objects. Holy water is kept in *stoups* near the doors of the church and sacristy so that we can make the sign of the cross with it to remind us that we enter the living Church through Baptism.

123. *The thurible* or *censer* is a metal bowl hanging by three chains from a disk. The cover, pierced to allow the smoke to rise, is usually held by a fourth chain, which passes through a hole in the disk, so that the server can raise it. A metal ring is often used to hold these chains together above the bowl. The thurible with a single chain is easy to use although liable to overheat and burn the server's hands!

124. *The incense boat* is shaped like a boat, with a hinged lid and a matching spoon. From the boat, the grains of incense are spooned onto the burning coals in the thurible.

125. *Processional candles* are held in tall candlesticks carried in procession by two servers. These are usually kept on the credence table during Mass. In some places, the altar candles are used for processions.

126. *Torches* may be used at a Solemn Mass or Benediction. They are tall candlesticks without a base, carried by torch bearers, who bring them before the altar during the Eucharistic Prayer to honor the Lord at the Consecration and elevations. In medieval times, they were simply very tall candles or even three candles fused together.

127. *The processional cross* is a large crucifix, set on a long staff, to be carried in processions and, in some churches, used as the altar cross at Mass.

128. *The bell*, known as the "sanctus bell" or "sacring bell", is rung by a server at Mass, at the two elevations and as a warning before the Consecration. It has a practical use, to draw attention to the most sacred moments of the liturgy. In some places, it takes the form of a set of bells. It is used during the Eucharistic blessing at Benediction.

129. *The missal stand* is placed on the altar at the Preparation of the Gifts. It takes various forms, a metal or wooden bookrest or a cushion.

130. *The communion plate* or *communion paten* is used in some churches, held by a server under the chin of those who receive Communion directly into the mouth. It must be used when Holy Communion is given by "intinction", that is, by dipping the Host in the Blood of the Lord. It is always used at the traditional Latin Mass.

The Vestments

131. In the sacristy, the priest may ask a server to get him a chasuble from the vestment cupboard. The server should know exactly what he means, so that there can be no embarrassing mistake.

132. *The amice* is a piece of white linen or similar fabric, with tapes or narrow ribbons attached to secure or tie it. It is the first vestment which the priest puts on before Mass.

133. *The alb* is a white garment reaching to the ankles. It derives from the ancient Roman tunic and is a sign of purity. The word "alb" comes from the Latin word for "white".

134. *The cincture* is a cord used to tie around the waist and gather in the alb. It may be white or the color of the main vestments.

135. *The maniple* is worn on the left arm by the celebrant, deacon, and subdeacon during the traditional Latin Mass. Originally it was a handkerchief or towel and may be seen as a symbol of service.

136. *The stole* is a distinctive sign of those who have received Holy Orders, worn when they carry out the ministry in sacrament and worship. It is of the color of the season or day. It symbolizes pastoral authority in the community. The priest wears the stole around the neck and hanging down in front. The deacon wears his stole on his left shoulder, crossing it like a sash under his right arm. The priest wears the stole crossed over his breast during the traditional Latin Mass.

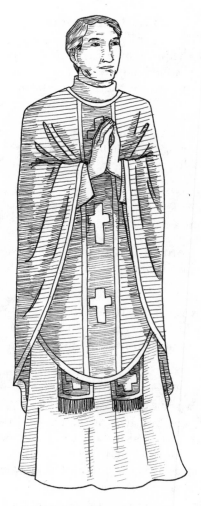

Celebrant Vested for Mass

Deacon Vested for Mass

Priest in Cope and Humeral Veil

A Bishop Vested for Solemn Pontifical Mass

137. *The chasuble* is the major Eucharistic vestment, worn over the stole and the alb. It is of the color of the season or day. There are various styles of chasuble: "ample", "gothic", "Roman", "conical". These styles developed over the years from the original form of outdoor cloak worn in the later Greek and Roman period. It stands for charity, the love of God, which covers all things, see Colossians 3:14.

138. *The dalmatic* is worn by the deacon. It resembles a square-cut coat, of the color of the season or day. It is worn over the stole and alb. The *tunicle* is a simpler form of dalmatic worn by the subdeacon in the solemn celebration of the traditional Latin Mass.

139. *The cope* is a large semicircular cloak, held at the front by a clasp or band of fabric. It is used for solemn celebrations of the sacraments and the Liturgy of the Hours and for Benediction of the Blessed Sacrament.

140. *The humeral veil* is a large white shawl, worn around the shoulders while carrying the Blessed Sacrament in procession and while giving the Eucharistic blessing at Benediction. It is worn by the subdeacon during the central moments of a traditional Latin Solemn Mass, and it matches the color of the vestments.

141. In addition to the basic vestments, the servers should know the vestments and regalia used by a bishop in our Roman Rite.

142. *The miter* is a double-pointed headdress, with two lappets hanging at the back. It has been used by bishops since the twelfth century and may also be worn by an abbot in his own monastic family. The ornate miter may be adorned with embroidery or gems and made of cloth of gold or silver. The simple miter is of plain white fabric. Servers who carry the miter cover their hands with a shawl, the *vimpa*, which functions like gloves.

143. *The crozier* or *pastoral staff* is usually curved at the top like a shepherd's crook. The bishop carries it to remind us that, like the Good Shepherd, he is the pastor and guardian of God's People. The hands of the server who carries it for him are covered with the *vimpa*.

144. *The ring* is worn at all times as a sign that, like Christ, the bishop is wedded to his Church as the faithful shepherd of the flock. In the solemn celebration of the traditional Latin Mass, the bishop wears a ring over his *gloves* during the Liturgy of the Word.

145. *The pectoral cross* is worn over the breast. When the bishop is vested or wearing choir dress, it hangs from a gold and green cord. When he wears his house soutane or a suit, it hangs from a chain.

146. *The episcopal dalmatic* is a lighter form of the deacon's vestment. It is worn under the chasuble on solemn occasions to remind us that the bishop possesses the fullness of the priesthood. In the solemn celebration of the traditional Latin Mass, the bishop also wears a subdeacon's *tunicle* under the dalmatic.

147. *The pallium* is presented to metropolitan archbishops as a sign of their unity with the pope. It is a narrow band of wool embroidered with small black crosses. It is pinned onto the chasuble for major occasions. Each pallium is made in Rome and blessed at Saint Peter's tomb by the Holy Father himself.

148. *The zucchetto* is the small violet skullcap. It is scarlet for cardinals, white for the pope. It is not worn during the Preface, Eucharistic Prayer, or Communion Rite.

149. *The cappa magna* is a large cloak with a train, which a bishop may wear in his own diocese on major occasions.

150. *The choir dress* of a bishop is: a purple soutane with a fringed purple cincture, a rochet (like a short alb), a purple mozetta (a short cape), a pectoral cross on a cord, a zucchetto, and a biretta (a square cap). Cardinals wear scarlet in place of purple. The pope wears white.

151. *The choir dress* of a priest consists of a surplice worn over soutane and collar or the religious habit of an Order or Congregation. A monsignor wears a rochet over a purple soutane. A canon wears a mozetta over his rochet, particularly when assisting in the cathedral.

The Server's Robes

152. As noted, the *General Instruction of the Roman Missal* expects servers to vest correctly when serving at the altar. The first form of dress suggested is the alb (*GIRM* 339). If the alb does not cover ordinary neckwear, an amice is used with it. It will need a cincture if it is not tailored. A surplice and soutane or cassock is the alternative form of dress. The color of the soutane varies from church to church.

153. Servers should take care of their robes, kept in their own vesting room. They should ensure that albs and surplices are always clean and neat. It is ridiculous to appear in the sanctuary in a short soutane or an alb that does not come to the ankles. The surplice should also be a sensible garment that fits the wearer properly. Standard footwear or at least dark shoes should be worn by servers as a team. Casual footwear—for example, sneakers or beach sandals—is not suitable.

A Bishop in Choir Dress

The Basic Actions

154. By "basic actions" we mean "how" we carry out our duties. But good techniques of serving also depend on knowing "why", the reasons for the actions we perform.

155. In going back to basics, older servers can take a refresher course. New servers will need to be taken through the basics before they can be allowed "on the altar".

156. New servers also learn by the example of older servers. The new server will pick up "customs" from the old hands on the job. If the older servers are slovenly in their way of serving, a bad tradition of thoughtless and even irreverent serving can be set up in a parish.

157. Older servers should ask themselves, "What sort of example do I set for the new servers? Will it be only a matter of months before these servers disregard the little things that are so important at the altar—because of my poor example?"

158. The great sculptor Michelangelo spent months making minor alterations to his statue of Moses. When someone asked why he spent so much time on these fine details, he replied, "Trifles make perfection, and perfection is no trifle."

159. What is described below may seem to be little things, or trifles, but when all these details are put together, we have good serving, efficient, reverent, and intelligent.

1. The Hands

160. Your hands must always be clean, with clean fingernails. Wash them before you serve because you will be handling things that are holy.

Hands Joined

161. *Joined hands* are held before the breast at 45°, palms together, fingers extended, thumbs crossed, right over left. This is the right way of holding your hands together, described in the *Ceremonial of Bishops*, art. 107, footnote 80.

162. The reason for joining hands in this way when you are walking, standing, or kneeling is quite simple. The joined hands are an expression of prayerful reverence and self-discipline. When all servers learn to hold their hands in the same way, a sense of harmony and reverence is achieved. It takes some practice. Make sure you keep your fingers together, and never let them droop forward. This way of joining the hands is only tiring if you press your hands together too hard and do not relax.

2. *The Sign of the Cross*

163. Your hands tell a story to the people. How carefully do you make the sign of the cross? This is our salute to God, an expression of our faith. So often we see people make it carelessly. But there is a correct technique.

164. Begin with your hands joined. Then, placing, the left hand below the breast (fingers extended and thumb flat), you take your right hand to the forehead, with fingers and thumb together and extended.

165. *"In the Name of the Father . . ."*

166. Now bring your right hand to the center of the breast, above the left hand, and touch the breast with the ends of the extended fingers.

167. *". . . and of the Son . . ."*

168. Now, with the end of the fingers of your right hand, touch your left shoulder and then your right shoulder.

169. *". . . and of the Holy Spirit . . ."*

170. Now rejoin both hands before your breast as before.

171. *"Amen."*

172. You also learn an important point from making the sign of the cross. Whenever your right hand is busy, handling the cruet, passing something, *always* keep your left hand flat below your breast, with fingers extended, thumb and fingers together. If your right hand is busy, you *never* let your left hand dangle beside you.

173. Before the Gospel, at the words, "A reading from . . .", you make the sign of the cross with your thumb on your forehead, lips, and breast. Make the signs clearly, without haste, keeping the fingers of your right hand together, extended, and your left hand resting as usual against your breast. These signs mean: "God be in my mind, God be on my lips, God be in my heart."

3. Sitting

174. Whenever you stand, you hold your hands together correctly. But what do you do with your hands when you sit down? When you sit, at once place your hands, palms down, on your knees, fingers together. To relax, bend your elbows in slightly. When you stand, join the hands again immediately.

175. When you sit down, keep your legs together. Never cross them and never sprawl about, as this looks untidy. Always sit up straight, and never lean back casually in your seat. When two or more servers sit down, they should sit at the same time and rise at the same time.

4. Walking

176. When walking, whether in procession or carrying out a duty, never hurry. There may be occasions when something has been forgotten, and you are sent to get it. Even in that situation, move with dignity and decorum, even if more swiftly than usual. But never walk backwards. Not only does this look foolish, but it leads to accidents. In ascending or descending steps, do not bother about your robes. They will not get in the way if you lift your feet, so there is no need to stare down.

177. If you are walking with other servers, try to keep in step. This is most important in *processions*. The secret of a good procession has three elements. (1) Spread out—do not crowd one another. There is plenty of room, and a procession looks more like a triumphant Christian parade if it is neatly arranged. The cross bearer must always stay well back from the thurifer to avoid making contact with the thurible! (2) Look straight ahead, and do not get distracted by anyone outside the procession. (3) Move at a steady pace, neither too fast nor too slow. However, for the procession with the coffin at the funeral rite and in a procession of the Blessed Sacrament, a slower pace is more appropriate. A "set" of servers—for example, the two servers bearing candles and thurifer, and the boat bearer—should always walk and act together, keeping in step.

5. Kneeling

178. Servers learn to kneel without the help of a bench, kneeling desk, or seat in front of them. When you kneel, practice so that you never have to put a hand to the ground to steady yourself. Learn to lower your whole body with dignity, first bringing your right knee to the ground, then your left knee.

Always keep your hands joined, as you would when standing. Kneel "up straight", that is, never rest back on your heels.

179. Whether you stand or kneel, your posture expresses prayer and devotion. Obviously it is wrong to stare around the church when serving at the altar. At the same time, be careful not to go into a daydream, because you may forget what comes next or you may be required for some unexpected duty.

6. Genuflections

180. A genuflection is a special sign of homage paid only to God. It is directed primarily to our Lord Jesus Christ, really present in the Blessed Sacrament. Do you know *when* and *where* to genuflect?

181. You always genuflect whenever you pass in front of the Blessed Sacrament reserved in the tabernacle. This rule applies, at the beginning and end of Mass, if the tabernacle is in the sanctuary. But during Mass, you bow whenever you pass in front of it. The cross bearer, candle bearers, and thurifer bow their heads instead of genuflecting (*GIRM* 274). If the Blessed Sacrament is located a long way back from the main altar, in what is really a separate area, it may be the local custom to bow to the altar rather than genuflecting at the beginning and end of Mass.

182. *To genuflect*: (1) Keep your hands joined correctly as you move, head erect. (2) When you reach the spot where you are to genuflect, stop, and bring your feet together, so that your genuflection is going to be a separate act from your movement forward. You may have to wait anyway, if there is a team of servers and clergy forming up before the altar. (3) Look straight ahead, body straight, and do *not* bow your head or bend your body. Your knee makes the act of adoration. (4) Now move your right foot back, as you bend your left leg, and bring your right knee to the floor, just about level with the instep of your left foot. Just pause for a moment, then stand up without any rush and move to wherever you are going. With practice, you will not lose balance or flop down or get into the bad habit of bobbing.

183. Here are some useful hints for those who are training young servers, who often find it hard to keep their balance.

184. a. As they genuflect, get them to look at a spot straight ahead of them at eye level. This helps them to keep the body erect.

185. b. If they look clumsy, check whether the right knee is in line with the instep of the left foot. You will need to explain what "instep" means and demonstrate the procedure.

186. c. Get them to walk a few steps before making the genuflection, so they get the idea of bringing both feet together before the act of genuflecting.

187. d. If possible, have them practice in the church, wearing robes, so they get used to normal conditions.

188. e. Take care to teach them the meaning of genuflecting, pointing out the purpose of the tabernacle and leading them in prayer to our Lord really present in the Blessed Sacrament.

7. Bows

189. There are two bows in the liturgy: a bow of the head and a bow of the body.

190. *You bow your head*, without any hurry and never too deeply, as a sign of respect when receiving any object—for example, a cruet—from the priest. You bow to a bishop whenever your duties require you to approach him or leave him during any celebration. You bow at the Name of our Lord and our Lady during any text that you recite—for example, in the Creed and Gloria. During the Liturgy of the Hours, you bow in honor of the Holy Trinity at the words, "Glory be to the Father, and to the Son, and to the Holy Spirit."

191. *You bow from the waist*, without any hurry, hands joined, when you reverence the altar itself, when passing the tabernacle with the Blessed Sacrament immediately behind and close to the altar. In such a sanctuary, you make the same bow whenever you pass the altar during serving duties. In the Creed, you bow at the words ". . . and by the Holy Spirit was incarnate of the Virgin Mary, and became man. . . ."

Movement in the Sanctuary

192. As noted in the section on walking, always move at a sensible speed, neither too fast nor too slow. When moving in pairs or groups, always move *together* as a team.

193. One important point is worth noting about moving in pairs. If you both have to turn around together to move in the opposite direction, turn *in* toward one another—for example, when two servers turn away after offering wine and water to the celebrant. You must watch carefully so as not to make a move too soon, just as you must never keep the priest waiting, by delaying or dreaming. Certain points during Mass are worth noting so you do not move too soon.

194. *When you bring the wine and water to the priest*, do not approach while he is offering the bread, but come to the altar when you have answered "Blessed be God forever" or, when the prayer is said quietly, as you see the priest placing the paten on the altar.

195. Do not approach to *wash the priest's hands* until he has finished the prayer for the offering of wine and placed the chalice on the altar.

196. *Never move during the time of the Consecration* unless it is really urgent. There are emergencies, and then you must use your common sense.

197. *At the end of Holy Communion*, if the priest has to replace a ciborium in the tabernacle, do not bring the water (and wine) to the altar, for cleansing the chalice, until the door of the tabernacle has been closed.

198. *Here are some more useful hints for those who are training new servers*. Under the heading of "walking", we noted the problem of steps. They are not a hazard to the experienced server, but new servers will need to practice in their robes, carrying objects, candles, cruets, etc.

199. *To move up a step*: 1. As you approach the step, glance down to get your bearings. 2. Then look straight ahead and keep hands joined, if not carrying anything. 3. Lift higher than normal the leg with which you happen to be stepping forward. 4. Move this "ascending" foot well forward on the step. This method definitely works, but you may have to practice at times.

Procedures during Mass

200. Certain basic movements need to be understood before serving Mass. In some slight details, these may vary from church to church, according to local custom. Care has been taken to give a practical account of those procedures that involve objects used in the liturgy.

Holding an Open Book

1. Books

201. If you carry a sacred book—for example, the Book of the Gospels—do so reverently, keeping both hands securely underneath it, especially if you are in a procession.

202. When you hold the missal or book of the chair for the priest, hold it at a suitable height. If he is a tall priest, you may have to rest the book on your forehead. However, it is better to hold the book so that you can still see the priest. He may want to give you a sign, and, if you are hidden behind the book, he will find it difficult to let you know. Keep the book still. Do not take it away until the prayer, etc., is finished. At an evening Mass, if the lighting in the church is unusual, make sure there is no shadow cast on the pages of the book.

203. Be careful where you put your fingers underneath the book, because you may hide the words of a prayer printed at the bottom of the page or at the edge of the paper. Hold the page flat. Remember that these books are valuable. Handle them with care, and do not wrench the pages back, because this may break the spine of the binding. Clean hands do not leave dirty marks on the book.

204. Two books are placed on the altar during Mass. The *Book of the Gospels*, or *lectionary*, may be placed on the altar, after the entrance, at the beginning of Mass, and taken from the altar for readings and/or the Gospel. After the Gospel, it does not return to the altar but is placed on a credence table, unless the priest or deacon wishes to use it during the homily. In some places, it may be taken out in the procession at the end of Mass. The *missal* is only placed on the altar at the Preparation of the Gifts. It remains there until after the priest has cleansed the chalice, unless it is the custom for him to say the Prayer after Communion and give the blessing at the altar.

205. In carrying the missal on its stand or cushion from the credence table, there is no need to turn it away from you. Keep

it in such a position that you could read it, if open, and place it on the altar, at an angle, to the left of the center.

2. *Candles*

206. The candle bearers carry two candles, to honor the cross in procession and to honor our Lord in his Holy Gospel. They are usually placed on the credence table, and they *remain alight* during Mass or other celebrations.

207. The basic rule is one hand around the knob, the other hand under the base, keeping the bowl to catch wax at eye level. For the pair of candle bearers, each server places his *outside hand* around the knob, his inside hand under the base, i.e., one server has his right hand around the knob of his candlestick, the other uses his left hand.

208. Hold the candles still when walking or standing. Make sure you pick them up and replace them together on the credence or altar. Hold them straight, to prevent wax from falling on the floor, and try to hold them at the same height, which is easier if servers are of the same stature.

209. These candlesticks should be at least 18 inches high, not the small objects used in some places. They should match the processional cross. In some churches, the altar candlesticks are used for processions and are designed to rest next to the altar. These would need to be at least a yard tall, but not too heavy.

Carrying a Processional Candle

3. Presentations

210. In giving an object to the priest, you are acting on behalf of the people. With clarity and reverence, let them see what you are presenting on their behalf.

211. *If you bring the priest a ciborium* containing hosts or a paten with the large host, hold it up at such a height that the people can see it. Do not let the altar hide it. This also applies when handing the priest the wine and water cruets. It is better manners to hand them to him rather than letting him serve himself from the tray. On the tray, the wine cruet should be located nearer the priest. If the cruets have handles, turn these toward him.

212. *In presenting a ciborium, paten, or cruets*, come close to the priest, so he does not have to stretch out to you. It may be best to hold them underneath. As you present cruets, do not jerk them forward suddenly. Reach out naturally. Be helpful and considerate.

213. *In receiving the cruets from the priest*, do not jerk them from his hand. Take them naturally, in your right hand, and bow your head to the priest before you return to the credence table—a sign of respect.

214. *If you are serving on your own*, it is customary to present the wine cruet first, with your right hand, then pass the water cruet to your right hand, receiving back the wine with your left hand, then handing the water cruet to the priest with your right hand, then passing the wine cruet to your right hand, and finally receiving the water back with your left hand. This sounds complicated, but it is a circular series of movements. Bow as usual before you return to the credence table.

215. *In presenting a cruet or any object* with your right hand, always remember to keep the left hand flat on your breast, thumb and fingers together.

4. Washing the Priest's Hands

216. *a. If there are two servers*, as soon as they have placed the wine and water cruets back on the credence (unless they must wait for the incensing), the first server (on the right) takes the pitcher and the dish; the second server (on the left) takes the towel. Both come to the side of the altar, perhaps not as close to the tabletop as when offering cruets, and wait for the priest, side by side. When he extends his hands, the first server holds the dish directly beneath them, and pours a reasonable amount of water over all his fingers, without leaning forward. The second server, holding out the *unfolded* towel, gives it to the priest to dry his hands and receives the towel back in both hands, then both servers bow their heads together to the priest and return to the credence, where the towel is folded neatly.

217. *b. If there is only one server*, first open out the towel and drape it over your left arm before you take the pitcher and dish to the priest. Pour water over the priest's hands, then raise your left arm, still holding the dish, so that the priest can take the towel and dry his hands. Take the towel back on the arm, bow, and return to the credence.

5. Preparing the Chalice on the Altar

218. At the beginning of the *Preparation of the Gifts* (a) the deacon, (b) an instituted acolyte, or (c) a *trained* server brings the chalice to the altar. As we shall refer to this later, in describing the Mass in detail, the procedure should be known as part of training. But the linen, etc., used to prepare a chalice in the sacristy and on the credence should first be known by name.

219. a. It is customary to place the linen cloth for cleansing, the *purifier* or *purificator*, over the bowl of the chalice, but still folded.

220. b. If the paten is not large, it is placed above the purifier, with hosts to be consecrated on it. (A large paten may be kept separate from the chalice.) Above the paten may be placed the *pall*, which is useful for keeping dust and insects out of the chalice. It is a card, about 6 inches square, covered with linen, often embroidered on its upper surface.

221. c. Unless it is kept in a large wallet called a *burse*, which always is placed last, the most important linen cloth, the folded *corporal*, is now placed above chalice and paten. The corporal is the cloth, folded into nine squares, on which the chalice, paten, and ciboria are placed for the Liturgy of the Eucharist.

222. d. The *chalice veil* ought to be placed next. It is made of the same material and color as the vestments of the Mass, or it may always be white. It is arranged so as to conceal the chalice when seen from the front.

223. e. If it is to be used, to keep the corporal fresh and neat, the burse containing the corporal is placed flat, on top of the veiled chalice. The burse and veil are always used during the traditional Latin Mass.

224. f. Except perhaps at a Mass without a congregation, the chalice as prepared should *not* be on the altar before Mass begins, nor should the priest carry it to the altar. It should be on the credence table. However, in the traditional Latin Mass, the priest carries it to the altar for a Low Mass. At a

Solemn Mass, it is arranged on the credence table covered with a humeral veil.

225. Assuming that a deacon, acolyte, or M.C. is not to bring the chalice to the altar, the server who brings it should be ready to move at the end of the Prayer of the Faithful, or the Gospel or homily, if this Prayer of the Faithful is omitted at a weekday celebration. Another server may bring the missal. Here is the procedure:

226. a. You may remove the chalice veil at the credence table and fold it neatly, also taking the corporal from the burse, if used. Next carry the chalice, corporal, etc., to the altar, your right hand around the knob of the chalice, your left hand flat on top of the corporal. If two servers prepare the chalice, one will carry the chalice, the other will carry the corporal, either in the burse or reverently, flat, on outstretched hands, palms up.

227. b. According to local custom, place the chalice either at the side of the altar, where it will receive wine and water, or to the right side of the center of the altar, allowing space to unfold the corporal.

Bringing the Chalice to the Altar

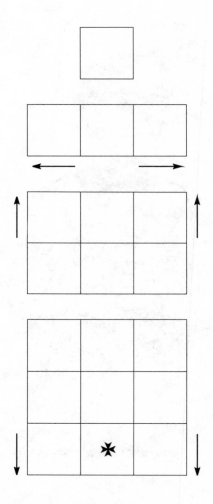

Unfolding the Corporal

64

228. c. Take the corporal reverently. Do *not* flick it open or shake it open in midair. Instead, (1) place it *flat* at the center of the altar, still folded, but nearer to the edge where the priest stands, approximately 6 inches from the edge. (2) Unfold it, first to your left, then to your right, revealing three squares. Next unfold the section furthest from you, away from yourself, making six squares visible. (3) Finally, unfold the crease that is nearest to you, toward yourself, making nine squares visible. (If there is a cross embroidered at the edge of a center square on the outside, move the corporal around so that this is nearest to the priest.)

229. d. If there is a pall on the chalice, remove it with your right hand, and place it just behind the chalice. If a small paten is used, this now leaves the large host ready for the priest at the Preparation of the Gifts. If a large paten is used and is not coming to the altar in a procession of gifts, this is now brought to the altar and placed near the corporal. If there is a procession of gifts with the paten and/or ciboria, these are placed on the corporal after the procession. The chalice is never brought to the altar in a procession of gifts, because it is not a gift.

6. Bells

230. Bells may be rung at certain times during the Mass to draw the attention of the people to the most sacred moments of the liturgy (*GIRM* 150). The times when they are rung depend on local custom, but they should be rung (a) as a "warning bell", when the priest extends his hands over the gifts, just before the Consecration, (b) once or three times at each elevation or showing of the Host and Chalice, after the Consecration, (c) perhaps as a signal for Communion or to tell the people to recite the Communion verse, as soon as the priest has received the Precious Blood.

Using Bells

231. Hand bells are easier to manage as you can continue to watch the priest while you ring the bell. A set of bells usually works best when rotated, not when shaken or swung in the air. New servers will need to be trained carefully in the use of the bell, how to ring it or strike it with best effect. Except in a large church, the bell should not be rung too loudly. A short sound is enough for the warning bell if used at this time. A longer sound is better to accompany the action of the elevation and showing of the Host and Chalice, and this should be reverently and carefully timed to accompany the actual moments of the raising and showing, *never* during the last words of Consecration. In the traditional Latin Mass, the bell is rung three times at each elevation: as the priest genuflects, as he raises the Host or Chalice, and as he genuflects again.

7. *The Use of the Thurible*

232. Incense is one of the richest signs of prayer and worship in our liturgy. It is a fragrant perfume only to be offered to God and to honor his holy People and the gifts they bring to the Lord. We read about "frankincense" in various parts of the Bible, especially as a gift of the three wise men who came to our Lord at Epiphany time (Mt 2:11). It has been used in Catholic worship since about the fourth century.

233. Incense is made from gum olibanum, a precious resin taken from the *boswellia carterii* bush in Southern Arabia. To this basic ingredient, other spices may be added, to vary the perfume. In Christian usage in both East and West, the grains or powder burn slowly on hot coals. The fragrance is at its best when the incense is first placed on the coals, so the *thurifer* (incense bearer) should take the thurible back to the sacristy after each of the four occasions when it is used during Mass. *Smoke alarms should be switched off at the times when incense is used.*

234. *Incense is used*:

1. during the Entrance Procession and to honor the altar and cross at the beginning of Mass;

2. to honor our Lord in the reading of the Holy Gospel;

3. at the Preparation of the Gifts to honor the offerings, the cross, the altar, and clergy, and the people sharing in the one Sacrifice;

4. finally, after each Consecration, to honor our Lord at the elevation or showing of the Host and Chalice.

235. The thurible is not brought back to the sanctuary unless it is to be used in some procession or rite that will immediately follow the Mass.

236. *a. Carrying the Thurible.* If you are tall, carry it in your right hand, just below the disk, fingers gripping the chains. It should swing gently beside you, to keep the coals alight. Before you leave the sacristy, make sure the coals are really alight. You may carry the boat and spoon in your left hand, against the breast. If there is a *boat bearer*, rest your left hand flat against your breast as usual. If you are not tall enough to let the thurible swing at full length, grip the chains with your right hand about one foot above the bowl and hold the disk and top of the chains against your breast with your left hand. Always let it swing *beside* your body, never at right angles across your body—which could trip you up!

237. *In a procession* to or from the sanctuary, it is customary to swing the smoking thurible beside you, as a sign of worship in that procession. If you are experienced, this may be carried out with dignity and skill, but it requires practice. Avoid "showing off"—for example, with exaggerated swings that might hit someone.

238. *b. Presenting the Thurible.* (1) Approach the priest with the boat bearer. At once, transfer the thurible to your left hand. (2) Slide the securing ring up the chains, approximately

Carrying the Thurible with One Hand

Carrying the Thurible with Two Hands

one foot. (Do not forget this!) (3) Pull the single chain, which lifts the lid, so that the lid comes up and is stopped by the ring. (4) Now grip that chain against the other three chains, in your left hand, at the disk, so the lid will not slide down again and close the thurible. (5) Grasp the chains at the securing ring with your right hand, at the same time lowering your left hand and the disk to your breast, and then extend the bowl and chains in your right hand at a level that is convenient for the celebrant. (6) The boat bearer (or deacon, M.C., or other minister) holds the boat open, with the spoon handle toward the celebrant, so he may easily spoon the grains onto the coals. When he is placing incense on the coals, keep the thurible still, making sure that the bowl is level and close to him. If he is seated, keep it at the level of his lap. If he is standing, keep it at the level of his waist.

239. *c. Closing the Thurible.* (1) With your right hand, lower the thurible until the three chains are extended. (2) Release your left-hand grip on the single chain at the top disk, and now lower the lid gently by your right hand. (3) When the lid is in place over the bowl, slide the securing ring back down the chains to hold the top of the lid in place. (4) If you are going to keep the thurible for a procession—for example, at the Gospel—transfer your grip from the left to the right hand, at the top of the chains, at the disk, letting your left hand rest against your breast, the thurible now swinging gently beside you. (5) However, if you are not tall enough for the single-handed way of carrying the thurible in procession or when moving about, just bring your left hand and the disk against your breast, gripping the chains with your right hand as usual one foot above the bowl, letting the thurible swing gently beside you.

Holding the Thurible Open to Receive Incense

Closing the Thurible

Giving the Thurible to the Celebrant

240. *d. Giving the Thurible.* (1) If you are to hand the thurible to the celebrant, deacon, or another minister, first make sure you have secured the lid. Then transfer the top of the chains and disk to your right hand and the chains held above the bowl to your left hand. (2) You can now present the thurible to the celebrant, deacon, or minister. Your right hand, with the top disk and chains, goes to his left hand. Your left hand, with the chains held above the bowl, goes to his right hand. This means that he is now able to use the thurible to incense the altar, the book, or the gifts. (3) At once, join your hands properly, turning and moving back a few paces, according to the situation.

241. *e. Incensations.* When the thurible is swung toward a person or object, this act of honor is known as *incensation, incensing,* or *censing.* There are customary rules for this action, and the basic procedure should be known for those times when the thurifer may have to offer incense.

242. To incense a person, first face the person and bow your head. Taking the chains in your right hand, approximately six inches above the bowl, holding the disk and top of the chains against your breast, raise the bowl to your eye level —never lower. (2) You will find it easier if your grip around the chains in your right hand has the chains running across your hand, with the bowl hanging over the side of your first finger, secured by your thumb. You can then "aim" and control the incensation. (3) Holding the bowl well out from your face, swing it toward the person, according to the customary number of swings. There is no need to let the bowl fall back and hit the chains, unless this makes it easier. (4) Finally, lower the bowl, moving it to your right side, and bow once more to the person you have incensed.

Incensing a Person

243. There are two kinds of swing, a *double swing* and a *single swing*. With a double swing, you swing the thurible out toward the person or object twice and then lower the thurible. With a single swing, you swing the thurible once and then lower it. You incense the celebrant with three double swings (after he has incensed the gifts and the altar), a group of concelebrants with three double swings, the deacon with two double swings, M.C. and servers with three single swings, and the people with three double swings (*Ceremonial of Bishops*, 92–96). To incense the people, come to the center, in front of the altar, bow to the altar, then face the people, bow, and swing (1) to the center, (2) to your left, (3) to your right. Bow again, face the altar and bow to it, then proceed to your place or to the sacristy.

244. At the elevation or showing of the Host and the Chalice, the thurifer, kneeling, incenses the Host and the Chalice with three double swings. At Benediction of the Blessed Sacrament, as the priest gives the Eucharistic blessing, kneeling, the thurifer incenses the Host with three double swings, making the incensations keep time with the action of blessing.

Carrying the Processional Cross

8. Carrying the Cross

245. A taller server should carry the processional cross. Because the Holy Cross is being carried, the *cross bearer* or *crucifer* does not bow or genuflect on approaching or leaving the altar. The figure of the crucifix always points out, away from the cross bearer. To keep control of the staff and to keep the cross straight and not swaying from side to side, you need to find a good grip on the staff.

246. The left hand should hold the lower part of the staff, with the right hand securing the upper part of the staff. You may find it helpful to keep the right hand before your eyes. Hold the staff out from your body so that your legs will not get tangled with the staff as you move. Hold the cross high so that it never trails on the ground, but do not hold it at an extreme height, because this looks foolish and you may lose control. Brackets or a socket hold the cross when not in use, either at the side of the sanctuary or, if it is used as the altar cross, in some position near the altar. Learn how these function. Never lean the cross against the wall, because this is disrespectful and it may slide down or fall over and cause harm.

Emergencies

247. Before we learn the details of serving Mass, we need to be aware of what to do when something goes wrong.

248. *If you make a mistake*, remember that you and the other servers may be the only people in the church who know it is a mistake. Just keep moving, and act calmly and with dignity! We all make mistakes. With practice we learn how to work through them or how to do the right thing immediately.

249. *If something unusual happens* among the congregation, do not stare or whisper. This rule applies strictly when people are distressed—for example, at a funeral. Look straight ahead, unless, of course, you are asked to help in any way—for example, by getting a glass of water.

250. *If another server faints* and you are nearby, loosen the collar and help the server to the sacristy at once. If you *feel* sick or *think* you might faint, do not delay. *Immediately* go to the sacristy or outside to get fresh air. Loosen your collar, sit down, put your head between your legs to allow blood to circulate. Someone will help you, just as you may help another server with this advice. If this problem continues, see the head server or whoever is in charge of servers. To avoid problems on a hot day or in a stuffy building, make sure you drink some water before Mass. It never breaks the fast for Holy Communion. Do not wear a jacket or sweater underneath your robes on a hot day.

Availability

251. The willingness to serve at the altar is your own way of doing the will of God. If you were at a weekday Mass and the priest came onto the altar without a server, you should go up at once and assist him. That is what availability means. But it can extend beyond your parish or school.

252. As a server, you are not restricted to serving in the church where you normally assist. For example, when on vacation, you may offer to serve in the local church, especially if you see that there are no servers or that they need help. Being available to support others is a sign of service of God and people.

4.

The Mass

253. Each server should know the structure of the *rite* of the Mass, not just "to know what comes next", but to understand the meaning of each step in the celebration of the Divine Liturgy and to cultivate the "spirit of the liturgy". The Mass itself is a drama, an action, moving steadily forward to its supreme moments, when heaven and earth meet in the great mystery of the altar.

The Structure of the Mass

254. There are two major parts in the rite of Mass: the *Liturgy of the Word*, which leads to the *Liturgy of the Eucharist*. Before the Liturgy of the Word, there are the *Introductory Rites*. After the Liturgy of the Eucharist, there is the *Concluding Rite*. These may vary in form, but the two major parts follow the same pattern, with texts varying according to the occasion, season, or feast, as set out in the *Roman Missal*.

1. Introductory Rites

255. *The Entrance Song* or *Introit* opens the celebration and accompanies the procession of priest and servers to the altar. It should be sung, to deepen our unity together and to introduce us to the mystery of the season or feast.

256. *The Veneration of the Altar and Greeting of the People* come after the entrance. As it is the sign of Christ himself, the

CEREMONIES EXPLAINED FOR SERVERS

center of the church and of our Eucharistic assembly, the altar is shown reverence by three traditional gestures: (a) the bow or customary reverence, (b) the priest and deacon's kiss, (c) the incensation, when incense is used. Having made the sign of the cross in the Name of the Holy Trinity, the Name that gathers us as one, the celebrant greets us. The greeting reminds us that we are one, in the power and grace of God.

257. *The Penitential Rite*, according to one of three forms, invites us to be sorry for our sins and takes away venial or minor sins that do not need absolution in private confession. We come to God in a spirit of contrition, so that we may celebrate the Holy Eucharist worthily and grow in grace.

258. *Lord, Have Mercy (Kyrie eleison)* is addressed to our Lord and is sung or said if not already included in the third form of the Penitential Rite.

259. *The Gloria* is an ancient hymn of praise, sung or recited on Sundays outside Lent and Advent, on solemnities and feasts, and at solemn local celebrations. We praise the Father and his Son, Jesus, the Lamb of Sacrifice, for we shall offer and receive him in the sacrificial mystery of the Eucharist.

260. *The Collect* is introduced with an invitation to prayer and a time of silent prayer. On behalf of the people, the priest offers this prayer, which expresses the occasion or season, in words addressed usually to God the Father, through Christ our Lord, "in the unity of the Holy Spirit". We all respond with "Amen", "so be it".

2. *The Liturgy of the Word*

261. *The First Scripture Reading* on a Sunday or Solemnity is usually taken from the Old Testament, its theme related directly

to the main reading, the Gospel. A lector should read this Old Testament reading and the Second Reading.

262. *The Responsorial Psalm* may continue the theme of the reading or express the mood of the season or occasion. It should be sung as a "responsory", that is, with the people making the responsive verse their own prayer and the cantor or choir singing the text of the psalm. It is incorrect to describe it as a "response to the readings".

263. *The Second Scripture Reading* on a Sunday or Solemnity is taken from any portion of the New Testament that is not a Gospel, especially the letters of Saint Paul. We should note that all the readings in the Liturgy of the Word come from the Bible. It is never permitted to use readings from other sources.

264. *The Alleluia* or *Gospel verse* should be sung, our joyous welcome of the words of the Lord himself in his Gospel. The word "alleluia" means "Praise God!" During Lent, "alleluia" is never used until the Easter Vigil.

265. *The Gospel* is the major reading of the Liturgy of the Word. We stand to show our reverence for the words of Jesus Christ and the events of his life, truly recorded in the sacred scriptural text. Christ is present through his Word read in the community of believers. Only the deacon or a priest may read the Gospel.

266. *The homily*, commonly, but not correctly, known as the sermon, is an explanation and proclamation of the readings of the liturgy. The ministry of preaching is entrusted to ordained men, because they speak for the Church.

267. *The Profession of Faith*, or Creed, is our act of faith, our assent to the teachings of the Church and the readings we have

heard. Therefore the Creed is our preparation in faith for the offering of the Eucharistic Sacrifice. The Creed must be said or sung on Sundays and Solemnities, and it may be used at important local celebrations.

268. *The General Intercessions* or *Prayer of the Faithful* were restored to the Roman Rite by the Second Vatican Council. After a brief introduction by the celebrant addressed to the people, the deacon or a lector announces the prayer intentions, also addressed to the people, and we respond with the petition, a verse asking God to hear us, or with silence. The celebrant sums up the set of intentions in a short prayer.

3. The Liturgy of the Eucharist

269. Up to this point, the liturgy has been celebrated at the chair and the ambo. For the offering of the Holy Sacrifice itself, the action now moves to the altar.

270. In the Liturgy of the Eucharist, the Church reenacts the Last Supper. In three steps, we obey the command of our Lord to "do this. . . ." (1) He took bread and wine—the Preparation of the Gifts. (2) He blessed, or gave thanks over, this food—the Eucharistic Prayer and Consecration. (3) He broke the Bread he had changed into his Body and gave his Body and Blood to his disciples—the Communion Rite. Whenever the Church reenacts the Last Supper, the one Sacrifice of Jesus Christ is offered in the visible form of a sacred banquet.

271. *The Preparation of the Gifts* may begin with a Procession of the Gifts of bread and wine, brought by representatives of the people, to show our involvement in the Sacrifice that is about to take place. This bread and wine that God has first given to us is given back to God, from whom everything comes. A collection, and especially gifts for the poor, show that we are all offered with the bread and wine. To set this food aside for its sacred purpose, the priest uses prayers similar to those used by a Jewish father at the beginning of a meal, prayers like those used by our Lord at the Last Supper.

272. After he has washed his hands, as a sign of purity and preparation for offering a sacrifice, the priest invites us to share in the offering, "Pray brothers and sisters. . . ." Then he gathers our prayers together in the *Prayer over the Offerings*.

273. *The Eucharistic Prayer* is the heart of our Mass, a prayer of thanksgiving, "Eucharist". It is a prayer of consecration, a priestly prayer of sacrifice. There are various steps in this greatest prayer, which begins with the *Preface*, when the priest leads us in offering thanks to God, with words that vary according to the season or occasion. In the *Sanctus*, we praise God the Holy Trinity, "Holy, holy, holy Lord God of hosts. . . ." We kneel for the central words of the Eucharistic Prayer.

274. At the *epiklesis*, the priest extends his hands over the gifts and asks the Holy Spirit to change them into the Body and Blood of Christ. The *narrative of institution* is the form of words, taken from the Last Supper, used for the *Consecration*. At this supreme moment of our Mass, the bread and wine are truly changed into the Body and Blood of Christ. By this real and permanent change, transubstantiation, the one Sacrifice of Christ is made present and offered. The priest shows us the Host and the Chalice at each *elevation*, and we adore our Lord. An *acclamation* follows the Consecration. We proclaim the "Mystery of Faith", that we believe in the Real Presence and the Sacrifice of the Eucharist, Christ giving himself up for us.

275. The priest continues the Eucharistic Prayer. In the *anamnesis* (Greek for "memorial" or "replay"), we remember the saving death and Resurrection of our Lord, made present here and now through the Eucharist. In the *offering*, the priest expresses what is happening, that we offer Christ the victim to God the Father, that we offer ourselves in him, the true Priest, that we become one in Christ. The *intercessions*, prayers for others, unite the Church on earth, the Church beyond death in purgatory, the Church in the glory of heaven, to this one Sacrifice offered for the living and the dead, enriched by the prayers of our Lady and the saints. Finally, in the great *doxology* (praise of God), the priest raises the chalice and paten, the Body and Blood of Christ, offering "through him and with him and in him . . .", and we all respond with the great "Amen."

276. *The Communion Rite* begins with the Lord's Prayer, when we ask for "our daily bread", provided especially in the Body of Christ, the food for those who have been redeemed and forgiven. In the *rite of peace*, we beg for peace and unity in the Church and the world. We show our love for one another, our preparation for Communion, by giving a *sign of peace*, a sign of the true peace that only Jesus can give us.

277. While we pray to the Lord as the "Lamb of God", the priest repeats the action of the Lord at the Last Supper by *breaking the Host*, so that the sacred Food can be shared in Holy Communion. ". . . [W]e who are many are one body, for we all partake of the one bread" (1 Cor 10:17). He places a fragment of the Host in the Chalice, an ancient custom that is a sign of the unity of the Body and Blood of Christ, who is alive and risen, present with us in the Eucharist.

278. After a quiet prayer of preparation, the priest shows us the broken Host, "Behold the Lamb of God. . . ." We respond by admitting we are not worthy for him to come into our

bodies, but his grace will heal our souls. The priest first receives Holy Communion and then distributes Communion to the faithful. A chant, hymn, or sacred song may be sung during Communion to express our faith and unity with the Lord and with one another. *Silent prayer* should follow the distribution of Holy Communion, a time for thanksgiving, for we are now united to Christ the Lord. A short *prayer after Communion* completes the Communion Rite. Brief announcements may follow.

4. The Concluding Rite

279. The celebrant gives *the blessing*, which may take either a simple form or a more solemn form, with prayers and responses, according to the occasion. As we began the Mass "In the name of the Father, and of the Son, and of the Holy Spirit . . .", so we conclude the Mass in the power of the Holy Trinity, making the sign of the cross on our bodies, a sign of faith, of belonging to the Church. In *the Dismissal*, the deacon or the celebrant sends us out into the world, glorifying the Lord by our lives, that is, by bringing his peace to other people, living out the Eucharist that we have offered and celebrated.

Serving at Mass

280. As a guide to the serving at Mass, five elements in serving have been selected: (1) *Mass with the People*, a typical form for Sunday Mass, adapted by local custom for weekdays. (2) *Concelebrated Mass*, when a group of priests celebrate at the same altar. (3) *The Blessing and Sprinkling with Holy Water*, which may take the place of the Penitential Rite on Sundays. (4) *Mass without the People*, when the priest celebrates with only one server present.

1. Mass with the People

281. This inclusive description of the procedures at Mass is written primarily for servers. In the *General Instruction of the Roman Missal* (2002), a distinction is now made between Mass without a deacon (*GIRM* 120–70) and Mass with a deacon (*GIRM* 171–86).

282. *Preparations.* Having vested and checked neat hair, clean hands, etc., the servers make sure that everything is ready, under the direction of a priest, M.C., or head server. Remember the main points of the action of the liturgy:

283. *The altar*: dust cover removed (if used), at least one cloth spread, candles lit (see appendix 1, *Lighting Candles*), nothing else on the altar at this stage except candles, flowers, crucifix, if these are arranged on the altar. Microphone, connected and ready, if it is set on or in the altar.

284. *The celebrant's chair*: in position, the missal or book of the chair nearby, a folder or book for the *Prayer of the Faithful* and notices nearby. Microphone, connected and ready.

285. *The ambo*: the lectionary, open and marked for the Mass (unless it is carried in procession). Text for the intentions of the *Prayer of the Faithful*. Microphone, connected and ready.

286. *The credence table*: covered with a cloth and on it the chalice(s) prepared (see chapter 3, *Procedures during Mass 5*), perhaps a large paten with bread, ewer, basin and towel, Communion plate(s), if used, and, *only* if there is no procession of gifts, cruets of wine and water, ciboria or patens with bread. If the vessels are to be purified on the credence table, during or after Mass, a second corporal is left, folded, on the credence. When extraordinary ministers assist in distributing Holy Communion and cleanse their fingers at the credence table, a small vessel of water and a purifier will be needed. The bell may be kept on the credence until it is needed and also the missal stand, unless kept elsewhere.

287. *The table of the gifts* set up as the starting point if there is a procession of gifts. It should be covered with a cloth, and on it will be the wine (and water), patens and/or ciboria with bread, and perhaps gifts for the poor, according to custom.

288. *The tabernacle*: if used during Mass, the key, a corporal spread on the surface of the altar, ledge, or table in front of it, two candles burning if it is in a separate chapel or area well away from the altar, the small vessel of water and purifier to cleanse the fingers of ministers of Communion, unless this is on the credence table.

289. *The sacristy*: vestments set out, or easily available, for celebrant and other clergy (see appendix 2, *Setting out Vestments*). If incense is to be used, charcoal should be prepared and lit about ten minutes before Mass, the boat checked to see that it is full of incense. In case extra quantities or specific objects are needed during Mass, each server should know where bread, wine, and altar linen are kept in the sacristy.

290. *Cell phones* must be switched off or set in silent mode. During Mass, it would be best to leave them in a secure place in the sacristy under the supervision of the sacristan or head server. But never leave any valuable possessions in the sacristy or vesting room. Servers should also be acquainted with the technology of the *sound system*, which varies from church to church. As noted above, when incense is used, *smoke alarms* in the sacristy and church should be switched off.

291. *Entrance Procession*. In the sacristy, all form up according to local custom. *Silence* is best before Mass, to reflect on the sacred duties we are about to offer to God, to be ready for

any last minute instructions. The practice of a prayer in common before serving is to be encouraged (see appendix 3, *Prayers for Servers*). When the signal to move is given, all bow to the sacristy cross and proceed in order to the altar, by whatever route is chosen. When incense is used, the thurifer approaches the celebrant either in the sacristy, before the procession, or during a pause in a porch or some other convenient place, *before* moving to the altar. Incense is prepared and blessed, and the thurifer leads the procession (with a boat bearer). An instituted acolyte carries the cross, if he is not the M.C.

292. If incense is not used, the cross bearer goes first (chapter 3, Procedures 8), flanked by two servers carrying lighted candles (chapter 3, Procedures 2). If candles are not carried, the cross bearer walks ahead of other servers. (Carrying the cross is strongly recommended, but not required.) If the deacon assists, he carries the Book of the Gospels. A lector walking in the procession comes between the servers and the celebrant and may carry the lectionary, or it may be carried by a server (chapter 3, Procedures).

293. *Introductory Rites.* On arrival in the sanctuary, form up according to local custom, but always so as to allow the celebrant the central space. All make the "customary reverence", the deep bow or genuflection. The cross bearer and candle bearers do not make the reverence. The cross bearer now places the cross in its position; the candle bearers place their candles either on the credence table or near the altar. From now on, they base themselves near or on either side of the credence table. When incense is used, the celebrant kisses the altar, receives the thurible, and incenses the cross and altar. The thurifer steps back while the altar is incensed, receives the thurible back, bows to the celebrant, and returns to the sacristy. If the Book of the Gospels or lec-

tionary has been carried in procession, the deacon, lector, or server places it reverently on the altar.

294. The celebrant goes to his chair, and servers go to their designated places. The book bearer approaches immediately with the missal or book of the chair (chapter 3, Procedures 1) so that the priest may begin the Introductory Rites. If needed, a candle bearer may act as book bearer, coming over from the normal position of the candle bearers, near the credence table. One server at Mass always acts as book bearer.

295. If *Penitential Rite 1* is used, all strike the breast with the right hand, by custom three times, at "through my fault . . .", placing the left hand below the breast. Servers should respond *clearly* during the responses at Mass, to give the people a lead. The book bearer will step back, according to local custom, during the *Kyrie* and *Gloria*, especially when these are sung, but must be in position for the *Collect*. After the response "Amen", the book bearer takes the missal or book of the chair to a credence table and goes to a seat. (The lectionary is taken to the lectern if necessary.)

A. THE LITURGY OF THE WORD

296. All servers sit, remembering the discipline of hands when sitting and standing. When incense is used, the thurifer goes to the sacristy to get the thurible during the Responsorial Psalm and sees that the charcoal is burning properly and is "on cue" *well before the Gospel.* The thurifer waits at a convenient position, near the credence table. As soon as the reading before the Gospel concludes, the thurifer goes directly to the celebrant, who remains seated. If there is no boat bearer, another server may assist with the boat, or the deacon or M.C. will assist. All stand for the singing of the *Alleluia* or *Gospel Verse.* This accompanies the preparation

of incense, the celebrant's private prayer, the blessing of the deacon, and the Gospel procession to the ambo.

297. *The Gospel Procession.* When the celebrant says his private prayer at the center, or when the deacon goes to be blessed, candle bearers take their candles and form up before the altar, either flanking the celebrant, if he is to read the Gospel, perhaps a few paces behind him, or waiting in the same position for the deacon, who takes the Book of the Gospels or lectionary from the altar. The thurifer stands between the candle bearers. An M.C. may stand next to the celebrant or deacon. All bow to the altar, and the candle bearers and thurifer *lead* the celebrant or deacon to the ambo.

298. During the reading of the *Gospel*, candle bearers stand on either side of the lectern, facing in toward the book, candles held at the correct level and kept still. The thurifer may stand on the right of the Gospel reader, with the M.C. nearby, ready to hand the thurible to the reader (chapter 3, Procedures 7). After the reader has incensed the book, the thurifer receives the thurible back and lets it swing gently at full length during the reading. At the end of the Gospel, all return to the center, bow to the altar, and go to their places. The candle bearers place the candles on the credence or near the altar. The thurifer takes the thurible back to the sacristy. All sit for the homily.

299. *The Creed* is said or sung, all standing and making the deep bow together at "and by the Holy Spirit was incarnate of the Virgin Mary, and became man". (At all Masses on Christmas Day and the Solemnity of the Annunciation, March 25th, everyone kneels at these words.) The book bearer may be required at the chair for the Creed and will assist with the book or folder containing the *Prayer of the Faithful*. If the deacon or lector announces the intentions, the text for the intentions should *already* be at or near the ambo.

B. THE LITURGY OF THE EUCHARIST

300. For the *Preparation of the Gifts*, the altar itself must first be prepared. A server takes the missal and its stand, placing it on the altar; slightly left of center, at an angle. Another server, perhaps one of the candle bearers at the credence table, unveils the chalice and takes the corporal (folded or in its burse). Another server may bring the chalice (with a paten and bread). Follow chapter 3, Procedures 5, the four steps of spreading the corporal and placing the chalice on the altar. These steps will be adapted when only one server is available. This server first places the missal on the altar and then brings the veiled chalice to the altar, unveiling it, spreading the corporal, and arranging the chalice in one action. The chalice veil may be left neatly folded, lengthwise, on the altar or taken back to the credence before the server assists with wine and water. When a deacon or acolyte assists, bring the corporal and chalice(s) to him at the altar so he can prepare the vessels.

301. When there is a *Procession of the Gifts*, the celebrant stands after the servers have prepared the altar and goes to the front of the altar, where two servers, or more if necessary, join him. All bow to the altar and turn toward the people, coming to a convenient position to meet the procession and receive the gifts. This procession should proceed reverently without haste, and at the right time, that is, *only* when the celebrant is waiting to receive the gifts, making sure that the hymn has commenced that is meant to accompany this action. In some churches, it is customary for the candle bearers *without candles* to go to the table of the gifts while the altar is being prepared and then lead the people who bring bread and wine to the altar. Alternatively, the cross bearer, without cross, goes to the table of the gifts during the preparation of the altar and leads the people. As the celebrant and deacon receive the gifts of bread and wine, these are given to the servers, who then *follow* the celebrant and deacon to the altar, so as to allow them to take their positions for the offering prayers.

302. *The Preparation of the Gifts* follows, the servers either presenting bread, wine, and water from the side of the altar, if there has been a procession of gifts, or bringing wine and water from the credence table. (chapter 3, Procedures 3). The cruets of wine and water are presented from the right side of the altar.

303. When incense is used, the thurifer goes to the sacristy to get the thurible during the *Prayer of the Faithful*, returning to a position near the credence once this prayer is completed. After the offering of wine, as the celebrant bows and prays quietly, the thurifer approaches the celebrant, with the boat bearer or another server, deacon, or M.C. to assist. The celebrant prepares incense at the center of the altar (chapter 3, Procedures 7b, c, d). The celebrant incenses the gifts, the cross, and the altar. He is incensed, either by the deacon, M.C., or the thurifer (chapter 3, Procedures 7e). Unless the deacon carries out the incensations, the thurifer incenses the M.C., servers, and the people (see Procedures 7e). The thurifer bows at the center and may go to the sacristy to attend to the thurible, returning with the thurible for the Eucharistic Prayer, or the thurifer may take a position near the credence table and wait there for the Eucharistic Prayer and carry out incensations from that place.

304. When two, four, or six torch bearers assist at the Eucharistic Prayer, the thurifer, having incensed the people, waits at the center (with boat bearer). The torch bearers come from their seats and form up according to the space available.

All bow to the altar, and the thurifer leads the team to the sacristy or another convenient place where they light the torches and wait until the *Sanctus*.

305. After the incensations, or after the offering of wine, if incense is not used, two servers approach the right side of the altar for the washing of the celebrant's hands (chapter 3, Procedures 4a). One server washes his hands according to Procedures 4b.

306. *The Eucharistic Prayer.* Servers now go to the places where they stand and kneel for the central prayers of the Mass. If not on a step, the bell is brought from the credence table. At the altar, the deacon or preferably the M.C. turns the pages of the missal for the Prayer over the Offerings, the Preface, and Eucharistic Prayer; otherwise, the celebrant turns the pages himself.

307. When torch bearers assist at the Eucharistic Prayer, the thurifer leads them from the sacristy at "Holy, holy, holy Lord. . . ." They carry the torches in their outside hands, the inside hand resting flat on the breast. On arrival in the sanctuary area, the whole team bows and then they kneel, unless they must wait awhile until the singing of the Sanctus is completed and the people kneel when the celebrant begins the prayer. There are two formations in which torch bearers may kneel, depending on the space available. They may kneel in a line across the sanctuary, with the thurifer at the center, or in two lines, leading toward the altar, with the thurifer at the center.

308. Servers kneel when the people kneel during the Eucharistic Prayer. A server rings the bell according to custom (chapter 3, Procedures 6). A candle bearer at the credence table may ring the bell. When incense is used, the thurifer takes a position either at the side near the credence table or at the center of the sanctuary, especially when there are torch bearers. The boat bearer, another server, or M.C. helps the thurifer place incense in the thurible, well before the Consecration, certainly *before* the "warning bell" is rung as the priest extends his hands over the gifts. The thurifer carefully incenses the Host and the Chalice at each *elevation* (chapter 3, Procedures 7e).

309. The servers respond clearly with the *acclamation* after the *Consecration*. All servers kneel during the Consecration and remain still, attentive, and reverent during this most sacred moment of the Mass. At the end of the Eucharistic Prayer, the Doxology, ". . . through him, and with him, and in him . . ." is said or sung by the celebrant(s), and servers respond with a clear "Amen."

310. From this point of the Mass, servers genuflect when passing in front of, or behind, the altar, to reverence the Blessed Eucharist now on the altar. After the "Amen", all servers stand. When incense is used, the thurifer genuflects and returns to the sacristy. If there are torch bearers, they genuflect, and the thurifer leads them back to the sacristy with the torches. They extinguish these candles and return to their places in the sanctuary. The thurifer leaves the thurible in the sacristy, carefully extinguishing the charcoal for the sake of safety, unless the thurible will be needed for a procession or rite immediately after Mass. The thurifer returns to a place near the credence table.

311. *The Communion Rite* begins with the *Lord's Prayer*. When the *Sign of Peace* is given, the servers use the gesture prescribed by local custom and greet one another. At least one server should go to the celebrant and deacon to receive the sign of peace. The sign of peace should be warm, reverent, but always orderly, because it is a *sacred* action, not just a handshake. Servers should only give the sign to those near them—i.e., it is not an excuse for wandering around the sanctuary or for waving, singing out, or hearty wringing of hands. A good procedure would be to turn to the server near you, clasp the right hand and say, "The peace of the Lord be with you always", a greeting that has the response "Amen" (*GIRM* 154). Servers do not leave the sanctuary and move about the church giving the sign to people.

312. The traditional procedure in the sanctuary has been to face one another; the one receiving the peace bows, the one giving it placing hands on the other person's shoulders, the one receiving placing hands under the elbows, and both bow the head forward so that their left cheeks are side by side at the words "The peace of the Lord be with you always". The response is "Amen." They step back slightly and, with hands joined again, bow to one another. This formality may be observed, but it is no longer the rule that the sign of peace is passed along in a kind of chain, beginning with the celebrant. However, that is the required procedure in the solemn forms of the traditional Latin Mass.

313. After the *Lamb of God* and breaking of the Host, all kneel, leading the people in "Lord, I am not worthy . . .". It may be a local custom to sound the bell when the celebrant drinks from the Chalice. If Communion plates are used, these must be brought from the credence table at once or, preferably, during *Lamb of God*. To receive Holy Communion conveniently, the servers should come to the center, or some other space, bow or genuflect together, and receive the Blessed Eucharist from the celebrant, who either passes along the line of servers or stands in position as the servers approach him, two by two.

97

314. *When Holy Communion is given under both kinds,* there are two usual procedures:

315. 1. The deacon, or a concelebrant, acolyte, or other minister, hands you the Chalice after you have received the Host from the celebrant. Respond with "Amen" to the words "The Blood of Christ", and, holding it firmly, drink carefully from the Chalice. The minister of Communion always wipes the Chalice after it has been handed back (*GIRM* 286).

316. 2. The celebrant or minister dips the Host in the Chalice prior to placing it directly into your mouth. This is called "intinction". The Communion plate is used during intinction, held under the chin of each communicant (*GIRM* 287). It is more convenient if a server holds the plate as people receive the Lord in this way. The plate is then given to the minister, who takes it to the altar or credence to be purified.

317. During intinction, the communicant never dips the Host in the Chalice, because this is self-service, and it causes accidents. It is never permitted for servers or the people to pass the Chalice around to one another, nor is it permitted for them to take the Chalice from the altar, or some other place, and help themselves, as if they were concelebrating priests. The Body and Blood of the Lord is always *given and ministered* to the lay faithful by those ordained or authorized to serve us in this way.

318. When there are no priests, deacons, or instituted acolytes to assist at Holy Communion, an authorized *Extraordinary Minister of Holy Communion* may assist. Remembering the principle in chapter 2 that roles and ministers must never be confused in the liturgy, a server should never act as a minister of Holy Communion unless needed in a real emergency situation. Nor should a server hold the Chalice during intinction.

319. At the conclusion of Holy Communion, if Communion plates have been used, these are placed on the altar, at the right-hand corner where the vessels will be cleansed, or on the credence, if the vessels will be cleansed there. The server(s) assisting with *the purification of the vessels* or *ablutions* must be prompt in either bringing the water (and wine, if the priest wishes to use it) to the altar or in attending at the credence table. According to local custom or the wishes of the priest, deacon, or acolyte, you pour wine first and/or a larger quantity of water second. You may pour the water over the celebrant's fingers. He may offer a ciborium instead of the chalice, and then he pours the water or wine into the chalice from that ciborium. Bow to him and replace the cruets.

320. *If the ablutions are carried out at the right-hand corner of the altar,* servers return to the altar and take the purified vessels back to the credence table. If the celebrant, deacon, or acolyte has not veiled the chalice and folded the corporal at the altar, a server carries out this duty at the altar (chapter 3, Procedures 5, preparing the chalice), and a server will then take the chalice to the credence table. If the ablutions are carried out at the credence table, this duty may take place there.

321. *If the ablutions are deferred until after Mass,* a server spreads a corporal on the credence table and arranges it conveniently so that there is room for the vessels when they are brought to the table after Communion. A server should return to the sanctuary after Mass to assist the celebrant, deacon, or acolyte in purifying these vessels and then take them back to the sacristy.

322. During Holy Communion, a server removes the missal and stand from the altar, unless the prayers after Communion and blessing take place at the altar. Once the ablutions are complete and the vessels and missal have been removed from the altar, servers sit during silent prayer after Holy Communion. The book bearer, however, must be ready with the missal or book of the chair, waiting near the celebrant. All stand for the *Prayer after Communion*. Then all sit if notices are read out.

C. THE CONCLUDING RITE

323. Servers stand for the *Blessing* and *Dismissal*, the book bearer attending the celebrant at the chair. It is best for the cross bearer and candle bearers to take the cross and candles and wait near the credence table during the Blessing. Then all form up in the area in front of the altar, waiting for the celebrant to kiss the altar. All make the customary reverence with him and return in order to the sacristy by the chosen route.

D. AFTER MASS

324. In the sacristy, all form up, bow to the cross, and wait for any instructions. Servers may be required to assist the sacristan and put away the vestments. Unless another Mass is to follow, vessels, cruets, books, etc., are brought back to the sacristy, altar candles are extinguished, and the dust cover is replaced on the altar. Check that microphones or a sound system are turned off and portable microphones are taken back to the sacristy. If incense has been used, make sure no charcoal is smoldering and that the bowl of the thurible is scraped clean. Servers put their robes away neatly and ensure that their own vesting room is tidy. Check the roster. Make a visit to the church for a prayer before you leave.

2. Concelebrated Mass

325. *Preparations.* Certain points need to be noted when a number of priests concelebrate Mass. Extra *chairs* will be needed according to the number of concelebrants. Extra *chalices* may be needed for Holy Communion, taken to the altar from the credence table at the Preparation of the Gifts. A set of booklets containing the Eucharistic Prayer, according to the number of concelebrants, should be in position near the altar on a credence table. Each priest should have his own *purifier*, and these may be on the credence table. Extra *wine* may be needed. In the sacristy or another room, sets of *vestments* are laid out for the concelebrants. Servers may be asked to help the sacristan set out vestments, see appendix 2, *Setting out Vestments*. If enough chasubles are available, each concelebrant should wear chasuble, stole, and alb (amice and cincture), or at least the stole over an alb. The principal celebrant always wears the complete vestments. Servers may help concelebrants to vest before Mass. A second M.C. may be needed to coordinate a major concelebration.

326. *Entrance Procession.* Everything proceeds as for *Mass with the People*, but the concelebrants come after the servers, in order, before the principal celebrant. If the deacon carries the Book of the Gospels, he leads the concelebrants; otherwise, he may walk next to the principal celebrant.

A. INTRODUCTORY RITES

327. On arrival at the sanctuary, form up according to local custom, but allow space for the concelebrants. When there are a large number of concelebrants, servers should make the customary reverence as a team and go to their places, while the concelebrants make the reverence two by two and kiss the altar. In other respects, the Introductory Rites proceed as for Mass with the People.

B. THE LITURGY OF THE WORD

328. If there is no deacon, a concelebrant reads the Gospel. Everything proceeds as for Mass with the People.

C. THE LITURGY OF THE EUCHARIST

329. Concelebrants may assist the principal celebrant at the Procession of the Gifts and in preparing wine and water in the chalice(s). Extra chalices are brought to the altar before the Preparation of the Gifts, together with purifiers, which may be placed neatly on each side of the corporal. If there are many concelebrants, extra corporals for the chalices may be spread on the altar, perhaps at each side of the altar. The wine and water may be poured into these chalices at the credence table even before Mass begins. Servers who carry prepared chalices to the altar must take great care to avoid an accident.

330. After the incensations or the washing of the principal celebrant's hands, a server or M.C. either gives concelebrants booklets with the text of the Eucharistic Prayer or places them on the altar, depending on the number of concelebrants and where they stand. Some concelebrants stand near the altar with the principal celebrant, but space must be kept to the right of the principal celebrant when a deacon assists. The concelebrants join in the Eucharistic Prayer, quietly saying together the major portions of the prayer. After the final doxology and "Amen", a server immediately collects the booklets used for the Eucharistic Prayer and places them on a credence table.

331. The concelebrants receive Holy Communion according to several procedures, depending on their number and position in the sanctuary. At a major concelebration in a crowded church, Holy Communion may have to be distributed at various positions in the building—for example, at the back of the church or in chapels. A server should accompany each concelebrant to these positions, especially if visiting clergy are uncertain where to stand to distribute Communion. This server will also lead the priest back to the altar and/or tabernacle. If there are extra chalices, the ablutions may be carried out on the credence table or a side altar, and servers assist.

D. THE CONCLUDING RITE

332. Everything proceeds as above in Mass with the People. Unless there are a great number of concelebrants, unable to be arranged in the sanctuary, it is better for servers and clergy to form up and make the customary reverence together before leaving the sanctuary. This is simpler than at the beginning of Mass, because *only* the principal celebrant and deacon(s) kiss the altar at the conclusion of concelebrated Mass.

E. AFTER MASS

333. Servers help concelebrants to divest and put away those vestments that belong to the sacristy of the church. If the ablutions have been deferred until after Mass, servers assist a deacon or concelebrant at the credence table or side altar as he purifies the vessels and then take them back to the sacristy. Otherwise, all proceeds as for Mass with the People.

3. The Blessing and Sprinkling with Holy Water

334. Water may be blessed and sprinkled over us before the Liturgy of the Word, as a reminder of our Baptism, our sharing in the saving events of the death and Resurrection of the Lord, and as a sign of sorrow for sin and protection

from evil. On all Sundays, and Saturday evening Masses for Sunday, this rite may take the place of the Penitential Rite at the beginning of Mass.

335. The structure of the rite is: (a) introduction to the blessing and invitation to prayer, (b) the prayer of blessing of the water, (c) the blessing and mingling of salt in the holy water, where customary, (d) the sprinkling of celebrant, clergy, servers, and people, (e) the short concluding prayer.

336. *Preparations.* Before Mass, a small table with the vessel of water, and/or the holy-water bucket and sprinkler will be placed near the celebrant's chair. The salt, on a dish, may be on the table. Salt should be used if the water is to be kept for some time and used for the stoups at the doors of the church. If water is to be blessed only for the sprinkling at this particular Mass, the table may not be necessary, and servers could bring the bucket, containing water, the sprinkler, and salt to the celebrant at the chair, holding these before him as required.

337. *The Rite.* After greeting the people at the beginning of Mass, the priest may explain the blessing of water and invite the people to pray. The book bearer is in position at the chair, with the missal or book of the chair open at the rite for the blessing of water. Servers may move the table into position, closer to the chair, or a server may hold the water before the celebrant.

338. Using one of the prayers in the missal, the celebrant blesses the water. If salt is used, he blesses the salt, and a server hands him the dish of salt that he mingles with the holy water in silence. A server gives him the sprinkler. Taking some holy water, he first sprinkles himself and the servers near him. Make the sign of the cross when you are sprinkled. The celebrant is accompanied by a server, carrying the

bucket, as he sprinkles the other servers, clergy, and choir and as he goes through the church, sprinkling the people. If you carry the bucket, hold it firmly, well within the priest's reach so he can place the sprinkler in it. During the sprinkling, an antiphon, set out in the missal, or a psalm or hymn is sung, expressing the meaning of this rite.

339. If a large amount of water has been blessed for later use, a server, the M.C., or the deacon fills the bucket from the larger vessel before the celebrant commences the sprinkling. When the celebrant returns to the chair, at the conclusion of the chant, the bucket and sprinkler are replaced on the table or held by a server, and the priest says the short concluding prayer. The Gloria of the Mass follows. After the Collect, servers remove the table and place it at the side of the sanctuary. The holy water may be left on it, placed on a credence table, or taken at once to the sacristy.

4. Mass without the People

340. The Roman Missal provides a simplified rite of Mass when a congregation is not present, that is, a Mass celebrated by a priest assisted by a server. It is not correct to call this a "private Mass" because every offering of the Holy Sacrifice is a public action of the whole Church.

341. *Preparations.* The server vests as usual. Two candles are lit at the altar, the dust cover is removed, and at least one cloth is spread. The missal is open at the Mass for the day, on its stand, at the left side of the altar, square with the edge of the altar. The chalice and paten, prepared as usual, may be on the altar, at the right side, or on the credence table. The cruets of wine and water, ewer, basin, and towel are on the credence table or, if there is no credence table, on the altar near the chalice. The bell may be on the altar step or at the credence. If there is an ambo, the lectionary should be

there, opened, or on or near the altar if there is no ambo, as may be the case at a side altar or in a small chapel.

342. When the celebrant has vested, bow to the sacristy crucifix and lead him to the altar. Standing at his right side, make the customary reverence, go to a place to the right of the altar, and join in the prayers of the *Introductory Rites*.

343. *The Liturgy of the Word* may take place at the ambo or at the altar. If the priest reads the first reading, you sit. If you read the first reading and responsorial psalm, the priest sits. Stand for the Gospel, making the responses, turned toward the celebrant. If there is a homily, sit. If the Creed is said, stand and say it with the celebrant. If there is a Prayer of the Faithful, you may announce the intentions and make the responses.

344. *The Liturgy of the Eucharist.* If the chalice is on the credence, bring it to the altar, spreading the corporal and setting out the purifier as usual. When the priest stands at the altar, hand him the paten and bread. If the chalice and paten are already on the altar, the priest attends to their preparation himself. Serve the wine and water as usual. Wash his hands as usual. If the bell is at the credence, take it to your place, at the step, at the right side of the altar, where you stand for the Preface of the Eucharistic Prayer. Kneel for the prayer, and ring the bell as usual.

345. Stand for the Lord's Prayer, etc. The celebrant may give you the sign of peace. Kneel while the celebrant prays before Holy Communion, and join in "Lord, I am not worthy. . . ." Come to the center if you receive Holy Communion. Bring the cruets to the altar, and assist the priest in the purification of the vessels, at the right side of the altar. If the chalice was on the credence at the beginning of

Mass, take it back to the credence. If there is a silent prayer after Communion, sit or kneel. Stand for the Prayer after Communion.

346. *The Concluding Rite* consists of the greeting and the final blessing. After the priest has kissed the altar, make the customary reverence with him and lead him back to the sacristy. Return to the altar, extinguish the candles, and bring the sacred vessels, cruets, missal, etc., back to the sacristy as usual.

5.

The Traditional Latin Mass

347. The original versions of the *Roman Missal* are in Latin, which is the universal language of the Church. Since the Second Vatican Council, most public Masses are celebrated in the "vernacular", the language of the people, which for us is English. But the popes have made it clear that Latin is to be used for various occasions, as a reminder of the universal community of the whole Church. Servers should be able to recite or sing the people's parts in Latin.

348. In 2007, Pope Benedict XVI published *Summorum Pontificum*, which restored the wide use of the traditional Latin Mass. He defined two forms of the Mass: the *Ordinary Form*, in the *Missale Romanum* authorized by Saint Paul VI in 1970, in light of the reforms of the Second Vatican Council. The previous chapter of this book is devoted to serving this Ordinary Form. Then he defined the *Extraordinary Form*, provided in the *Missale Romanum* authorized by Saint John XXIII in 1962. The original edition was authorized by Saint Pius V in 1570 and prepared in light of the reforms of the Council of Trent. In this book, the Extraordinary Form is described as the "traditional Latin Mass".

Pronouncing Latin

349. Whatever form is used when Mass is celebrated in Latin, the server will need a booklet to read the responses. The only problem is how to pronounce Latin correctly. There are some easy rules, and with practice it is not difficult to pronounce Latin. Because we are used to Mass in English, it is also easy to get to know the meaning of the basic words and phrases.

"a"   is always "a"—as in "ah!"

"e"   is either a short "e", as in "get", or a longer "e"— "ay", as in "they", especially at the end of a word like *Domine*, meaning "O Lord . . .".

"i"   is always a short "i" as in "pin".

"o"   is either a short "o", as in "ox", or a longer "o"— "oh", especially when it comes at the end of a word, *Deo*, meaning "to God".

"u"   is usually a short "u", as in "push".

"r"   is rolled on the tongue, as in Spanish or Italian.

"ae"   is always as in "bay".

"c"   is usually "ch", as in "charge", but becomes a hard "c", as in "cat", when it is a double "c", *peccata*, meaning "sins", or when it comes after a vowel combination, such as in *saecula*.

350. *Basic Latin responses* should be known by heart. For example —*Dominus vobiscum* (The Lord be with you)—*Et cum spiritu tuo* (And with your spirit)—*Verbum Domini* (The word of the Lord)—*Deo gratias* (Thanks be to God), but note that the "t" sounds like an "s" with a "t" before it, "grahtsiahs". The "Lord have mercy" in Greek, *Kyrie eleison*, is "keereeay elayeeson"; *Christe eleison* is "kreestay elayeeson".

351. The Gospel responses: "Glory to you, O Lord", *Gloria tibi, Domine*, and "Praise to you, Lord Jesus Christ", *Laus tibi, Christe*, but note that *Laus* sounds like "house".

352. At the Preparation of the Gifts: "Blessed be God for ever", *Benedictus Deus in saecula,* and the more complicated response to "Pray brethren . . .", *Orate fratres. . . . Patrem omnipotentem—Suscipiat Dominus sacrificium de manibus tuis ad laudem et gloriam nominis sui, ad utilitatem quoque nostram totiusque Ecclesiae suae sanctae.*

353. At the Preface: *Sursum corda* (Lift up your hearts)—*Habemus ad Dominum* (We lift them up to the Lord)—*Gratias agamus Domino Deo nostro* (Let us give thanks to the Lord our God) —*Dignum et iustum est* (It is right and just).

354. The response to the prayer *"Libera nos . . ."—Quia tuum est regnum, et potestas, et gloria in saecula* (For the kingdom, the power, and the glory are yours, now and forever).

355. The dismissal: *Ite, missa est* (Go forth, the Mass is ended). —*Deo gratias.*

Serving at Mass

1. Low Mass

356. One server usually assists at Low Mass. The celebrant faces "east", that is, by facing the altar, he leads the people, standing with them in prayer. As we face it, the left side of the altar is called the *Gospel side*: the right side is called *the Epistle side*. There is a mat or cushion on each side where the server kneels at various times during the Mass. The top step at the altar is called the footpace, or *predella.* The area in front of the steps is the pavement.

357. After vesting, check that the altar is prepared: dust cover removed, two candles lit, missal stand on the Epistle side of the altar, square with the edge, the three altar cards or charts set up, cruets of wine and water, ewer, basin and towel

on the credence table, bell on the lowest step, Epistle side. You will need a people's missal or booklet to make the responses. The chalice and paten with bread (covered with the burse and veil) and the missal marked for the Mass are prepared in the sacristy.

358. After he has vested, the celebrant puts on his biretta and takes up the veiled chalice and paten. Take the missal in both hands, holding it underneath, resting on your chest. With the priest, bow to the sacristy cross and lead the way to the altar, pausing to offer some drops of holy water to him from the stoup at the sacristy door.

359. On arriving at the altar, take the biretta from the celebrant and genuflect as he genuflects or bows. Place the biretta on the credence table or chair, and then set the missal on its stand, closed, with the spine of the book on the right side of the stand. Return to the center, genuflect, and wait there while the celebrant places the chalice on the altar and opens the missal. When he comes to the center of the pavement, kneel on his left and answer the Prayers at the Foot of the Altar, striking your breast three times at "*mea culpa* . . ." in the Confiteor.

360. *Mass of the Catechumens.* As the celebrant goes up to the altar, stand, go to your kneeling mat on the Gospel side, and kneel and respond to *Kyrie eleison*. After the Collect, watch while he reads the Epistle. As soon as he lowers his right hand to the altar (as a signal), say *Deo gratias*, go to the center, genuflect, and ascend to the missal at the Epistle side. As the celebrant goes to the center, take the missal on its stand, descend the steps to the center, genuflect, ascend the steps, and place the missal and stand on the Gospel side of the altar, toward the end of the altar and at an angle. Wait there as the celebrant begins the Gospel, making the signs of the cross on forehead, lips, and breast, then return to the

center, genuflect, and stand at your mat on the Epistle side facing him while he reads the Gospel. Say *Laus tibi Christe* at the end. At a public Mass, a sermon may follow and you go to your seat.

361. *Mass of the Faithful.* Return to your place on the Epistle side, and kneel for the Creed, if said, bow as the celebrant genuflects at *"et incarnatus est. . . ."* Respond to *Dominus vobiscum*, and go to the credence table as soon as the celebrant removes the chalice veil to commence the Offertory prayers.

362. Take the wine cruet in your right hand, the water in your left. Ascend the side steps, and wait until he brings the chalice to you, then bow and present the wine with your right hand (first kissing the cruet), transfer the water to your right hand, receive back the wine and present the water to him (first kissing the cruet). Transfer the wine cruet back to your right hand. Receive back the water cruet, bow, and take the cruets to the table. For the Lavabo, drape the unfolded towel over your left arm and take the ewer in your right hand and basin in your left. Ascend the steps, bow, and pour water over the celebrant's hands, then present the towel so that he can dry his hands. Receive it back on your arm, bow again, and take the ewer and basin to the credence. Go to your mat on the Epistle side and kneel, ready to respond to *"Orate fratres. . . ."*

363. Remain kneeling for the Secret Prayer and the Preface, making the responses. As the celebrant says *"Sanctus, sanctus, sanctus"*, ring the bell three times in harmony with these words. Then he begins the Canon. Watch carefully until he extends his hands over the chalice and paten at *"Hanc igitur"* and ring the bell once. As the Consecration draws near, take the bell, go to the center, genuflect, ascend the steps, and kneel behind him on his right, bowing reverently as he consecrates the bread. Ring the bell once as he genuflects,

then raise the end of his chasuble with your left hand, and with your right hand ring the bell again as he elevates the Host. Let go of the chasuble, and ring the bell a third time as he genuflects. Bow reverently as he consecrates the wine. Ring the bell once as he genuflects, then raise the end of his chasuble with your left hand, and with your right hand ring the bell again as he elevates the chalice. Let go of the chasuble, and ring the bell a third time as he genuflects. Stand, go to the center, genuflect, and return to your place with the bell. Kneeling, make the responses at the end of the Canon, for the Lord's Prayer, and for the prayers that follow.

364. Before he receives Communion, the celebrant holds the broken Host over the paten and, bowing, says three times, *"Domine, non sum dignus."* Ring the bell three times in harmony with these words. After he has received Communion, he may give Communion to you and to the people. If so, he turns and holds a Host over the paten or ciborium saying, *"Ecce, Agnus Dei. . . ."* You may join in *"Domine non sum dignus"* three times. If you are to receive Communion, take the Communion plate from the credence, come to the center, genuflect, and kneel at the center on the step below the priest's step while he places the Host onto your tongue. Stand and return to your place, unless you assist him at the altar rail by holding the Communion plate under the chin of people receiving our Lord, then hand him the plate at the end of Communion.

365. Go to the credence table, and take the cruets of wine and water. As the celebrant extends the chalice to you with his right hand, pour some wine into it. Wait while he consumes this first ablution. When he comes to the Epistle side, pour a little wine and a larger quantity of water over his fingers, bow, and take the cruets back to the credence table. Go to the center, genuflect, ascend the side steps on the Gospel

side, take the missal and stand, come down to the center, genuflect, and bring them up to the Epistle side, setting the stand square with the edge of the altar. Go to the center, genuflect, go to your mat on the Gospel side, and kneel for the final prayers of the Mass, making the responses to "*Dominus vobiscum*", "*Ite missa est*", and the blessing. Stand as he reads the Last Gospel from the altar card, make the required responses, and genuflect as he genuflects, saying "*Deo gratias*" at the end. Go to the credence or chair and get the biretta, then take the closed missal from its stand and come to the center. Genuflect with the celebrant, hand him his biretta, and precede him to the sacristy, carrying the missal. Bow to the sacristy cross and assist as usual after Mass.

2. *Low Mass with Two Servers*

366. Two servers may assist at Low Mass, dividing the duties of one server between them. Server 1 is based at the Epistle side; server 2 is based at the Gospel side.

367. On arriving at the altar, server 1 takes the biretta. After the *Epistle*, server 2 transfers the missal. At the *Offertory*, server 1 presents the wine and server 2 presents the water. At the *Lavabo*, server 1 presents the towel, and server 2 pours the water. At the *Sanctus*, server 1 rings the bell. At the *Hanc igitur*, server 1 rings the bell. At the *elevations*, server 1 raises the chasuble and rings the bell. Server 2 raises the chasuble with server 1. At the *ablutions*, server 1 pours the wine, and server 2 pours the water. At the transfer of the missal, server 2 transfers the missal, and server 1 transfers the chalice veil, meeting together and genuflecting at the center of the pavement before placing the missal on the Epistle side and the veil on the Gospel side. During the Last Gospel, server 1 gets the biretta and hands it to the priest once all have genuflected.

3. Solemn High Mass

368. The detailed description of Solemn Mass may be found in Adrian Fortescue, J. B. O'Connell, and Alcuin Reid, O.S.B., *Ceremonies of the Roman Rite Described* (London and New York: Burns & Oates, 2009). What follows is a general guide.

369. The priest celebrant is assisted by a deacon and a subdeacon. An M.C. supervises the ceremonial. The two candle bearers are called "acolytes". The thurifer may be accompanied by a boat bearer. Two, four, or six servers act as torch bearers. On major occasions, it may be the local custom for a cross bearer or crucifer to lead the procession to and from the altar, flanked by the acolytes, but this is normally reserved for when Solemn Mass is celebrated by a bishop.

370. The usual preparations are made: six candles are lit, the altar cards set up, the missal on its stand on the Epistle side of the altar, square with the edge and open at the Introit of the Mass. On the covered credence table are prepared: the veiled chalice and paten with a priest's host, purifier, pall, corporal in the burse, with cruets for wine and water, a ciborium containing people's hosts, if needed. The subdeacon's humeral veil covers the vessels. A ewer and basin are provided with a towel. The bell may be on the table or on a step nearby. Toward the back of the table, space on each side is needed for the acolytes' candles. On the right side of the pavement of the sanctuary, three seats, the sedilia, are provided for the celebrant, deacon, and subdeacon.

371. On arriving at the pavement, all genuflect. The acolytes place their candles on the credence, and, with the thurifer, they are based there during Mass. All kneel as the celebrant, deacon, subdeacon, and M.C. say the Prayers at the Foot of the Altar. Incense is prepared and blessed at the altar before the celebrant incenses it. During Mass, the deacon and subdeacon take positions behind the celebrant, beside him, or on each side of him, according to the action or prayer.

372. The Epistle is intoned by the subdeacon facing the altar on the pavement on the Epistle side. The choir sings the Gradual or Tract. On the pavement on the Gospel side, the Gospel is sung by the deacon from the Book of the Gospels. The subdeacon holds the book, the M.C., acolytes, and thurifer assist. A sermon may follow. At the center of the altar, the celebrant intones the Creed, which is sung on prescribed days; all genuflect at *"et incarnatus est"*.

373. The Offertory begins when the subdeacon brings the chalice and paten to the altar. Assisted by the deacon, the celebrant offers the bread and wine and incenses the offerings, cross, and altar. Then he is incensed, followed by the deacon and subdeacon, M.C., and servers, (choir), and the people. After the Secret Prayer, the celebrant chants the Preface, the choir sings the Sanctus, the bell is rung as at Low Mass, and the torch bearers enter and arrange themselves on the pavement. The celebrant commences the prayers of the Canon in very quiet voice, and the bell is rung at *"Hanc igitur"*. The deacon raises his chasuble at the elevations, an acolyte rings the bell, and the thurifer offers incense. The Pax, sign of peace, is given from the altar, starting with the celebrant and deacon. It is then passed along among the servers and choir.

374. Communion proceeds in much the same way as at Low Mass. An acolyte rings the bell three times at *"Domine, non sum dignus"*. After he has received Communion, the celebrant gives Communion to the deacon, subdeacon, and servers, who first join in *"Domine non sum dignus"* three times. Servers come to the center in two's, genuflect, and

kneel on the step below the footpace to receive Communion. They assist the celebrant, deacon, and other clergy at the altar rail by holding the Communion plate.

375. After the ablutions and Prayer after Communion, the deacon sings the Dismissal "*Ite missa est*". The celebrant gives the blessing and goes to the Gospel side of the altar to read the Last Gospel as at Low Mass. Directed by the M.C., all form up on the pavement, genuflect, and return in procession to the sacristy.

4. Sung Mass

376. When a deacon and subdeacon are not available, a simplified version of Solemn Mass may be celebrated. The major differences are: the humeral veil is not used, so the paten remains on the altar, the priest chants the Gospel at the altar with the M.C., acolytes and thurifer standing near him. Throughout a "simple High Mass", the M.C. plays a key role standing at the altar near the missal, assisting the celebrant.

5. The Asperges Ceremony

377. In the traditional rite, the sprinkling with holy water is a separate ceremony before the main Mass begins on Sundays. It is known as the *Asperges*, from the first word of the Latin antiphon that is sung while holy water is sprinkled over the people: "*Sprinkle me with hyssop, O Lord, and I shall be cleansed; wash me and I shall be whiter than snow.*" The *Asperges Ceremony* is set out in *Ceremonies of the Roman Rite Described* (pp. 109–11). The holy water has already been blessed privately, so it is brought to the sanctuary in the procession. The celebrant wears a cope, but not the chasuble and maniple, because this is not part of the Mass. Before a Solemn Mass, he is assisted by a deacon, subdeacon, and an M.C.

6.

The Sacraments

378. The seven sacraments are contained within the Liturgy of the Church, as the *Catechism of the Catholic Church* (nos. 1077–1108) teaches. Each sacramental rite may be incorporated in the Mass or a Liturgy of the Word, even the Anointing of the Sick. Penance may be incorporated in a Liturgy of the Word, but in practice Penance usually takes a private form. Altar servers play their part in the public celebration of the sacraments as assisting "ministers".

379. For this chapter, the five sacraments selected are those usually celebrated by a priest in a parish: (1) *Baptism*; (2) *Holy Eucharist*; (3) *Penance and Reconciliation*; (4) *Matrimony*; (5) *Anointing of the Sick*. The other two sacraments, *Confirmation* and *Holy Orders*, are set out in chapter eleven, *Serving the Bishop*, because the bishop celebrates these sacraments.

What Is a Sacrament?

380. In assisting in the celebration of sacraments, we remember that these are the chosen ways Jesus Christ comes to us here and now, working for our salvation by bringing us his free gift of grace. Each sacrament is a human action charged with divine power, or, more than that, a divine act clothed in the words and actions of human beings. We see the human action, a visible sign: water, oil, bread, wine, human gestures, and we hear words. We cannot see the presence of the Lord, using the visible sign, water, and word for Bap-

118

tism, bread and wine as the matter to become the Eucharist, oil and action and word for the Anointing of the Sick.

381. In these holy signs, Jesus Christ gives us *grace*, the presence and work of the Holy Spirit. In faith, we welcome his grace, and in turn the sacraments nourish and strengthen our faith. This is why the server always treats the sacraments with reverence and respect. You are able to show this in the way you handle any of the objects or material used for a sacrament and in the way you concentrate on the rite, knowing what comes next, ready to assist when needed. But before describing the duties of servers when each sacrament is celebrated, it is necessary to understand what the sacrament means, what God is doing for us in these sacred actions, these means of grace.

Baptism

382. You were baptized. In this first *Sacrament of Christian Initiation*, God adopted you as his son or daughter. To become his son or daughter, you were born again, freed, and cleansed from Original Sin, raised to God's new life of sanctifying grace. By water and the Holy Spirit, you were "born again" into the family of God, becoming a member of the Church. Through Baptism, you have access to God, the right and the power to share in the worship and sacraments of his Church by the permanent effect or *character*. You are filled with the goodness of God, justified, and the good deeds you perform are pleasing to God and helpful on your way forward to heaven. The gift of faith given in Baptism gradually grows in us. If you are true to these great gifts of Baptism, one day you will live with God forever.

383. The *matter* of Baptism is water, which should be blessed. The candidate is immersed or washed while the minister says the *form* of Baptism, which in the Roman Rite is "N, I baptize you in the name of the Father, and of the Son, and of the Holy Spirit." The *minister* of Baptism is a bishop, priest, or deacon, or, in an emergency, any person who knows how to baptize.

384. Baptism is the first part of *Christian Initiation*, followed by Confirmation and the Holy Eucharist. In practice in our parishes, infant Baptism is the typical beginning of Initiation. Therefore, infant Baptism is set out first for the convenience of servers.

1. The Rite of Baptism of Children

385. Children may be baptized either during Mass or in a rite separate from Mass. There are four steps in the rite: (1) *Reception of the Children (or Child)*; (2) *Liturgy of the Word*; (3) *Celebration of the Sacrament*; (4) *Concluding Rite*. When Baptism is celebrated during Mass, the Reception of the Children takes the place of the Greeting and Penitential Rite. After the Liturgy of the Word, the rite of Baptism continues, with the Celebration of the Sacrament and the minor ceremonies. The Liturgy of the Eucharist follows the Baptism, and at the conclusion of Mass, the priest may use one of the final blessings from the rite of Baptism.

386. *1. Reception of the Children*. The celebrant welcomes the children in a public ceremony, with members of the community present. He questions the parents, and godparents as to their responsibilities toward the children. The celebrant, parents, and godparents make the *sign of the cross* as a sign of welcome and the claim of Christ on this child.

387. *2. Liturgy of the Word*. If celebrated during Mass, the Sunday readings are usually followed, otherwise a reading or readings from the rite of Baptism, chosen to explain the meaning and power of the sacrament. In a homily, the celebrant helps those present to realize what is happening, the beginning of a new life of faith, a life to be lived in the community of God's People.

388. The *Intercessions* ask God to be with the children and their families. This prayer concludes with invocation of the saints, including the names of the saints chosen for these children. In the *Prayer of Exorcism*, the priest claims the children for Christ, who delivers us from the power of Satan. This is underlined in the *Anointing before Baptism* with the Oil of Catechumens, the oil of those about to be initiated. Just as athletes were anointed with oil in ancient times before a race or contest, so the sign of strength is given before the struggle of Christian life begins.

389. *3. Celebration of the Sacrament.* The celebrant blesses the water for each celebration of Baptism, except during the Easter season, when the water blessed at the Easter Vigil is used. The beautiful prayers of blessing bring together the many signs and symbols of Baptism in the Bible, leading to the cleansing quality of water and the true cleansing from sin by baptismal washing.

390. In the *Renunciation of Sin and Profession of Faith*, the parents and godparents speak on behalf of the children, first rejecting Satan and his influence and, then, accepting the faith into which the children are to be baptized, the faith that they receive as God's gift. Having stated their own wish that these children should be baptized, the parents and godparents present the children for the *Baptism*. Using the form of words, the celebrant may either immerse the child in the water or pour water on the head of child. The font may be either a large bowl or a pool with still or running water.

391. Four ceremonies follow the Baptism. The *Anointing with Chrism* shows us that, through Baptism, the Christian becomes a member of "a chosen race, a royal priesthood, a holy nation, God's own people" (1 Pet 2:9). The *Clothing with the White Garment* reminds us of the dignity of Christian life, for we are clothed with the risen Christ, washed clean in his Blood. "For as many of you as were baptized into Christ have put on Christ" (Gal 3:27). The giving of the *Lighted Candle*, kindled from the Paschal candle, is a sign of the light of faith, kindled from the risen Christ, the faith of the "children of the light". The *Ephphetha* (meaning "be opened") is a touching of the mouth and ears of each child who will receive the faith and proclaim the faith and by listening and speaking. This reenacts Christ healing the man unable to hear or speak recorded in Mark 7:32–35.

392. *Concluding Rite.* In the *Procession to the Altar*, the parents and godparents bring their children to the center of the Eucharistic community, where one day these children will be nourished by the Blessed Eucharist. The *Lord's Prayer* reminds all present of the basic duty of Christian prayer, as they thank God the Father for adopting these children in Baptism. The *Blessings* are bestowed first on the mother and father of each child and then on the whole community that has shared in the celebration of Baptism.

2. Serving Baptism of Children

393. Because Baptism is meant to be a *public* celebration, servers should assist the priest or deacon who administers the sacrament. When Baptism is given during Mass, they assist the priest celebrant, but servers should also be rostered for public celebration of Baptism outside Mass—for example, at a regular time on a Sunday. At least two servers should assist at Baptism, outside or during Mass. One server holds the book, so that the celebrant may keep his hands free for actions such as anointing. The other server brings objects used in the ceremonies to the celebrant, parents, and god-parents. If a deacon or instituted acolyte assists, he may take over certain parts of the rite itself. To enrich the celebration with what is called "exterior solemnity", that is, to make it more festive, a cross bearer and two candle bearers may also assist, especially when there is singing with the processions as advised in the ritual. Incense may be used at a Mass during which Baptism is celebrated, but it is not used during a celebration of Baptism outside Mass.

394. In describing the rites of Baptism, (A) denotes *Baptism outside Mass*; (B) denotes *Baptism during Mass*.

395. *Preparations*. Having vested, servers check that everything is ready for Baptism.

396. *The altar*: candles lit, (B) ready for Mass.

397. *The ambo*: (A) lectionary open at readings for Baptism, unless the ritual is to be placed on the ambo because it contains these texts; (B) lectionary open for readings for Baptismal Mass or Mass of the Day, unless a Book of the Gospels is carried in.

398. *The font*: (A) and (B), the cover removed, the bowl filled with clean water (unless running water is used), a vessel for pouring water (unless the babies are to be immersed), towels, Sacred Chrism in an oil stock, cotton balls (if required), baptismal candles, and baptismal robes (unless it has been arranged for the families to supply them). These objects may best be set out on a covered table near the font. The Paschal candle, lit, should be near the font, in its stand or bracket. *Note*: During the Easter season, the font is to be filled only with the water blessed at the Vigil, usually

kept in a vessel in the sacristy or baptistery (the chapel set aside in some churches for the font). During this season, the Paschal candle is set up near the ambo. Therefore, if the ambo is some distance from the font, the candle will either be brought to the font for the ceremony of Baptism (by a server during the procession to the font) or placed at the font before the whole celebration and replaced at the ambo after the celebration.

399. *The credence table*: (A) and (B), Oil of Catechumens, cotton balls (if required).

400. *The sacristy*: the ritual (unless the celebrant prefers to have this book ready near the chair), vestments, for the celebrant, priest, or deacon, (A) alb or soutane and surplice, stole, and cope, white or a festive color; (B) alb, stole, chasuble; and for an assisting deacon, (A) alb, stole, dalmatic if available; or soutane, surplice and stole; (B) alb, stole, dalmatic if available.

401. The celebrant takes care of the baptismal register and certificates, either in the sacristy or some other place. Also in the sacristy, if to be used, (A) and (B) processional cross and candles and, for (B), any other requirements for Mass.

402. *Entrance Procession*. Having bowed to the sacristy cross, servers and celebrant proceed either to the entrance of the church or to the sanctuary. The celebrant may receive the children either at the church door, at the entrance to the sanctuary, or at the chair. In (B), it will be more usual to commence Mass at the chair or entrance to the sanctuary, the *Reception of the Children* taking the place of the Penitential Rite.

403. *Reception of the Children*. For (A) and (B), the book bearer holds the ritual during the questions. Unless a deacon stands

on the celebrant's right, the other server may take this position, but slightly back from the celebrant. If the children are received at the church door, after they have been signed with the cross, there is a procession to the sanctuary, or (A) another area where the Liturgy of the Word takes place. The order of procession: cross and candles (if used), servers (deacon or acolyte), celebrant, parents with children, godparents, usually arranged in family groups.

404. *Liturgy of the Word.* For (A), a reading or readings from the ambo in the sanctuary or at a lectern in the baptismal area or chapel. Candles may be used for the Gospel, as at Mass. For (B), the rite of Mass continues with the Gloria (if prescribed), the Collect, readings for the Mass of the Sunday or Baptism, with the customary ceremonies of Mass.

405. The *homily* follows for (A) and (B). The book bearer attends the celebrant with the ritual for the *Intercessions* and invocation of saints. In (B), the Creed is omitted, because of the later baptismal profession of faith, and other petitions for the Church and world are added to the *Intercessions*, before the invocation of saints. A reader may lead the intentions in (A) and (B), but not the invocation of saints.

406. The book bearer holds the ritual during the *Prayer of Exorcism*, for which either the celebrant approaches the children or they are brought before him at the chair. During the exorcism, the other server brings the Oil of Catechumens from the credence table, or other convenient place, to the celebrant (or deacon or acolyte, if assisting). If a deacon or acolyte is not assisting, the server unscrews the top of the stock, if necessary, before handing it to the celebrant for the *Anointing before Baptism*. The server may offer the celebrant cotton balls or give this to the deacon or acolyte to wipe away extra oil. After the anointing, the server receives

the oil stock, bows, replaces the cap, if necessary, receives cotton balls, if used, and takes the oil back to the credence.

407. *Celebration of the Sacrament.* For (A) and (B), the *procession to the font* depends on the design of the church. If there is a separate baptistery or the font is located at some reasonable distance from the place where the preceding ceremonies were celebrated, then the procession may be led by cross and candles (and/or Paschal candle during the Easter season). The same order of procession is followed as set out for the *Reception of the Children.* The congregation may join in this procession to a baptistery if they cannot see the Baptism from their places in the seats. However, if the font is in the same area as the sanctuary, only the servers and celebrant may need to go to the font, family groups remaining in the front seats. Singing should accompany the procession.

408. At the font, the book bearer holds the ritual while the celebrant blesses the water. The other server may stand near the table, ready to assist at the ceremonies that follow. An assisting deacon or acolyte stands on the celebrant's right. For the *Renunciation of Sin and Profession of Faith*, the celebrant either remains at the font or approaches the family groups, the book bearer attending as usual.

409. For the *Baptism*, the celebrant invites each family group to the font. As they begin to approach, the other server hands the celebrant the pouring vessel, unless Baptism is by immersion. The book bearer steps back after the question, "Is it your will . . . with you?" The other server hands a towel to the celebrant (or assisting deacon or acolyte), receiving it back after the children have been dried, with the usual bow. At the conclusion of the Baptisms, the server replaces the pouring vessel, along with used towels, on the table. Unless the deacon attends to it, the server unscrews the Chrism stock and reverently hands it to the celebrant for the *Anoint-*

ing with Chrism. If cotton balls are used, the server takes it from the table, ready to hand it to the celebrant (or deacon or acolyte). The book bearer attends with the ritual.

410. The celebrant goes to each child, held by the mother, for the anointing. If there are many children to be anointed, other priests or deacons present may anoint some of the children. The other server receives the Chrism, and cotton balls if used, bows, replaces it on the table, also screwing the lid onto the stock.

411. For the *Clothing with the White Garment*, the book bearer attends during the short address to the children, stepping back if the celebrant himself places the garments on the children. The other server hands each garment to the celebrant (or deacon or acolyte), taken from the table, or the godparents clothe the children, either with these white garments or with those provided by the family.

412. As each child is clothed, the other server brings the baptismal candles from the table, giving a candle to each father (or family representative), unless the fathers have brought family candles to the church. The celebrant (and deacon or acolyte) with the book bearer goes to the Paschal candle at its stand near the font. He takes the candle in his hand or lifts it from the stand and offers the flame of faith to the fathers, who light the baptismal candles. The book bearer steps forward as the celebrant reads the explanation of the candle to the family groups.

413. If the *Ephphetha* is to follow, either the mothers bring the children to the celebrant, or the celebrant goes to each family group for the touching of the ears and mouth. The book bearer attends. If there are a large number of children, the celebrant need only read the formula, omitting the touching of the ears and mouth.

414. During the ceremonies of the *Celebration of the Sacrament* in a baptistery, if the cross and candles led the procession, the cross bearer and candle bearers may stand behind the font, if there is room, or to one side, in a line facing the font, bearing the cross and candles. If this is thought to be tiring, the cross and candles should be placed in a suitable position until needed for the procession to the altar at the conclusion of baptistery rites.

415. *Concluding Rite.* In (A), this follows immediately, the procession returns to the sanctuary, or the servers and celebrant lead the families from the font area to the center of the sanctuary. The fathers carry the lighted candles. In (B), after the baptismal ceremonies, the fathers extinguish the candles and Mass continues in the usual way with the Preparation of the Gifts. According to local custom, families may be involved in the Procession of the Gifts. The *Concluding Rite* may replace the blessing at the end of Mass.

416. For (A) and (B), the book bearer attends with the ritual as the celebrant stands in front of the altar. The other server may stand to his right, unless the deacon or acolyte assists. For (B), the other server first lights the candles held by the fathers, if the celebrant chooses to bless the parents at the conclusion of the Mass. For (A) and (B), servers and celebrant form up as usual before the altar, make the customary reverence, and return to the sacristy.

417. After the Baptism, the celebrant registers each child, usually in the sacristy. Servers bring everything used for the ceremonies back to the sacristy, especially collecting baptismal garments if these belong to the parish. Make sure that the font is covered, that the Paschal candle has been extinguished, baptismal booklets collected, microphones off, baptismal register not left out if the children were registered in the church, and, for (B), that the usual procedures after Mass have been completed. Used baptismal water is either poured into the font drain or the sacrarium in the sacristy.

3. Christian Initiation of Adults

418. An important part of the liturgy is the Rite of Christian Initiation of Adults, as developed in the first centuries of the Church. Adults and older children who have not been baptized prepare for Baptism by passing through a series of stages leading to Baptism, Confirmation, and first Eucharist, the three sacraments of Christian Initiation, celebrated during the Easter Vigil.

419. The way in which these stages of initiation are celebrated depends on the local culture of the people. In various situations, the steps are reduced and adapted, even delayed over a long period of time, so that the catechumens can be properly instructed. The role of servers is the same as in celebrations of Infant Baptism, adapted to the rites that take place at separate times marking the stages or steps of adult initiation.

420. *Rite of Acceptance into the Order of Catechumens.* Those who wish to become Christians are received as *catechumens*, people learning about the faith, under instruction. They are welcomed; they express a first promise (renounce pagan worship, if necessary); they are signed with the cross (given a new Christian name, if necessary) and led into the church for a celebration of the Liturgy of the Word. A Mass may follow. You will see that this is the full form of what is stage 1, *Reception of the Children*, in the rite of Infant Baptism, and with most of stage 2, *Liturgy of the Word*, added to explain and celebrate the occasion. Therefore, you serve in the same way as these steps in the rites explained above. One point to note: after the homily, the celebrant may present the new catechumens with books of the Gospels, perhaps a New Testament, and with crucifixes. The second server will bring these to the celebrant immediately after the homily.

421. *Rite of Sending for Enrollment* and *Rite of Election or Enrollment of Names*. These rites mark the point when the catechumens have finally decided to become full members of the Church. After the first rite of becoming a catechumen, they have received instruction, passed through various minor rites of blessing and exorcism, leading to the time of their enrollment in the Church, celebrated at the beginning of Lent. Their chosen godparents appear for the first time in these rites, which take place usually during a Sunday Mass. The book bearer attends the celebrant, who may lead the rite from the chair or in front of the altar, after the homily.

422. As the "elect", the catechumens keep Lent as a period of purification and enlightenment or illumination, leading to the sacraments. There may be three *Scrutinies*: (1) on the Third Sunday of Lent, (2) on the Fourth Sunday, (3) on the Fifth Sunday. The scrutinies are rites of exorcism and prayer to purify and strengthen the elect, who come before the celebrant after the homily, either at the chair or in front of the altar, the book bearer attending as usual with the ritual.

423. After the scrutinies (or, if appropriate, even before Lent), these rites are celebrated: receiving the Creed and the Lord's Prayer, reciting the Creed, the rite of *Ephphetha*, the opening of ears and mouth as in the infants' rite, a rite of choosing a Christian name, if necessary, exorcisms, and finally *the anointing with the Oil of Catechumens*, if this is not to take place just before the Baptism itself, during the Easter Vigil. If these rites are celebrated during Mass, perhaps in Holy Week, servers assist after the homily. The sec-

ond server brings the oil from the credence table, as in the infants' rite.

424. *Celebration of the Sacraments of Initiation.* The final step is Baptism, Confirmation, and the Eucharist, in the context of the Easter Vigil ceremonies. As described in chapter 10, "Holy Week", the candidates and godparents come to the font before or during the Litany of the Saints. The positions of servers are set out in chapter 10, for the Baptism of adults or infants during the "Easter Vigil in the Holy Night". The book bearer and another server or deacon or acolyte assist in virtually the same way as for the Baptism of Children. However, when adults are initiated, Baptism is followed by the Sacrament of Confirmation, celebrated usually in the sanctuary by the bishop or priest. In that situation, the Chrism will be on the credence ready for Confirmation. In the first Mass of Easter, these new Christians, who have died and risen with Christ, filled with the Holy Spirit, receive the Body and Blood of the Lord for the first time.

4. A Simple Rite of Adult Initiation

425. For various reasons, the long process of initiation may not be suitable for some wishing to become Christians as members of the Catholic Church. All the above steps can be celebrated in one rite, in a form almost identical to the Baptism of Children, usually during a Mass. This rite is served in the same way as (B) or (A) for the Baptism of Children, but the godparents are given the baptismal candles, which they light from the Paschal candle and then give to the newly baptized. The Chrism will be on the credence table for the Confirmation that follows Baptism, usually in front of the altar. The server (or deacon or acolyte) brings it to the celebrant.

426. The adult rites may also be adapted for children who are old enough to take instruction and speak for themselves. Servers assist in the same way as for the Baptism of infants or adults.

5. The Reception of a Baptized Christian

427. It often happens that God calls members of the separated Churches and communities into full membership of the Catholic Church. Because they have been baptized already, these Christians are reconciled to the Catholic Church without Baptism, but through an act of faith, Confirmation, and the Eucharist. They go to confession before the rite of reception because the Sacrament of Penance renews the effects of Baptism. In a case when Baptism is doubtful, a conditional Baptism is first given privately.

428. Even if the candidate chooses to be received privately, at least two servers should assist in the ceremony and serve the Mass. The candidate may choose to be received during a public Mass.

429. The rite takes place after the homily. The book bearer attends with the ritual, either before the altar or at the chair. The candidate is called forward, welcomed, and invited to make a public profession of faith, the Nicene Creed, said by all, to which the candidate adds a short expression of Catholic faith. The priest then receives the candidate into the Church, with a laying on of hands, unless Confirmation follows. For Confirmation, a server (or deacon or acolyte) brings the Chrism from the credence table, taking it back to the credence after the anointing. After the new Catholic has been welcomed by the priest, Mass continues with the Prayer of the Faithful. The sponsor and other members of the community present, including the servers, may welcome the new Catholic after the Prayer of the Faithful, in which case the sign of peace is omitted from the Mass. The new Catholic may receive Holy Communion under both kinds.

The Eucharist outside Mass

430. You receive Jesus Christ in the Eucharist. In Holy Communion, you are united with God in the most wonderful way possible in this world. You are united with other Christians to be the community of the Church. Jesus Christ nourishes us with his Body and Blood, because he is really, truly, and substantially present under the appearances of bread and wine. As the true "Bread of Life", we are joined to him, offering himself to the Father, strengthening us to live as Christians day by day, feeding us with supernatural Food for eternal life in heaven. The Eucharist is the third *Sacrament of Christian Initiation.*

431. The *matter* of the Eucharist is wheat bread and grape wine. In our Roman Rite, the bread is unleavened, made without yeast. The *form* of the Eucharist is found in the essential words of Consecration: "This is my body . . . this is the Chalice of my blood. . . ." The *minister* of the Eucharist is a bishop or priest, who alone may consecrate the Eucharist as well as give Holy Communion. A deacon may give Holy Communion as may an instituted acolyte or an extraordinary minister, a lay person licensed to give Holy Communion when needed.

432. The Church reserves the Blessed Sacrament in a tabernacle for two purposes: (1) so that those unable to come to Mass may receive Holy Communion from the reserved Sacrament, and (2) so that we may all come to adore our Lord really present in our churches in the Sacrament of his love. Two liturgical practices reflect the purpose of the reserved

Sacrament: (a) *Holy Communion outside the time of Mass*, (b) *public adoration*, known as exposition and Benediction.

1. Holy Communion outside Mass

433. People may not be able to come to Mass, or they may be in a place where Mass can only be offered now and again. The clergy arrange for a suitable time when the people can gather for a rite of Holy Communion and receive Hosts reserved in the tabernacle from an authorized minister of the Eucharist.

434. Even when they receive Communion in these ways outside Mass, the faithful are united with the Sacrifice of the altar. They share in the sacred banquet with all the graces and blessings of Holy Communion, just as if they were receiving in the normal way, during Mass.

435. Communion may be given outside Mass on any day and at any hour, according to pastoral needs. For servers, two rites are described: (A) *Holy Communion outside Mass*, in a church or chapel, at which servers should assist, (B) *Communion of the Sick*, at which servers are not usually present.

436. *Preparations.* Having vested, servers check that everything is ready for (A) *Holy Communion outside Mass*.

437. *The altar*: two candles—lit, dust cover removed, altar cloth spread, corporal spread.

438. *The ambo*: lectionary open at the readings. If the Communion Rite takes the place of Sunday Mass, then the Sunday readings may be used.

439. *The chair*: the ritual containing the Communion rite.

440. *The tabernacle*: the key, vessel with water, and purifier for fingers.

441. *The credence table*: if not at the tabernacle, vessel with water, and purifier for fingers or, if the ciborium is to be cleansed, a cruet of water and a purifier. If used, Communion plate(s) also on the credence.

442. *The sacristy*: if the minister of Communion is a priest or deacon, amice, alb, cincture, stole or soutane, surplice, stole; if the minister is an acolyte, amice, alb, cincture. An extraordinary minister of Holy Communion should vest as an acolyte or in attire approved by the bishop. At least one server assists. In churches where a deacon, acolyte, or minister leads the rite in the place of Sunday Mass, it would be appropriate to have other servers carrying the cross and candles.

443. The entrance is made as for Mass. A server holds the ritual as the minister greets the people and leads a penitential rite. The server sits while the minister or a lector reads the chosen readings. (If this rite takes the place of Sunday Mass, the deacon or minister may read Sunday readings, including a Gospel, and deliver a homily, if authorized.) A *Prayer of the Faithful* follows the readings. If a *Shorter Rite* is preferred, there is only one short reading.

444. *The Communion Rite* is celebrated at the altar. The server may stand to the side of the altar, near the credence table or in front of the altar on the credence side. The server places the ritual (open at the rite of Communion) on the altar, to the left of the corporal, and kneels while the minister brings the Blessed Sacrament from the tabernacle to the altar. After the minister has genuflected, the server stands for the Lord's Prayer and the sign of peace and kneels as the minister shows the Host to the people, "Behold the Lamb of God. . . ." The server takes the Communion plate (if used) from the credence and comes to the center to receive Communion and assist, if necessary, with the plate at the Communion of the people.

445. At the conclusion of Communion, the server takes the plate to the minister and brings the vessel of water and purifier from the credence, or the water cruet and purifier, if a ciborium is to be cleansed as well as the minister's fingers. (The minister may prefer to cleanse fingers at the tabernacle, after replacing the ciborium.) The server bows after any cleansings and takes vessels back to the credence. After a time for thanksgiving, the server stands while the minister says the concluding prayer and gives the blessing (or, if not ordained, the minister invokes God's blessing) and dismisses the people. (These final prayers are said at the altar, but a priest or deacon could lead them at the chair, a server attending with the ritual.) Having made the customary reverence, server and minister return to the sacristy.

446. After the rite, having extinguished candles, the server folds the corporal and brings it to the sacristy, unless it is kept in a burse near the tabernacle or on the credence.

2. Communion of the Sick

447. In every parish there are sick or frail people at home or living in a seniors' residence, a hospital, hospice, or some other institution for care. The priest, deacon, or another authorized minister takes the Blessed Eucharist from the tabernacle to these people and celebrates a simple Communion Rite with them.

448. Communion of the Sick who cannot come to church is allowed on Holy Thursday and Good Friday, but others may receive Communion only at the ceremonies. On Holy Saturday, Holy Communion may only be given as *Viaticum*, "Food for the journey", that is, Communion for the dying.

449. It is not customary in English-speaking countries for the Blessed Sacrament to be taken to the sick in a procession with servers attending. However, a vested server may assist at the Communion of sick people in a hospital, home for seniors, boarding school, or similar place. The server kneels as the minister takes the Eucharist from the tabernacle and then leads the minister to the sick people. The server may carry a candle and sound a small bell to alert people that the Blessed Sacrament is being brought to the sick. The server accompanies the minister from room to room, or bed to bed, if a number are to receive the Lord, joining in the prayers. The server leads the minister back to the chapel, kneels while the Eucharist is reposed in the tabernacle, stands, genuflects, and returns to the sacristy.

450. *Setting up a Sick Room.* Every server should know the correct way to prepare a room for the Communion of the Sick at home. In a convenient position, on a table covered with a cloth: two candles, lit as soon as the minister of the Eucharist arrives, and a bowl of water and small towel. To these may be added a crucifix, flowers, and, if the minister does not bring it, a vessel of holy water and a sprinkler or small branch. If the *Anointing of the Sick* forms part of the rite, there should also be cotton balls or tissues on a small plate.

451. The minister brings the Eucharist in a pocket pyx and uses a small ritual, unless prayers are said from memory. Booklets may be provided for those present who assist in the rite.

A priest or deacon wears a miniature stole over his street clothes.

452. Unless someone else has this duty, meet the minister at the door, but do not engage in conversation with someone who is carrying the Blessed Sacrament. Lead the minister to the room. The minister greets those present and places the pyx on the table. All kneel in silent adoration. Those present are sprinkled with holy water as a sign of Baptism. If the sick person wishes to go to confession, leave the room and shut the door, returning after the confession. A penitential rite may take the place of this confession. (If the sick person is dying, the priest adds the *Plenary Indulgence* for the dying.) A *Baptismal Profession of Faith* may follow. (If the *Anointing of the Sick* is to be given, it is introduced with a *Litany* and *Laying on of Hands*.)

453. After the Lord's Prayer, kneel as the minister shows the sick person the Host, "Behold the Lamb of God . . .", and gives Holy Communion. The minister may cleanse the pyx and fingers. After a short prayer, there is a *final blessing*. If there is still a Host in the pyx, a priest or deacon gives a silent *Benediction* with the pyx instead of the blessing, and you kneel as he does this.

454. After the rite, water used for cleansings is poured onto clean earth, not down the sink, and cotton balls or tissue used for the anointing is burned. The clergy need to be notified beforehand if anyone else wishes to receive Holy Communion with the sick person.

3. *Public Adoration of the Blessed Sacrament*

455. "The Master is there! Everyone, go to him!" The words of Saint Peter Julian Eymard encourage us to come before the tabernacle to adore our Lord, always present in the Sacra-

ment of his love. Each of us may choose to "make a visit" to the Blessed Sacrament whenever we can come to the church or school chapel. That visit is a private form of prayer, a free and personal act of devotion to Jesus in the Blessed Eucharist.

456. The Church also encourages us to adore the Blessed Eucharist as a community, outside the time of Mass, in acts of public devotion. Servers play an important part in public adoration, which takes three beautiful liturgical forms: (A) *Exposition of the Blessed Sacrament*, which usually includes (B) *Benediction*, the Eucharistic blessing, and on certain special occasions there is (C) a *Eucharistic procession*.

457. Each of these liturgical actions is a kind of extension of the celebration of Mass, designed to celebrate the Real Presence of our Lord and to give us a chance to adore him. Servers assisting in these sacred rites must always be reverent, prayerful, and well aware of procedures.

4. Exposition of the Blessed Sacrament

458. The term "exposition" means to show the reserved Sacrament outside the tabernacle as the focus for our adoration. During exposition, the whole church becomes a Eucharistic shrine of prayer. Exposition must cease during Mass celebrated in that church, even if the Host will be exposed once more at the end of the Mass, as in the Forty Hours Devotion, two days of adoration celebrated in various parishes.

459. *The first form of exposition is with the monstrance*, the Host being visible in a lunette, which fits into the center of the monstrance. The monstrance is placed either on a corporal spread on the altar or on a corporal spread on a throne or "tabor stand", placed on or behind the altar for a more solemn form of exposition. Extra candles and flowers are arranged near the monstrance during the time of exposition. Incense is used when exposition begins.

460. *The second form of exposition is with the ciborium*, which is taken from the tabernacle and placed on a corporal, spread on the altar. At least two candles should burn on or near the altar, and incense may be used.

5. Benediction of the Blessed Sacrament

461. The term "benediction" means a blessing, in this context a *Eucharistic blessing* given with the monstrance or ciborium, *Benediction of the Blessed Sacrament*. This rite is celebrated during or at the conclusion of exposition, with servers assisting. The Host may never be exposed simply to give Benediction. Before Benediction, there must be silent adoration and/or devotions in the form of prayers, singing, and readings—for example, novena prayers. The Liturgy of the Hours may be combined with exposition and Benediction.

462. A priest, deacon, authorized acolyte, extraordinary minister, or appointed member of a religious community may expose the Blessed Sacrament. Only a priest or deacon may give Benediction. In describing the rites for servers, (A) *Exposition* is combined with (B) *Benediction*. To this description is added the procedure of exposition at the end of Mass, which leads to (C) a *Eucharistic procession*.

463. *Preparations.* Having vested, servers check that everything is ready for exposition and Benediction, if it is to be given.

464. *The altar*: if the monstrance is used, four or six candles lit (or more, according to local custom); if the ciborium is used, at least two candles lit, dust cover removed, corporal either spread or in a white burse folded. If a throne is used, the corporal is spread on the place where the monstrance rests.

If this throne is behind the altar, there will still need to be a corporal on the altar. According to custom, flowers may be on or near the altar, and a white frontal may be used. The monstrance stands to the left of the corporal, and it may be covered with a white veil.

465. *At the altar step*: a book containing Benediction prayers, the bell, and incense boat (unless it is carried to the altar).

466. *Near the altar*: for Benediction, a white humeral veil, draped on a stand or folded on the credence table.

467. *The ambo*: a lectionary or another book for any readings or litanies.

468. *The chair*: any books required for a celebrant, if devotions are to be presided over from the chair or if the Liturgy of the Hours is celebrated.

469. *The tabernacle*: the key.

470. *The sacristy*: vestments required: for a priest or deacon celebrant, amice, alb, cincture, stole, and cope, or soutane, surplice, stole, and cope; for an assisting deacon, amice, alb, cincture, stole, and dalmatic, if available, or, for a simpler rite, amice, alb, cincture, stole, or soutane, surplice, and stole. The cope may not be required for the beginning of exposition if the Eucharist is exposed for some time and Benediction follows later. Others permitted to expose the Eucharist wear amice, alb, and cincture or soutane and surplice or appropriate religious habit, according to the bishop's directions. The stole and cope are white, unless another color is used for the Liturgy of the Hours. The humeral veil must always be white. Also in the sacristy: a thurible prepared, the boat, unless it is at the step of the altar, and, if required, two, four, or six torches for torch bearers. (The cross and processional candles may be used if the Liturgy of the Hours is celebrated during exposition.)

471. At least two servers are required for (A), preferably more for (A) and (B). The liturgical action usually takes place in front of the altar, all facing the altar of exposition.

472. *Note*: A simple genuflection is made when you pass the Blessed Sacrament exposed, but in Australia a "double genuflection" is still required, a practice widely followed in other countries, such as the United States, the United Kingdom, Ireland, and Canada. You make a double genuflection when you enter or leave the area where the Blessed Sacrament is exposed: (1) Look straight ahead, body straight, and do not bow your head yet or bend your body. (2) Move your right foot back as you bend your left leg, and bring your right knee to the floor, and immediately bring your left knee to the floor. (3) In that kneeling posture, bow your head and the upper part of your body reverently, then stand up without any rush, and move to wherever you are going.

473. *Entrance Procession*. Having bowed to the sacristy cross, servers and celebrant proceed to the sanctuary. The thurifer may keep the thurible slightly open; incense is not put on the coals until exposition begins. The thurifer goes first (cross and processional candles follow, if used), two, four, or six torch bearers (if [B] is to follow [A]) bearing lighted candles in their outer hands, the M.C. or acolyte, the deacon if assisting, the celebrant coming last. The deacon or two servers may walk beside the celebrant holding his cope.

474. *Exposition*. All form up in front of the altar and make the customary reverence. Torch bearers should be arranged across the sanctuary facing the altar or in two lines, one behind the other on either side. All kneel. If there is a deacon or assisting priest, he is on the celebrant's right. The thurifer kneels

at the center once the celebrant has passed. The other server or M.C. is on the celebrant's left. The celebrant, deacon, or assisting priest goes to the tabernacle, takes the lunette, and exposes the Blessed Sacrament.

475. If the tabernacle is some distance from the altar, in a chapel, the priest or deacon has the humeral veil placed around his shoulders as he kneels before the tabernacle. Preceded by servers bearing candles (i.e., the torch bearers) or even by members of the congregation bearing candles, he brings the lunette to the altar of exposition and exposes the Host. Therefore, servers and celebrant could go first to that chapel and then proceed to the altar of exposition, or they could kneel before the altar and wait while the priest or deacon and several servers go to bring the Host to the altar from the chapel.

476. A Eucharistic hymn may be sung as exposition begins. At a suitable point during the hymn, the celebrant stands and turns to the right. The thurifer stands at once, goes to the right of the celebrant, opens the thurible, and faces him, holding it at a convenient level. The deacon, M.C., or another server stands between the celebrant and thurifer, back a few paces, holding the open incense boat, the handle of the spoon directed to the celebrant. Incense is placed in the thurible. The thurifer closes it and hands it to the deacon, M.C., or another server, who hands it to the celebrant *only* when all are kneeling once more. The celebrant incenses the Blessed Sacrament with three double swings. All bow before and after the incensation. Those on either side of the celebrant should hold back his cope, to free his arms. Therefore, the thurifer or M.C. should go to the celebrant's left, if there is not already another server or assistant there. The celebrant returns the thurible, either to the deacon or M.C. or directly to the thurifer, who may either stay in

position at the step (if [B] is not to follow [A]) or go and kneel at the center, behind the celebrant flanked by torch bearers (if [B] follows [A]).

477. If this is the beginning of a *Holy Hour* or a long period of exposition, after some silent prayer, all stand, make the genuflection together, and return to the sacristy in the same order as at the entrance. Silence must be kept strictly in the sacristy, so that the people adoring the Blessed Sacrament in the church are not disturbed or distracted. Servers should not leave as soon as they have divested but should spend some time before the Blessed Sacrament in personal prayer. If it is a Holy Hour, and you are to serve the final Benediction, there is no need to divest, and you will join in the devotions either at a seat to the side of the sanctuary or in the body of the church, but be ready to return to the sacristy in time to prepare for Benediction.

478. *Benediction.* If (B) follows (A), servers remain in the sanctuary. If there are readings, hymns, novena devotions, etc., the celebrant may preside from his chair, the book bearer attending where necessary. If *Evening Prayer* or *Vespers* is celebrated, servers follow the directions in chapter 8. If the celebrant goes to the chair or if there is to be preaching or readings from the ambo, servers go to their seats in the sanctuary, all having genuflected together first. They return to the altar step for the final Benediction. If there are shorter devotions, litanies, or silent prayer, all remain kneeling in position in front of the altar of exposition and Benediction follows at once.

479. A suitable *Eucharistic hymn* is sung once the celebrant and servers kneel in their positions at the altar step, after they have come either from the sacristy, from their seats in the sanctuary, or on a signal by the celebrant or M.C. if they are already kneeling in position. During the hymn, the Blessed

Sacrament is incensed in the same way already described above. (If the hymn "Tantum Ergo" is sung, it is customary to bow at the words of the second line of the first verse, "veneremur cernui". Incense should be placed in the thurible at the end of the first verse.)

480. All remain kneeling as the celebrant stands and sings the *Benediction Collect*. Toward the end of the prayer, a server brings the humeral veil, unfolds it, and takes it by the clasps or ribbons in each hand. The server comes behind the celebrant, genuflects, and places it around the celebrant's shoulders as he kneels, putting the clasps or ribbons into his hands so he can easily secure the veil. The server steps back, genuflects, and kneels at the same place as before. The celebrant stands, goes to the altar, genuflects, takes the monstrance, and gives the *Eucharistic blessing*, slowly making the sign of the cross over all present, saying nothing. While the celebrant gives the Eucharistic blessing, the thurifer incenses the Host with three double swings. Another server or the M.C. rings the bell three times, keeping pace with the sign of the cross. If a deacon or another priest assists, he comes to the altar with the celebrant, genuflects, hands him the monstrance, kneels during the blessing, then stands to receive the monstrance after the blessing. After the Eucharistic blessing, it is customary for the Divine Praises to be said or sung before the Blessed Sacrament is reposed in the tabernacle.

481. *Reposition*. After the Eucharistic blessing, all remain kneeling as the celebrant, deacon, or assisting priest reposes the Blessed Sacrament in the tabernacle. If the Blessed Sacrament was brought from a chapel for exposition, it is taken back to that chapel, either with all the servers escorting the celebrant and then returning from the chapel to the sacristy or with several servers escorting the celebrant, deacon, or

assisting priest and then returning to the altar of exposition before going back to the sacristy. In either case, as at
the beginning of (A), a server first places the humeral veil
around the shoulders of the priest or deacon before he takes
the lunette back to the chapel. During reposition, an antiphon and psalm or an acclamation or hymn is sung. After
reposition, before the altar of exposition or the chapel altar,
all form up, make the customary reverence, and return to
the sacristy, in the same order as at the entrance. Servers
return to extinguish candles and bring objects back to the
sacristy.

482. However, during a long period of exposition, Benediction
may take place during exposition but without reposition,
because adoration is to continue. In this case, after the Eucharistic blessing and during a final hymn, all stand, genuflect, and return to the sacristy.

6. Exposition at the End of Mass

483. The way the liturgy is extended by adoration is clearer when
a Host consecrated at Mass is exposed in the monstrance
after Holy Communion. On the Solemnity of the Body and
Blood of the Lord, *Corpus Christi*, this is the best way to
introduce the Eucharistic procession. On Holy Thursday,
this procedure is followed for the transfer of the Holy Eucharist or procession to the altar of repose.

484. For exposition following Mass, in addition to the usual
preparations for Mass, the requirements for (A) and (B) are
carried out, but the monstrance will be kept on the credence
until needed. After Holy Communion and the cleansing of
vessels, a server removes the missal and stand. The deacon,
acolyte, or server brings the monstrance to the altar, placing
it to the left of the corporal, which remains spread on the
altar because the Host, on a paten or already in the lunette,

rests upon it. The celebrant, a concelebrant, or the deacon comes to the altar, genuflects, and exposes the Host in the monstrance, placing it on the corporal.

485. The Prayer after Communion follows, at the chair, the book bearer attending as usual. The Blessing and Dismissal are omitted. The celebrant comes to the center, with the deacon, servers forming up as for (A). All genuflect and then kneel. A hymn may be sung, and the Blessed Sacrament is incensed, as described for (A) and (B).

486. If a throne is placed on the altar for exposition, a server brings this from a credence table as soon as the Prayer after Communion has been said. The server places it at the center of the altar, genuflects, and returns to the step at the front of the altar. The celebrant or deacon lifts the monstrance from the corporal onto the throne before the hymn and incensation.

487. Unless a procession or devotions follow, all stand, genuflect, and return to the sacristy. Benediction may never follow Mass immediately but must at least be distinct from the Mass by way of devotions, readings, or silent prayer. Extra candles, lamps, and flowers are best arranged after Mass.

7. The Eucharistic Procession

488. A majestic act of public homage to Jesus Christ in the Blessed Sacrament is the Eucharistic procession, which witnesses to the faith and devotion of the Christian people. An annual procession on or near the Feast of Corpus Christi may have special importance and meaning for the pastoral life of a parish, town, or city. It proceeds from the church through the streets or through some other suitable area outdoors. At various Eucharistic shrines, or at different churches or chapels, the monstrance is placed on a

decorated table or altar and Benediction may be given. The procession either returns to the church whence it began or concludes at another church, always with solemn Benediction. The bishop has authority over the time, place, and circumstances of a Eucharistic procession.

489. *"It is fitting that a eucharistic procession begin after the Mass in which the host to be carried in the procession has been consecrated. A procession may also take place, however, at the end of a lengthy period of adoration"* (Sacred Congregation for Divine Worship Decree *Holy Communion and the Worship of the Eucharist outside Mass* [June 21, 1973], 74).

490. Servers must be carefully trained and rehearsed before a Eucharistic procession. They should move at a reverent pace and should keep perfect formation. The procession is led by the cross (or a Eucharistic banner) flanked by candle bearers. Other servers without specific duties walk behind the candle bearers. Clergy in choir dress, deacons, and concelebrants precede the canopy carried over the celebrant. There may be a second thurifer, but the thurifers come immediately before the celebrant carrying the monstrance. Each thurifer swings the thurible by the inside hand to honor the Blessed Sacrament. A boat bearer provides more incense for the thuribles if the procession is long.

491. The canopy carried over the celebrant is held by four or six servers or by other people trained to keep it steady. Torch bearers, two, four, or six, should escort the Blessed Sacrament, grouped around the canopy but not beneath it. As this is usually an outdoor procession, they should carry torches with glass protectors or lanterns. All other members of the procession, whether clergy, servers, or congregation, may carry hand candles during the procession, according to custom. If other groups such as the Knights of Columbus, soldiers, or flower girls assist, they are not mingled with the servers but are grouped as an escort in front of or around the procession as it moves forward. Only the celebrant carrying the monstrance, with a deacon or deacons holding back his cope, may walk beneath the canopy. Bishops and other prelates in choir dress walk behind the canopy, followed by the laity who wish to join the procession. Those not in the procession should kneel as the Blessed Sacrament passes by.

492. If the procession follows Mass, after the Prayer after Communion, the celebrant at the chair may remove his chasuble and a server brings him a white cope. He comes to the front of the altar. All genuflect, and the Blessed Sacrament is incensed as described above. (A second thurifer brings a thurible from the sacristy and joins the servers in front of the altar, perhaps leading the torch bearers from the sacristy with torches or lanterns. Incense is placed in both thuribles just before the incensation.) Hand candles may now be distributed among the clergy and the faithful. Other servers remain kneeling. The humeral veil is placed around the celebrant's shoulders. He goes to the altar and takes the monstrance from the deacon or another priest or concelebrant. He comes to the front of the altar. On a signal from the M.C., all stand, genuflect, and turn toward the main door.

493. Unless the canopy joins the procession outside the main door, it is now brought forward by the bearers so that the celebrant may walk beneath it. Torch bearers move to their positions beside the canopy or in front of it, if the aisle is too narrow. Preceded by the cross bearer, candle bearers, servers, clergy, deacons, concelebrants, and thurifers, the celebrant slowly moves forward toward the main door, as the first hymn is sung. Directed by an M.C., prelates and the congregation fall in behind him, and the procession goes forward in whatever order is planned for the occasion.

494. If Benediction is given at various shrines or churches on the way, the directions for (B) are followed. When the procession returns to the church or reaches another church as the final destination, it moves to the sanctuary, servers taking positions to the side to allow the canopy through, unless it leaves the procession at the church door. All genuflect together and then kneel as the celebrant places the monstrance on the altar. He comes to the front of the altar, and a server takes away the humeral veil. Solemn Benediction follows as for (B), and then the Blessed Sacrament is reposed in the tabernacle. All make the customary reverence and return in order to the sacristy.

Penance and Reconciliation

495. You go to confession. In the Sacrament of Penance, you are reconciled to God and reconciled to his Church. You are freed from your sins, and you know the pardon and peace of our merciful Father, the redeeming love of his Son who died for us, the forgiving grace of the Holy Spirit. You are absolved, set free from your sins, and your Baptism is renewed, and you are in a state of grace, the way God wants us to be. We need faith to receive this first *Sacrament of Healing* so that it can bear fruit in our lives.

496. The *matter* of Penance is the confession of sins by a penitent, a Christian who has sorrow for sins, contrition. The form of Penance is the absolution, in the Roman Rite, at least, "I absolve you. . . ." The minister of Penance is a bishop or a priest duly authorized by the bishop.

1. The Rites of Penance

497. There are three forms of the Rite of Penance: (1) *The Rite for Reconciliation of Individual Penitents*, the usual form of private

confession to a priest; (2) *The Rite for Reconciliation of Several Penitents with Individual Confession and Absolution*, private confession to a priest celebrated within a penitential service; (3) *The Rite for Reconciliation of Several Penitents with General Confession and Absolution*, when people are absolved together because, for the time being, they cannot receive personal absolution.

498. You should be familiar with Rite 1 by going to confession regularly. However, you only assist, as a server, in the public celebration of Rite 2, or perhaps in the unusual situation when Rite 3 may be used. Therefore, only Rite 2 is described for servers' duties.

499. In the second rite, there are four steps that provide a community setting for individual confession, with attention to good preparation for confession and thanksgiving for the sacrament. The four steps are: (1) *Introductory Rites*, (2) *Celebration of the Word of God*, (3) *Rite of Reconciliation*, and (4) *Concluding Rite*. This Sacrament of Penance may never be combined with the celebration of Mass, but you will see that the shape of the whole rite is modeled on the Eucharistic liturgy.

500. *Introductory Rites.* After a suitable entrance hymn, the celebrant greets the people; then he, or another priest or deacon, explains the purpose of the celebration of Penance. An opening prayer follows, asking God to give those present the grace of sincere repentance.

501. *Celebration of the Word of God.* The readings from the Scriptures express God's call to repentance and conversion, how we are reconciled through Jesus Christ our Redeemer, and how God regards sin, especially in its community context. The readings may follow a pattern similar to the Liturgy of the Word at Mass. A homily follows, explaining the readings and preparing the people for the sacrament. In the examination of conscience, in silence, and perhaps with guidance from one of the clergy, all present personally reflect on how they have sinned and what they need to confess to the priest.

502. *Rite of Reconciliation.* There are four steps for this central part of the celebration of Penance: (a) all kneel or bow during a general confession, usually the Confiteor, "I confess . . ." from the Mass; (b) all stand and say or sing a litany asking for forgiveness; (c) the Lord's Prayer is said or sung, with a prayer added to it, as at Mass; (d) the individual confessions are now heard by priests, who give a penance and absolution.

503. *Concluding Rite.* The celebrant invites all present to join in a psalm, hymn, or litany in praise and thanksgiving for the sacrament of mercy and peace. After a prayer of thanksgiving, he blesses the people. The rite concludes with a dismissal.

2. Serving Rite 2

504. *Preparations.* Having vested, servers check that everything is ready for the celebration of Penance.

505. *The altar*: candles lit.

506. *The ambo*: lectionary open at the first reading, violet fall.

507. *The chair*: the ritual, marked for Rite 2.

508. *The sacristy*: vestments for the clergy: celebrant, amice, alb, cincture, violet stole (violet cope, if desired), or surplice, soutane, and violet stole. Other priests hearing confessions wear a violet stole over amice, alb, and cincture or surplice and soutane. A deacon assisting wears the same vestments

and may wear a violet dalmatic only if the celebrant wears alb and cope. The processional cross and candles should be used. The Book of the Gospels or lectionary may be carried in procession. Incense may be used for the Gospel. At least one server is needed, to hold the ritual at the chair.

509. *Entrance Procession.* Having bowed to the sacristy cross, servers, priests, (assisting deacon), and celebrant proceed to the sanctuary, while a suitable hymn is sung. Having made the customary reverence, priests and servers go to their seats in the sanctuary. The book bearer attends the celebrant at the chair. An assisting deacon stands on the celebrant's right.

510. *Introductory Rites.* When required for the greeting and the opening prayer, the book bearer holds the ritual at the chair.

511. *Celebration of the Word of God.* Servers remain seated for the readings. However, if there is to be a Gospel and processional candles are used, the candle bearers go to the center, as at Mass, and wait for the priest or deacon who reads the Gospel. If incense is used, it is blessed by the celebrant as usual. Candle bearers stand in the usual position at the ambo, returning to the center after the Gospel, and replace their candles on the credence table or near the altar. The homily and examination of conscience follow.

512. *Rite of Reconciliation.* Servers kneel or bow, according to local custom, during the general confession. They stand for the litany and the Lord's Prayer. If the celebrant directs these prayers, the book bearer attends at the chair or holds the ritual for the deacon or another priest. The priests now go to the confessionals or other suitable places where they will hear confessions. Servers sit at their places in the sanctuary during confessions. It would be good manners for servers

wishing to go to confession to go to the priests last, that is, after the people.

513. *Concluding Rite.* Servers stand for the thanksgiving hymn. The book bearer goes to the chair, where the other priests are standing with the celebrant. He attends the celebrant with the ritual for the final thanksgiving and blessing. The deacon or the celebrant or another priest dismisses the people. All form up in front of the altar, make the customary reverence, and return in order to the sacristy.

514. *Rite 3.* General Absolution. Collective absolution of all present by one priest, and/or a collective penance, is never permitted in Rite 2. But General Absolution may be given in unusual emergency situations, when by unforeseen circumstances the priest finds that he cannot hear a large number of confessions. Such a situation could never be advertised or planned, but if servers happen to be present, they should serve it in the same way as for Rite 2, described above. A formula of General Absolution takes the place of the private confessions in Rite 2. A server present at such an unusual occasion should remember the directive of the Church that, "A person who receives general absolution from grave sins is bound to confess each grave sin at his next individual confession" (*Rite of Penance*, 66) and that such a person is "strictly bound, unless this is morally impossible, to go to confession within a year" (*Rite of Penance*, 34).

Matrimony

515. God calls most members of his Church to the Sacrament of Matrimony. He unites husband and wife in a holy and inseparable union, giving them a special grace to live together in happiness, to form a family, and to bring up their

children in true reverence and love of God. Christian marriage is a vocation.

516. The bond of Christian marriage cannot be broken except by the death of husband or wife. Our Lord taught, "So they are no longer two but one. What therefore God has joined together, let no man put asunder" (Mt 19:6). Remaining faithful in body and in mind, in good times and in bad, married people live the sacrament day by day, sharing its graces and strengthening the bond of their promises and self-giving.

517. The *matter* of Matrimony is the outward giving of the rights of married life. The *form* of Matrimony is the external expression of the acceptance of these rights by way of consent and promise. The *ministers* of the Sacrament of Matrimony are the husband and wife. An authorized priest or deacon is the official witness of the validity and lawfulness of the sacramental contract because he presides over the celebration of this *Sacrament at the Service of Communion.*

1. The Rite of Marriage

518. There are two forms for the celebration of Marriage: (A) *Nuptial Mass*, the rite of Marriage during Mass, and (B) *Marriage outside Mass*, celebrated with a Liturgy of the Word.

519. According to the choice of those to be married, the Mass may be celebrated in solemn form, concelebrated, with a deacon assisting, choir, incense, etc., or in a simpler form. There should always be at least two servers. This Mass is a festive occasion, the normal way the Sacrament of Matrimony is meant to be celebrated within the community of the Church. The word "nuptial" comes from a Latin word for "wedding". The *rite of Marriage* is celebrated after the homily of the Mass. It consists of the questions, the consent, the blessing, and exchange of rings. The Mass continues, and, after the Lord's Prayer, the *Nuptial Blessing* is given to the couple.

2. Serving Nuptial Mass

520. *Preparations.* Having vested, servers check that everything is ready for the Nuptial Mass. The altar, ambo, chair, credence, and sacristy are prepared as for any Mass, depending on the solemnity desired. Additional requirements should be noted.

521. *The credence table*: a plate for ring(s), holy water and sprinkler (if it is to be used), the ritual, marked at the rite of Marriage.

522. *In the sanctuary*: two chairs with kneeling desks (prie-dieux) or cushions, for the bride and groom, microphones as required.

523. *In the sanctuary or in the sacristy*: a suitable table with the civil papers and register and a pen for the signing of certificates.

524. *The sacristy*: white vestments for the celebrant, concelebrants, and deacon. Booklets or prepared programs that should be given to the congregation before Mass.

525. *Entrance Procession.* Having bowed to the sacristy cross, servers and celebrant proceed either (a) to the sanctuary, to join the groom, best man, etc., as the bride enters the church and comes to the altar, or (b) to the entrance of the church, to meet the bride and groom and lead them both to the altar. Whatever procedure is chosen, servers and celebrant make the customary reverence on arrival at the sanctuary. The celebrant or M.C. may guide the bride and groom to their chairs. If incense is used, the altar is incensed as usual.

526. *The Introductory Rites and Liturgy of the Word* are served as usual. The readings are taken from those provided for Marriage, except on a Sunday of Advent, Lent, or the Easter season, a solemnity, Ash Wednesday, or in Holy Week.

527. *The rite of Marriage* comes after the homily. Unless their chairs are already in front of the altar, the bride and groom come to the center at the front of the altar. Other members of the wedding party are usually grouped near them as witnesses and attendants. The celebrant comes to the center. The book bearer brings the ritual and stands on the celebrant's left with the book open at the rite. The deacon, M.C., or another server stands on his right, back a pace or two.

528. The celebrant introduces the rite and asks the questions that express the intention of the bride and groom. He then invites them to join their right hands and declare their consent according to a form of words or a question. He receives their consent. The server on the celebrant's right or another server immediately brings the rings on the plate and the holy water from the credence table. Unless there is a deacon, and he takes the plate, the server holds out the plate with his right hand as the celebrant blesses the rings. If holy water is used, he then offers the holy water so that the celebrant may sprinkle the rings, unless another server brings the holy water.

529. The celebrant (deacon, M.C.) and book bearer return to the chair for the Prayer of the Faithful. If necessary, the

bride and groom return to their chairs. If it is a solemnity or Sunday, the Creed follows.

530. *The Liturgy of the Eucharist* is served as usual. At the Procession of the Gifts, the bride and groom may bring the bread and wine to the altar, servers assisting. The *Nuptial Blessing* comes after the Lord's Prayer. The prayer "Deliver us . . ." is omitted, and the celebrant introduces the blessing. He extends his hands toward the bride and groom during the prayer of blessing that is in the missal. (However, if Mass is not celebrated facing the people, a server either brings the ritual to him or takes the missal from the altar, holding it as he faces the bride and groom during the prayer of blessing.) The married couple may receive Communion under both kinds. If intinction is the method chosen for Communion, a server holds the Communion plate during their Communion. Mass concludes with a special blessing, the book bearer assisting at the chair.

531. *Civil papers and the register* are usually signed after the ceremony, either at a table in the sanctuary (never on the altar) or in the sacristy or some other convenient place. If the papers are signed in the sanctuary, after the final blessing, servers should go to their seats and wait until the signing is finished. They stand as the bride and groom leave the church, then come to the center, make the customary reverence with the celebrant, and return to the sacristy. If the papers are signed in the sacristy, after the final blessing, servers form up at the center of the sanctuary, waiting for the bride and groom to join them. All make the customary reverence and go to the sacristy, servers first, then the celebrant and bride and groom with the witnesses. Servers will wait in their own vesting room until the signing is finished and the bride and groom have left the church.

Do *not* extinguish candles or bring vessels and equipment back to the sacristy until the bride and groom have left the church.

3. Serving Marriage outside Mass

532. For various reasons, it may not be possible to celebrate Marriage during a Nuptial Mass. In place of the Mass, a Liturgy of the Word is celebrated, using the same readings as those provided for Mass. There should be at least two servers assisting at the ceremony. In certain circumstances, Holy Communion from the tabernacle may be given at the conclusion of the rite. The *rite of Marriage* is celebrated after the homily of the Liturgy of the Word. It takes the same form as Marriage during Mass, but the *Nuptial Blessing* is given at the end of the Prayer of the Faithful, followed by the Lord's Prayer and the final blessing.

533. *Preparations.* Having put on their robes, servers check that everything is ready for the celebration of Marriage:

534. *The altar*: candles lit (dust cover removed if Holy Communion is to be given).

535. *The ambo*: lectionary open at the readings for Marriage.

536. *The chair*: the ritual, marked at the Marriage rite, Opening Prayer.

537. *The credence table*: a plate for ring(s), holy water, and sprinkler.

538. *In the sanctuary*: as for Nuptial Mass above.

539. *The sacristy*: for the celebrant, amice, alb, cincture or soutane, surplice, with a white stole and white cope. Booklets or prepared programs should be given to the congregation before the celebration. Incense is never used for Marriage outside Mass, but if greater solemnity is desired, there may be servers with the cross and candles. (If Holy Communion is to be given, the usual preparations will also be made for Communion outside Mass.)

540. *Entrance Procession.* Servers follow the same procedure as for Nuptial Mass.

541. *The Introductory Rites* and *Liturgy of the Word* are served as for Nuptial Mass, the book bearer attending at the chair for the first prayer.

542. *The rite of Marriage* comes after the homily and is served in the same way as Nuptial Mass. However, the celebrant remains at the center with the bride and groom and wedding party for the Prayer of the Faithful, the book bearer attending with the ritual.

543. *The Nuptial Blessing* is added to the Prayer of the Faithful in place of the concluding prayer. The Lord's Prayer and final blessing complete the rite. (If Holy Communion is to be given, the celebrant goes to the tabernacle after the Nuptial Blessing, brings the Blessed Sacrament to the altar, and celebrates the rite of Communion outside Mass, beginning with the Lord's Prayer.)

544. The civil papers and register are signed as for Nuptial Mass, and other procedures are followed as for after Nuptial Mass.

Anointing of the Sick

545. When a Christian suffers serious illness, the frailty of age, or danger of death, Christ our Lord comes in this second *Sacrament of Healing*. He comes to strengthen and raise up the sick person with a healing of soul, and even of the body, if that is God's will. Freed from sin and strengthened against temptation by the grace of the Holy Spirit, the sick person is also prepared, if need be, to accept death, knowing that this is not the end of life, but the way to a new life in Christ. Anointing of the Sick, formerly known as *Extreme Unction*, is mentioned in Mark 6:13 and, in detail, in James 5:14–15: "*Is any among you sick? Let him call for the elders of the church, and let them pray over him, anointing him with oil in the name of the Lord; and the prayer of faith will save the sick man, and the Lord will raise him up; and if he has committed sins, he will be forgiven.*"

546. The *matter* of the Anointing of the Sick is olive oil (or another vegetable oil where it is difficult to obtain olive oil), blessed by a bishop or an authorized priest. The *form* of anointing in the Roman Rite is: "Through this holy anointing may the Lord in his love and mercy help you with the grace of the Holy Spirit. May the Lord who frees you from sin save you and raise you up." The *minister* of Anointing is a bishop or priest.

1. The Rite of Anointing

547. Unless given in emergency, the rite of Anointing follows a clear pattern of prayers and readings, usually combined with Holy Communion of the Sick, ministered by a priest. After the greeting, penitential rite, and reading from Scripture, perhaps with a short homily, the priest says a *Litany for the*

Sick. He then performs the *Laying on of Hands* in silence, a sign of prayerful blessing, seeking the healing grace of God for the sick person.

548.   If the oil has not been blessed already by the bishop, the priest may bless the oil for the sacrament. Usually he brings oil already blessed by the bishop. After the laying on of hands, he offers a *Prayer of Thanksgiving* to the Father, Son, and Holy Spirit, said over the blessed oil, praising the Father who sent his Son to save us, the Son who wills to heal us, the Holy Spirit who heals us with his mighty power.

549.   The *Anointing* is carried out by the priest. He traces a cross with the holy oil on the forehead and the palms of the hands (if possible), saying the form: "Through this holy anointing. . . ." The words of the form are divided into two sentences so that those present may respond with "Amen" twice, joining their prayers to this powerful "prayer of faith".

550.   A *Prayer after Anointing* asks God to continue his healing work in the sick person, as strength to recover or to accept suffering as a share in the Cross, or as strength to accept old age or death. The prayer is selected according to the condition of the sick person. Holy Communion of the Sick follows, introduced as usual by the Lord's Prayer. The final blessing, if a Eucharistic blessing is not given, recalls the theme of healing.

551.   Servers would not normally assist, as servers, at the rite described above. But the Church provides for a liturgical setting for the Anointing of the Sick: (A) *Anointing during Mass* and (B) *Anointing outside Mass*. As with Marriage, the sacrament is incorporated into the celebration of Mass after the homily, servers assisting as usual.

2. *Serving Anointing during Mass*

552. A Mass during which Anointing is given may be offered either in a church, usually with a number of sick and elderly people to be anointed, or in a hospital, home, or some other institution, for those confined there, or in the house where a sick person is confined. For the celebration in a church, people are needed to bring the sick and aged to church, which involves the parish community in a generous work of charity and care.

553. *Preparations*. Having put on their robes, servers check that everything is ready for Mass and Anointing. The altar, ambo, chair, credence, and sacristy are prepared as for any Mass, depending on the solemnity desired. Additional requirements should be noted.

554. *The credence table*: oil stock(s) with the Oil of the Sick for the priest(s), cotton balls (if they are to be used), cards with the form of anointing printed clearly on them for the priests, a dish containing sliced lemon, soap, a suitable ewer and bowl, towel.

555. *The ambo*: the lectionary, open at the readings for Mass for the Sick, unless other readings from the rite are chosen or the Mass for the Sick is not permitted.

556. *The chair*: the ritual marked at the rite of Anointing.

557. *In the sanctuary*: chairs for concelebrants and/or assisting priests.

558. *In the nave of the church*: reserved seats or places for those to be anointed.

559. *The sacristy*: white vestments for the celebrant, concelebrants, deacon; and/or assisting priests, amice, alb, cincture, white stole, or soutane, surplice, white stole. Booklets or prepared programs should be given to the congregation before Mass.

560. *Entrance Procession.* When those to be anointed are in their places in the church, having bowed to the sacristy cross, servers and celebrant (with any concelebrants, deacons, or assisting priests) proceed to the sanctuary. All make the customary reverence and proceed with Mass.

561. *The Introductory Rites* and *Liturgy of the Word* are served as usual. After the greeting and introductory words, the celebrant addresses those to be anointed, *"the reception of the sick"*. The book bearer may hold the ritual at this point, if the celebrant chooses to read from it. The readings are taken from those provided for Mass for the Sick or the rite of Anointing, except on a Solemnity or on a Sunday of Advent, Lent, or the Easter season, Ash Wednesday, and the days of Holy Week.

562. *The rite of Anointing* comes after the homily. The celebrant presides over the rite, either at the chair or at the center of the sanctuary in front of the altar, depending on circumstances and the number to be anointed and where they are located. A microphone may be needed at the center. If he stands at the center, the book bearer is on his left, with the ritual, the deacon on his right; concelebrants or assisting priests who will also anoint may gather behind him.

563. The *Litany for the Sick* is said (unless a Prayer of the Faithful is preferred, after the anointing). Then the celebrant (and other priests who will also anoint) perform(s) the *Laying on of Hands*, in silence, going to the sick and/or waiting for those who can come to the sanctuary. Each priest imposes hands on the sick people he will later anoint.

564. The celebrant returns to the chair or his position at the center and offers the *Prayer of Thanksgiving* over the blessed oil or, if necessary, blesses oil for the sacrament. While the laying on of hands is proceeding, the deacon and/or servers bring the oil to the chair or to the center. The deacon and/or servers will hold the oil before the celebrant as he offers the Prayer of Thanksgiving or as he blesses it. For the *Anointing*, the celebrant (and other priests who will also anoint) take an oil stock each from the servers and go to anoint some of the sick and/or wait for those who can come to the sanctuary to be anointed. Servers may be needed to accompany each priest, especially if many are to be anointed: (a) to hold a card, brought from the credence, with the form of anointing printed on it, for the priest to read as he anoints, and (b) to help with cotton balls, if used after the anointing. Hymns are usually sung during the anointing.

565. After the anointing the deacon and/or servers take the Oil of the Sick back to the credence table as well as cards and cotton balls, if used. The celebrant returns to the chair and sits. Two servers bring the lemon, soap, ewer, bowl, and towel to him, and he washes his hands, taking the lemon juice to break down the oil first and then holding his hands over the bowl as water is poured (with soap, if desired) and drying his hands. Servers bow and take the vessels back to the credence. If other priests have assisted with the anointing, servers may go to each priest at his chair to cleanse his hands. If many priests have assisted, there should be a second set of vessels at the credence or at a second credence, and two servers will attend there as the priests come to have their hands cleansed after the anointing.

566. The celebrant stands at the chair. If the Litany for the Sick was *not* said at the beginning of the rite of Anointing, the book bearer holds the folder or book containing a *Prayer of the Faithful*, prepared for the occasion. The celebrant leads the Prayer of the Faithful, a deacon or lector assisting. It always concludes with a *Prayer after Anointing*, taken from the ritual. If the Litany for the Sick was said at the beginning of the rite of Anointing, the celebrant says only the Prayer after Anointing.

567. *The Liturgy of the Eucharist* is served as usual, beginning with the Procession of Gifts and the Preparation of the Gifts. Those who have been anointed and all present may receive Holy Communion under both kinds. After Mass, servers bring the Oil of the Sick back to the sacristy so that the priest may replace it in the repository, ambry (a small wall safe), or other secure place where the Holy Oils are kept. If cotton balls have been used, it is burned. Water used for the cleansings is poured down the sacrarium.

3. Serving Anointing outside Mass

568. For various reasons, a simpler rite may be desired, without the celebration of Mass. The Anointing takes place after the Liturgy of the Word as in the Mass. The Prayer after Anointing may be replaced by the Lord's Prayer. The rite concludes with one of the special blessings of the sick, as in the ritual, and with the Dismissal.

569. *Preparations.* The same procedures and preparations as for Mass with Anointing of the Sick, but without the usual preparations for Mass. If solemnity is desired, the processional cross and candles should be used.

570. *Entrance Procession.* Servers proceed as in the Mass.

571. *Reception of the Sick* and *Penitential Rite* are directed from the chair by the celebrant, the book bearer attending with the ritual. The Liturgy of the Word is served as usual.

572. *The rite of Anointing* comes after the homily and is served as described for the Mass. The book bearer attends at the chair for the final blessing taken from the ritual.

573. After the rite, the same procedures are followed as for the Mass. If the liturgical Anointing of the Sick is celebrated in a private home, hospital, or some other place, with or without Mass, servers follow the above directions, adapting to the situation.

Other Celebrations

574. Servers assist at other celebrations that are not sacraments. These are described in the following chapters. First, there are frequently occurring celebrations such as *funerals* (chapter 7). In monastic churches, or parishes with a developed liturgy, the *Liturgy of the Hours* or *Divine Office* (chapter 8) is celebrated regularly, even daily. *Other ceremonies* (chapter 9) include certain occasions when public *blessings* take place and those with their own liturgical form: the *Blessing of Candles* on February 2nd, Feast of the Presentation of the Lord, and the *Blessing of Ashes* on Ash Wednesday, marking the beginning of Lent. The *Way of the Cross* is a popular devotion during Lent.

7.

Funerals

575. For Christians, the word "celebration" is a good word to use to describe a funeral. When we die, we pass through death into life. For us, "life is changed, not ended" (*Preface I for the Dead*). If we have been faithful and not chosen to turn from God by grave sin, we will enter the joy of eternal life in God, enjoying the vision of God for all eternity. We will share in the Resurrection of Jesus Christ. We will be raised up, body and soul, so that we may each share as complete persons in the glory of heaven.

576. At the same time, we know that death is a time for sorrow and mourning. Death is always a tragedy, brought about by human sinfulness and frailty. We know that we may not be worthy to enter heaven immediately. First, we may have to pass through the merciful process of purgatory, so that God may prepare us and perfect us for heaven. We know that we will need the help of the prayers of the Church.

577. The Catholic funeral liturgy therefore expresses all sides of the mystery of death. With Easter joy, we celebrate the hope of resurrection for the person whose mortal body lies before the altar. Jesus Christ has freed us from the corruption of sin and death. With Christian sorrow, we mourn the death of a fellow human being, remembering that each of us must die one day. But in charity and confidence, as the Church on earth, we offer Masses and prayers for the souls of the departed, that they may enjoy "light, pardon, and peace" forever.

578. In the prayers, readings, and ceremonies, the Catholic funeral expresses hope and confident faith, as well as mourning and sorrow. As you serve funerals, you can see that there is a strong sense of being able to do something to help the dead. Our rites, especially the Mass for the dead, are not mere memorial services. In the Communion of Saints, we are joined to millions of believers who have died before us. We can help them by our prayers. They can pray for us. We hope that one day we will all rejoice together in heaven.

The Various Funeral Rites

579. Because of many different situations and customs, there are different ways of celebrating a Catholic funeral. There may be prayers at the home of the deceased person or the funeral home, the "wake" before the funeral. Either at the church or in the funeral home, there may be a vigil, a night celebration of prayers and readings. The rosary may form part of this vigil. On the day of burial, there should be a funeral Mass, also known as Mass of Christian Burial, or, commonly, as Requiem Mass, from the Latin word for "rest" in the entrance verse, "Give them eternal rest, O Lord." If it is not possible to offer Mass, a Liturgy of the Word is celebrated. At the conclusion of the Mass or Liturgy of the Word, in the church or even at the grave, there is the Final Commendation and Farewell. At the grave or tomb, there will be the brief prayers of Christian burial, supplemented in some countries with other devotions.

580. Servers assist in the church and sometimes at the grave or tomb. In describing the duties of servers, a typical plan of the funeral has been selected. But this may need to be adapted in different situations.

581. *The Vigil for the Deceased* is celebrated at the church on the night before the funeral. The body may be received at the church as part of this vigil. The prayers and readings emphasize the time for mourning, personal preparation for the funeral, and prayer for the dead. The body may rest in the church during the night, after a viewing, if this is requested.

582. *The Mass of Christian Burial or Funeral Mass* is the center of the funeral rites. It is offered for the repose of the soul of the deceased person and to console and encourage those present with the hope of Easter, so that "the prayers which bring spiritual help to some may bring to others a consoling hope" (*Rite of Funerals*, Introduction 1).

583. *The Final Commendation and Farewell* is celebrated at the conclusion of the Mass (or a Liturgy of the Word). This rite at the coffin or casket is no longer known as the "absolution", because it "is not to be understood as a purification of the dead—which is effected rather by the eucharistic sacrifice —but as the last farewell with which the Christian community honors one of its members before the body is buried" (*Rite of Funerals*, Introduction 10). The cross is carried as a sign of the saving death and Resurrection of the Lord. Holy water is sprinkled as a sign of Baptism, which gives us the promise of eternal life. Incense is used to honor the body as the temple of the Holy Spirit and as a sign of prayer.

584. *Prayers at the grave or vault* with a Christian burial complete the funeral rites. The mortal body of the deceased is reverently committed to a blessed grave or tomb. After cremation, the ashes of the deceased must also be committed to a blessed place. The final rite not only expresses our respect for the mortal remains, our prayer for the dead and for those who mourn, but our sure and certain hope of the general resurrection of all the dead.

585. The rites are adapted in words and theme for the funerals of children and in circumstances where cremation is permitted. In the United States, certain customs are authorized, and these are described below as alternatives.

Serving a Funeral

586. Servers play an important role in the celebration of funerals, indeed, some of the earliest historical references to assisting ministers are descriptions of the funerals of Christian martyrs. You can be of great consolation to the relatives of the deceased by your reverent assistance at a funeral. Some funerals have a tragic atmosphere of grief and sadness. Some people can become very emotional. The trained server learns how to take this kind of funeral calmly—*never* staring at mourners and showing no reaction at all to any display of emotion. This self-discipline can help tone down difficult times of human grief when the strong faith of the Church is needed, with the dignity and peaceful assistance of the servers providing a simple sign of this faith.

1. The Vigil for the Deceased

587. Servers may be required for the Vigil for the Deceased, although in places where it is only a rosary with prayers, servers may not be needed. If Mass is celebrated as part of the vigil, all preparations are made as for Mass. If the body is to be received, the processional cross and candles should be used. Where it is customary to carry the Paschal candle, it should be held in a convenient metal socket that fits into the large candlestick, and precautions should be taken to avoid spilling wax. The casket or coffin should be arranged before the altar so as to leave ample space for ceremonies.

588. *Preparations.* Having vested, servers check that everything is ready for the Vigil for the Deceased.

589. *The altar*: candles lit and, if used, antependium of the color of funerals.

590. *Before the altar*: (a) *If the casket or coffin has been brought privately to the church already*, it is set on the *catafalque* (a stand for the casket or coffin), the feet of the corpse toward the altar (but toward the people if the deceased is a priest or bishop). A funeral pall, black, violet, or white, should cover the casket completely, falling to the ground. (In the United States, a folded white pall is nearby to be placed over the casket as a special rite.) The Paschal candle is set on a stand, and/or two, four, or six candles arranged near the casket; these should be lit before the people arrive (unless lighting the Paschal candle is part of the rite). According to custom, a Bible or cross, or a sign of Holy Orders for the ordained (stole, miter, etc.), may be placed on the coffin. (b) *If the coffin is to be received at the door of the church*, the catafalque will be in position, candles lit according to custom, the pall folded nearby. (In the United States, a white pall is brought folded to the door of the church for the rite of reception of the body.)

591. *The ambo*: lectionary open at chosen readings for the vigil, antependium of the color of funerals.

592. *The credence table*: prepared for Mass, if necessary, and, if the coffin is already in position, holy water.

593. *The chair*: if prayers are not to begin at the casket, the ritual, marked for vigil rites.

594. *The sacristy*: if prayers begin at the casket or if the body is received at the door, the ritual, marked for the rites; vestments, for the celebrant, priest, or deacon, amice, cincture, alb or soutane and surplice, stole of the color of funerals (black, violet, or white), and a cope of the same color, especially if the body is to be received, and for an assisting deacon, amice, cincture, alb, stole (dalmatic, if the priest wears a cope)—or Mass vestments, if Mass is to be offered. For the servers: processional cross, candles (or Paschal candle), thurible prepared, any objects to be placed on the coffin (in the United States, a folded white pall), and holy water if the body is received at the door or sprinkled at the beginning of prayers.

595. *Entrance Procession.* Having bowed to the sacristy cross, servers and celebrant proceed either to the sanctuary, if the body is already in place, or to the door of the church, if the body is to be received there.

596. *If the coffin or casket is already in place*, the celebrant goes to the chair to preside over a Liturgy of the Word, the book bearer attending with the ritual. The readings follow as usual, according to choice, perhaps with a homily. Intercessions and/or the rosary may follow. The celebrant may say final prayers for the deceased, at the casket, and a server will attend with the holy water for sprinkling. A blessing may conclude this rite, and all return to the sacristy.

597. *If the body is received at the door of the church*, the cross bearer and candle bearers move to the right, to allow the celebrant to meet the coffin. They then come in behind the celebrant, facing the door, so that, when they turn to face the altar, they will lead the procession to the catafalque. The thurifer goes first. If the celebrant sprinkles the coffin at the door, the holy water is presented by a server, who has brought it from the sacristy. If prayers are said at the door, the book bearer attends with the open ritual.

598. In the United States, when the vigil is celebrated, the celebrant follows the *Rite at the Church Entrance*. After the greeting and short Scripture reading, he sprinkles the casket saying the formula of blessing. A server attends with the holy water, another carries the ritual. A server brings the white pall, which the celebrant now places on the coffin, assisted by members of the family of the deceased or those in charge of funeral arrangements. After a short prayer, the procession goes forward to the catafalque: incense (if used), cross, Paschal candle, servers with the ritual and holy water, servers with any object to be placed on the casket, celebrant, deacon, coffin. If the casket has already been placed on the catafalque privately, the rite of sprinkling and placing the pall could be celebrated at the casket as the beginning of the vigil rite or Vigil Mass.

599. After the reception of the body and procession to the catafalque, the customary vigil devotions follow, the celebrant presiding from the chair as usual. If the vigil devotions are replaced by a *Vigil Mass*, this follows the same pattern as the funeral Mass described below, except that Mass concludes as usual with the Blessing and Dismissal, and the *Final Commendation and Farewell* is not celebrated. If the body is to rest in the church overnight, servers will follow directions as to whether candles or lamps remain alight or whether they must be extinguished.

2. The Mass of Christian Burial or Funeral Mass

600. The center of the celebration of a Catholic funeral is the Holy Sacrifice. Servers assist as at any other Mass, according to the degree of solemnity desired. There should be *at least* six servers for the Mass and the rite that follows, the *Final Commendation and Farewell*: Cross bearer, two candle bearers, book bearer, holy-water bearer, thurifer. One server could replace the candle bearers or act with them, if the Paschal candle is carried.

601. *Preparations*. Having vested, servers check that everything is ready for the funeral Mass.

602. *The altar*: candles lit for Mass as usual, antependium of the color of funerals.

603. *The chair*: the missal or book of the chair, marked for Mass, a book or folder for the Prayer of the Faithful.

604. *Before the altar*: The catafalque set up as described above for the vigil. Paschal candle or candles lit, if the body is already in position.

605. *The ambo*: the lectionary, open and marked for the Mass (unless it is carried in procession), microphone; fall of the color of funerals.

606. *The credence table*: prepared for Mass with the holy water for the sprinkling of the casket.

607. *The table of the gifts*: to be set up as usual if there is a Procession of Gifts.

608. *The tabernacle*: prepared as usual for Mass.

609. *The sacristy*: vestments set out for Mass, depending on whether there is an assisting deacon and/or concelebrants, the color either black, violet, or white, according to local custom or occasion. If the cope is to be worn for the final prayers, it should be in some convenient place in the sanctuary so that there is no need for a return to the sacristy before the final prayers. Incense is always used, at least for the final prayers.

If it is used during Mass, charcoal is prepared as usual about ten minutes before Mass. The funeral attendants distribute booklets or programs for the people.

610. *Entrance Procession.* All procedures are followed as for *Mass with the People* (chapter 4).

611. *If the body is not already in position*, the Entrance Procession goes to the door of the church: thurifer, cross bearer, candle bearers (or bearer of the Paschal candle), servers (deacon), celebrant. Cross bearer and candle bearers move to the right to allow the celebrant to meet the coffin. They come in behind the celebrant, facing the door, so that when they turn to face the altar, they will lead the procession to the catafalque, led by the thurifer. If the celebrant sprinkles the coffin at the door, a server presents the holy water. If incense is used, the thurifer approaches and the celebrant places incense in the thurible for the procession to the catafalque, led by the thurifer, in the same order as for the entrance to the door, the celebrant coming immediately before the coffin. Once the coffin or casket is placed on the catafalque, servers may assist in covering it with the pall, unless this is done by the family or friends of the deceased. If the Paschal candle has been carried, it will be placed carefully on its stand.

612. In the United States, the celebrant may follow the *Rite at the Church Entrance*, as described above for the vigil, sprinkling the casket and covering it with the pall before the procession to the catafalque. However, if the body is already in position before the altar, this rite could be celebrated in place of the Penitential Rite. Even if celebrated at the door, the *Rite at the Church Entrance* replaces the Penitential Rite, so that the priest, on arrival at the altar, kisses it, incenses it, if incense is used, and goes to the chair, where the book bearer attends for the appropriate Collect.

613. Mass proceeds as usual, according to the degree of solemnity. In the United States, the priest may incense the body at the Preparation of the Gifts, immediately after incensing the gifts and the altar. The thurifer (deacon, M.C., or acolyte) should accompany him as he incenses the coffin, all making the customary reverence together to the altar before and after incensation. If the body is incensed at this point, the incensation is omitted from the *Final Commendation and Farewell*.

614. If incense is not used until the final prayers, the thurifer should prepare the thurible during Holy Communion and bring it with the boat to the credence table in time for the Prayer after Communion. If the celebrant wears a cope for the final prayers, a server brings this to the chair as soon as the prayer has been said or sung. The Blessing and Dismissal are omitted. The celebrant removes his chasuble, assisted if necessary by a server, who drapes it over the chair. He puts on the cope, assisted by a server.

3. *The Final Commendation and Farewell*

615. At the catafalque, the rite of Final Commendation and Farewell is celebrated. The celebrant comes to the center of the sanctuary, to be joined by (deacon, M.C., acolyte) thurifer, book bearer and holy-water bearer. The candle bearers (or bearer of the Paschal candle) and cross bearer come and form up behind the celebrant and the others. All face the altar and make the customary reverence.

616. The cross bearer and two candle bearers (or bearer of the Paschal candle, having taken the candle from its stand, unless this is taken up after the prayers) go to the other end of the coffin, nearer the doors of the church. They turn and stand facing the altar. The candle bearers flank the cross,

but all stand back several paces from the coffin to allow the celebrant room for the sprinklings and incensation.

617. The celebrant (and deacon, M.C., acolyte) comes to a central position and faces the casket or coffin. The book bearer stands on his left, the thurifer and holy-water bearer on his right. The book bearer holds the ritual open at the prayers. The thurifer and holy-water bearer should face across the church, standing several paces away from the celebrant. Any concelebrants may join the celebrant, usually grouped behind him, all facing the coffin. The celebrant introduces the rite. Silent prayer follows. A chant of farewell is sung while the body is sprinkled and incensed. (In the United States, the sprinkling and incensation may be omitted, having already taken place during the Mass.)

618. For *the sprinkling of the coffin or casket*, the thurifer first comes to the celebrant, opens the thurible, and incense is prepared and blessed. The thurifer returns to the previous position, keeping the thurible slightly open and moving. The holy-water bearer comes to the celebrant, who takes the sprinkler (and bucket, if customary) and proceeds to move around the coffin, counter-clockwise, sprinkling it. If a deacon assists, the server gives him the sprinkler and bucket, and he offers the sprinkler to the celebrant. If the celebrant is wearing a cope, during the sprinkling the right side should be held back by the deacon, M.C., acolyte or holy-water bearer, to free the right arm. As he sprinkles the coffin, he may be accompanied by the deacon or a server, who also holds the bucket, unless he chooses to hold it himself. On reaching the far end of the catafalque, the celebrant and attendants turn together and bow to the processional cross before proceeding to the other side of the catafalque.

619. For *the incensation of the coffin or casket*, the thurifer comes to the celebrant (or deacon) as soon as he returns the holy water to the bearer and hands the thurible to the celebrant (or deacon). The celebrant moves around the coffin, incensing the body. He may be attended by the deacon, M.C., and/or servers, holding back the cope as he moves. Again, all turn and bow to the processional cross before proceeding to incense the other side of the catafalque. After receiving the thurible, the thurifer bows to the celebrant and goes to the far end of the coffin, to a position *behind* the cross bearer, that is, so as to be ready to lead the final procession out of the church.

620. At the conclusion of the singing, the celebrant says the final prayer, the book bearer attending. All now form up for the final procession. (1) The holy-water bearer, book bearer (bearer of the Paschal candle, carrying the candle), deacon, M.C., acolyte, any concelebrants, and the celebrant proceed to the foot of the coffin and fall in behind the thurifer, cross bearer, and candle bearers (unless the Paschal candle takes the place of the two candle bearers). Incense, cross, and candles must move forward *immediately* to allow ample room for clergy and servers, but they must not proceed as if the procession had already begun. (2) All turn to face the door of the church, if not already facing that way. All wait until the casket has been raised by the bearers and the M.C. or funeral attendant gives a signal for the procession to begin. (3) However, if there are many concelebrants or clergy in choir dress, they *either* start moving out of the church in procession before the incense, cross, servers, and celebrant, or the thurifer, cross bearer, and candle bearers (or bearer of the Paschal candle) may lead them out, slowly, while the celebrant and other servers wait until the casket is raised and wheeled or carried at a suitable time.

621. Concelebrants or clergy in choir dress or members of the Armed Forces or a Catholic Order may form up as a guard

of honor outside the church while the casket is carried to the *hearse* (funeral car). (4) On arrival at the car, thurifer, cross bearer, candle bearers (or bearer of the Paschal candle) move to a convenient place on one side, depending on the position of the hearse. The celebrant (deacon, M.C., acolyte), book bearer, and holy-water bearer may either move to the same side, standing in front of the thurifer, cross bearer, candle bearers (or bearer of the Paschal candle), or they may move to the other side. All face inward toward the coffin as it is placed in the hearse. The celebrant may sprinkle the coffin just before it is placed in the car. In some places, servers and clergy do not leave the church, but remain in the porch or narthex of the church, moving to each side and facing the coffin as it is carried out of the church to the car.

622. Once the coffin or casket is placed in the car, after a brief pause, the servers and clergy return to the church. Clergy may remain to comfort the family of the deceased, but servers return to the sacristy, still keeping the formation of the procession, but taking some other convenient route rather than the main aisle, because people will be coming out of the church. Under the direction of the M.C. or senior server, the servers replace every object used at the funeral Mass. If servers are to go to the cemetery for the burial, they follow the directions of the celebrant, M.C., or senior server. However, if the body is to be buried immediately in the churchyard or a cemetery close by the church, the funeral procession continues to move directly to that place, following the directions below for serving a burial.

4. Prayers at the Grave

623. The rite of Christian burial may be of a simple form, depending on circumstances. What is described below is an ideal situation—for example, when those who served the

funeral Mass are able to assist at the grave. The same procedures are followed for the Christian burial or placing of
ashes after *a cremation*. The ashes are treated in exactly the
same respectful way as the body of a deceased person, that
is, the ashes are permanently set in a blessed place where
people may come and visit and pray. Ashes may never be
scattered about or kept at home.

624. *Preparations.* Unless the funeral procession moves directly
from the church to the grave, vestments, robes, and liturgical equipment are brought to the cemetery. The following
objects are required: vestments, for the celebrant, amice,
alb, cincture or soutane, and surplice, stole, and cope, of
the color of funerals; for an assisting deacon, amice, alb,
cincture, stole, and dalmatic (if available), or soutane, surplice, and stole, robes for servers, the cross and candles,
prepared thurible and boat with incense, holy-water bucket
and sprinkler with water, the ritual.

625. On arrival at the cemetery, servers vest and prepare the candles and incense. They should be ready with the celebrant
to meet the car, or, if they traveled in the funeral procession by car, they proceed immediately to the hearse, forming up for the procession in the order outlined above as in
the church. All face the car while the casket is taken from
it. All turn and proceed, once the bearers have raised the
casket for the procession to the grave or vault.

626. If it is possible to stand on all sides of the grave, the cross
bearer and candle bearers stand at the head of the grave.
The celebrant (deacon, M.C., acolyte), book bearer, holy-
water bearer, and thurifer stand at the foot of the grave.
The book bearer attends on the celebrant's left. An assisting deacon stands on the celebrant's right, with the thurifer
and holy-water bearer farther to the right slightly behind
him or facing across. The positions are the same as for the

Final Commendation and Farewell. Relatives, other mourners, and funeral attendants sit or stand on each side of the grave.

627. If it is not possible to gather around the grave, as for example if the body is to be interred in a wall vault, the cross bearer and candle bearers move to the right side as the casket is brought to the vault, and they may best form up behind the celebrant, all facing the casket or vault for the prayers.

628. *If the grave has not been blessed*, after the blessing prayer, the thurifer approaches the celebrant and incense is blessed as usual. The thurifer steps aside with the thurible and waits while the holy-water bearer approaches the celebrant, who sprinkles the body and the grave or vault. The holy water bearer steps aside, the thurifer gives the thurible to the celebrant (deacon, M.C., acolyte), and the grave or vault is incensed. The thurifer receives back the thurible, bows, and steps aside. During the incensation and sprinkling, if the celebrant wears a cope, the deacon, M.C., or another server holds back the right side to free the celebrant's arm.

629. *The prayers* follow, according to local custom. The coffin or casket is lowered into the grave or placed in the vault at some chosen moment during or after these prayers. Where it is customary, a funeral attendant offers the celebrant some earth in a suitable vessel to be scattered over the coffin or casket after it has been lowered into the grave. If the *Final Commendation and Farewell* was not celebrated at the conclusion of the Mass in the church, it follows the prayers, usually before burial. The same ritual is observed as set out in no. 3 above.

630. Further prayers may be offered for the mourners. In the United States, the body is usually interred at the conclusion of the prayers. In Ireland and Australia, the rosary, or

part of it, may be said. A hymn or antiphon of our Lady may conclude the rites of Christian burial. At the end of prayers, or during the hymn, the procession forms up and returns to the point where it began. Servers follow the directions of the celebrant, M.C., or senior server.

5. *A Funeral without Mass*

631. When it is not possible to celebrate a funeral Mass, the rites should be arranged in such a way that a Mass for the deceased is offered apart from the funeral, that is, without the body present. At the funeral rite, the same number of servers is required as for a funeral with Mass, but in practice this may be reduced. In place of the Mass, a Liturgy of the Word is celebrated, servers assisting as for the Liturgy of the Word in a Mass. After the homily and Prayer of the Faithful, the *Final Commendation and Farewell* is celebrated as described above.

8.

The Liturgy of the Hours

632. The constant and perpetual "Prayer of the Church" is the *Liturgy of the Hours*, or celebration of the *Divine Office*. Those in Sacred Orders and members of religious Orders, congregations, and institutes are bound to pray the Office each day, according to their situation and their rule. Many lay people freely choose to pray the Office, in whole or in part, using the same Office book or "breviary" of the Roman Rite, the *Liturgia Horarum*, available in English translations or in the original Latin.

633. The Liturgy of the Hours is the prayer of Jesus Christ to the Father, the prayer of his Mystical Body, the Church. It is derived in form from the daily synagogue and Temple prayer of Israel, offered by our Lord during his earthly life. Centered around the psalms of Israel, the new People of God pray in union with Christ, making holy the whole day, raising praise and prayer at every moment around the earth. Whether prayed privately alone or in groups or ideally in community, the Liturgy of the Hours is always a corporate communal prayer, the work of the Holy Spirit, who leads us through the Son to the Father.

634. There are two main "hinges" on which the daily Office depends, *Morning Prayer*, or *Lauds*, and *Evening Prayer*, or *Vespers*. These are to be considered the major "hours" and are celebrated as such, with public liturgy, where possible— for example, in abbeys, monasteries, convents, and certain large churches and cathedrals.

635. The *Office of Readings* centers around two, or more, extensive readings, chosen from Scripture, the Fathers of the Church, conciliar or papal documents, lives of the saints, etc. It is a prayerful time for meditation and reflection on the treasures of revelation in Scripture and tradition contained in the chosen readings. This Office of Readings is also adapted as a vigil celebration—for example, before Christmas Midnight Mass.

636. The lesser hours are *Terce*, *Sext*, and *None*, shorter forms of prayer, spaced out to sanctify the day between the major hours of Lauds and Vespers. When not recited in community, only one of these lesser hours need be said, unless a particular rule or custom requires all three. It is known as *Prayer during the Day*.

637. *Compline* or *Night Prayer* is the final prayer of the day, usually offered before sleep. It is a short hour, commending us to the care of God, concluded by an antiphon of our Lady, a hymn invoking the protection of the Mother of the Church.

638. Servers are required to assist at a solemn celebration of either of the major hours, Morning Prayer and Evening Prayer, when presided over by a bishop, priest, or deacon, with singing and incense at the Gospel canticle. For this purpose, Evening Prayer has been chosen as a typical form of the solemn celebration of the Office because Morning Prayer is served in exactly the same way. Directions are also given for combining Evening Prayer with Mass and with exposition and Benediction.

The Structure of Morning and Evening Prayer

639. *Introductory verse* invoking the help of God as we begin to pray.

640. *The hymn* is sung to express the theme of the season or feast.

641. *Three psalms* at Morning Prayer are chosen from the Old Testament psalms and canticles and at Evening Prayer are chosen from the Old Testament with a final canticle from the New Testament. Short *antiphons* are sung or recited before and after each psalm, according to the day, season, or feast.

642. *Reading of the Word of God* is either a short reading or a longer reading, perhaps with a homily in a public celebration. Silent reflection may follow the reading or homily.

643. *A short responsory*, or responsorial song, usually follows the reading.

644. *The Gospel Canticle* is the high point of the celebration, in praise of God, Creator and Savior. At Morning Prayer, it is the *Benedictus* (Lk 1:68–79). At Evening Prayer, it is the *Magnificat*, the song of our Lady (Lk 1:46–55). At a solemn celebration, the altar, clergy, servers, and people are incensed during the canticle. The antiphons for the canticle vary according to the liturgical day, season, or feast.

645. *Intercessions*, similar to the *Prayer of the Faithful*, follow the canticle. At Morning Prayer, these prayers consecrate the day to God. At Evening Prayer, they are petitions for the needs of all people, living and dead.

646. *The Lord's Prayer* is sung or said.

647. *The Collect* is sung or said, according to the day, season, or feast.

648. *The Blessing and Dismissal* conclude a public celebration of the major Hours.

Serving Solemn Vespers

649. *Preparations.* Having put on their robes, servers check that everything is ready for the celebration of Evening Prayer.

650. *The altar*: candles lit (preferably six for solemn Vespers), antependium of the color of the season or day.

651. *The ambo*: an office book or lectionary, open for the reading, a fall of the color of the season or feast.

652. *The chair*: an office book, marked for the celebration, a second chair or chairs for assisting deacon(s), or two chairs, on each side of the celebrant, for priests assisting in copes; the microphone connected.

653. *Servers' seats*: office books.

654. *The sacristy*: vestments: the celebrant, amice, alb, cincture (or soutane and surplice, only if a deacon does not assist in dalmatic), stole and cope of the color of the season or day; the assisting deacon(s): amice, alb, cincture, stole, dalmatic; two assisting priests vest in copes, as may other priests assisting on major solemnities when other deacons may also wear dalmatics. Cantors wear choir dress unless it is the local custom for them to wear matching copes. For the servers: processional cross, and candles lit, prepared thurible and boat.

655. *Entrance procession*: Having bowed to the sacristy cross, the servers and clergy proceed to the sanctuary in the following order: thurifer (without the thurible), cross bearer, candle bearers, member of a robed choir, clergy in choir dress, cantors, book bearer, M.C. or acolyte, deacons in dalmatics, priests in copes, the celebrant, with assisting deacon(s) or two priests in copes beside him, holding back his cope as he walks.

656. If the choir is seated formally in stalls or seats in front of or behind the altar, members of the choir make the customary reverence in pairs and enter the seats. Unless they wait for the clergy, the cross bearer and candle bearers place the cross and candles in the appropriate positions as for Mass. The old custom of placing the candles on the pavement or lowest step in front of the altar, on each side, may be observed. On arrival before the altar, clergy and servers make the customary reverence together. The celebrant and his assistants kiss the altar before going to the chair. Servers go to their seats.

657. At the chair, attended by the book bearer with the open office book, the celebrant intones the *introductory verse*, and all make the sign of the cross and bow during "Glory be to the Father . . . Spirit. . . ." All remain standing during the singing of the *Office hymn*. All remain standing as the celebrant or cantors intone the antiphon for the first of the *psalms*. All sit once the cantors or choir have intoned the first line of the first psalm, up to the asterisk. All remain seated during the psalms, bowing at the end of each psalm during "Glory be. . . ." After the last antiphon has been sung, the lector comes to the center, makes the customary reverence, bows to the celebrant, and goes to the ambo.

658. During the *reading of the Word of God*, all remain seated. (However, if on an exceptional occasion a longer reading is chosen from the Gospels, to be read by the deacon, an assisting priest, or the celebrant, all stand and the ceremonial of the Gospel at Mass can be observed. The thurifer brings the thurible and boat from the sacristy toward the end of the third psalm, returning to his position at the credence table after the Gospel, if there is no homily.) All sit for the homily.

659. All remain seated while the cantors or choir lead the *short responsory*. During the singing, the thurifer brings the thurible and boat from the sacristy and takes a position in front of the credence table. All remain seated while the antiphon for the *Magnificat* is intoned and sung. The thurifer approaches the chair, and the celebrant prepares incense as usual, the deacon, and a priest or M.C. assisting with the boat and spoon. An assistant may hold back the cope as he places incense in the thurible and makes the sign of the cross. All stand as soon as the *Magnificat* begins, making the sign of cross at the first words.

660. The celebrant, deacon(s) or assisting priests, M.C., and thurifer move to the altar, directly, if seated behind it, or coming to the center of the pavement in front of it, then together they make the customary reverence and ascend the step(s) to the footpace. The thurifer steps back after giving the thurible to the deacon, an assisting priest, or M.C., and the celebrant incenses the altar as at Mass. The deacon and M.C., or the two assisting priests or the M.C. and thurifer, accompany him and hold back his cope as he walks around the altar. At the end of the incensation, the thurifer receives back the thurible. The celebrant and his assistants bow to the altar and return to the chair, if it is located directly behind the altar, or come down to the pavement, make the customary reverence, and return to the chair. (During the incensation of the altar, the candle bearers may follow the

custom of standing in front of the altar on each side, facing the altar, but without their candles, which remain on the credence or on the ground near the altar.) In some churches, after the incensation of the main altar, it is customary to go and incense the altar of a saint on his or her feast day. This is done in the same way as the incensation of the main altar, and candles should be lit at this altar.

661. Standing at his chair, the celebrant is incensed by either the deacon, the first assisting priest (with the second standing next to him), the M.C., or thurifer (if the others are not present). The thurifer incenses the deacon or the assisting priests, then any clergy in choir, then the M.C., the servers, and the people, as at Mass. Having made the customary reverence, the thurifer waits at the center, facing the altar, swinging the thurible at full length, while the "Glory be . . ." of the Magnificat is sung, then reverencing the altar and returning to the sacristy during the antiphon.

662. During the antiphon, the candle bearers may take their candles from the credence or the altar step and come to the celebrant at the chair, to stand flanking him, facing one another, when he leads the *Intercessions* for Vespers. All remain standing. The book bearer attends the celebrant during these prayers and the *Our Father* and *Collect*.

663. The deacon or another priest may proclaim the petitions of the *Intercessions*, at the ambo, but the celebrant must introduce the Lord's Prayer, sing the Collect, and give the blessing. If the deacon assists, he gives the dismissal. After the dismissal, the celebrant and deacon(s), or the celebrant, deacon(s), or two assisting priests go to the altar and kiss it, then all form up as usual in front of the altar, make the customary reverence, and return to the sacristy in the same order as for the Entrance Procession. If there is a formal choir, the thurifer (without thurible), the cross bearer, and candle bearers lead them out first, while the celebrant and his assistants and servers wait for a suitable moment before making the customary reverence and joining the procession. It may be the local custom for all to stand before the altar while an *antiphon of our Lady* is sung before they make the customary reverence and return to the sacristy.

Mass with Evening Prayer

664. The celebration of the Liturgy of the Hours may be combined with the celebration of the Eucharistic liturgy. Taking Evening Prayer as a major hour that may be combined with evening Mass, the shape of the celebration is as follows:

665. The liturgy begins with either the usual *Introductory Rites* of Mass or the entrance song and procession, or the introductory verse and office hymn of Evening Prayer, with servers following the procedures described above. The three *psalms* of Evening Prayer replace the Penitential Rite and "Lord have mercy" of Mass. Servers follow the procedures above. If required for the day, the *Gloria* is sung or said, followed as usual by the Collect of the Mass.

666. The *Liturgy of the Word* follows as usual at Mass. The *Prayer of the Faithful* is said as usual. On ordinary weekdays, the *Intercessions* of Evening Prayer may replace the Prayer of the Faithful. The *Liturgy of the Eucharist* is celebrated as usual. But after Holy Communion, the *Magnificat* is sung. If incense is used, servers follow the procedures set out above. The Prayer after Communion and *Concluding Rite* of Mass complete the celebration.

667. Evening Prayer may also be added to Mass immediately after the Prayer after Communion. The psalms are followed by the Magnificat and its antiphon and the final prayer of

Evening Prayer, Blessing, and Dismissal. All other elements in Evening Prayer are omitted.

Vespers and Benediction

668. Provided there is suitable time for Eucharistic prayer and silent adoration, Benediction of the Blessed Sacrament could follow Evening Prayer. This popular rite is known as *Vespers and Benediction*. The Blessing and Dismissal are omitted, and exposition begins after the final prayer as described in chapter 6.

669. Evening Prayer may also be celebrated before the Blessed Sacrament exposed, so that the Office and adoration are combined. After the Host is exposed, the celebrant goes to the chair, and Evening Prayer is celebrated as usual. But before incensing the altar itself, the celebrant and any assistants kneel on the edge of the footpace, and the celebrant incenses the Blessed Sacrament with three double swings, bowing before and after, his cope held back by assistants.

670. The celebrant may choose to lead the Intercessions kneeling with assisting clergy and servers in front of the altar of exposition. After the final prayer, the rite of Eucharistic Benediction could begin with the hymn as usual. Unless the Blessed Sacrament is to remain exposed on the altar, reposition follows as usual, according to chapter 6.

9.

Other Ceremonies

Blessings

671. *People, places, and objects* may be blessed privately in a simple form. For example, the priest may make the sign of the cross over rosary beads, blessing them in the name of the Holy Trinity, so that they may be a sacred sign and help, a "sacramental" for the use of God's People. However, there are more formal blessings, celebrated in a liturgical way— for example, to mark the opening of a new school or to bless some new furniture or a statue in a church. These are set out in the *Book of Blessings*.

672. If a blessing is not given during Mass (after the homily or after Holy Communion), the liturgical rite is as follows:

673. The *entrance song, sign of the cross*, and *greeting* by the bishop or priest who blesses.

674. A brief *introduction* or explanation of the ceremony.

675. A *scriptural reading* appropriate for the occasion. If a Gospel passage is used, the reader is a priest or deacon. A responsorial hymn follows.

676. A brief *homily*, which may be omitted if there are speeches later.

677. The *Prayer of Blessing*, from the *Book of Blessings* or another approved source.

678. The *sprinkling with holy water* of the place or object blessed.

679. The *Prayer of the Faithful*, suitable for the celebration.

680. The *Lord's Prayer*, introduced by the bishop or priest.

681. The *blessing* of the people and the dismissal.

682. At least a book bearer and holy-water bearer should assist the celebrant at a blessing liturgy. To add solemnity to the occasion, a cross bearer and two candle bearers may assist. A thurifer may be required for some blessings. If the bishop blesses, there will also be a miter bearer and a crozier bearer who walk behind him in procession. A deacon, acolyte, or M.C. may assist in directing the rite. Other priests may sprinkle the holy water if a large building is being blessed or may place crucifixes in the classrooms of a school that is being blessed.

683. *Preparations.* Having vested, servers check that everything is ready for the blessing, either (a) in the church or (b) in another place. The full form of the ceremonial is described below.

1. A Blessing in the Church

684. *The altar*: candles lit.

685. *The lectern*: the lectionary open for the chosen reading.

686. *The chair*: a folder with the prepared text of the rite, a second chair for an assisting deacon, other chairs for priests assisting.

687. *The credence table*: the holy water and sprinkler.

688. *The sacristy*: vestments: for the celebrant, (a) a bishop: amice, alb, cincture (or violet soutane and rochet), pectoral cross, stole and cope, ornate miter, crozier, that is, unless the bishop chooses to wear his choir dress and a stole; (b) a priest: amice, alb, cincture (or surplice and soutane), stole and cope for an assisting deacon, amice, alb, cincture (or surplice and soutane, if the celebrant wears a surplice or rochet), stole, and dalmatic, if the alb is worn. For the servers: processional cross and candles lit (prepared thurible, if incense is required). Programs for the people

2. *A Blessing in Another Place*

689. All the above preparations are made, but adapted to the situation. Clergy and servers may vest in a suitable room. There must be a chair for the celebrant, chairs for assisting clergy, guests, etc. A lectern is needed for the reading, and there may be some kind of "altar" or symbolic focus for the celebration and a suitable table for a credence. Microphones are necessary if the blessing involves a large congregation, especially outdoors.

690. Servers and clergy proceed in the usual order of procession either to the sanctuary or to the place of blessing. If the bishop is celebrant, the miter bearer, crozier bearer, and book bearer come last in the procession behind the bishop, receiving the miter and crozier on arrival at the sanctuary or place of blessing.

691. The book bearer attends at the chair for the *sign of the cross* and *greeting*. He may remain if the celebrant introduces the rite, or another priest, deacon, or lay person may give an *introduction* at the ambo or lectern. If a priest or deacon reads from the Gospel, servers may assist with candles and incense as at Mass, otherwise a lector reads this scriptural reading from another part of the Bible. A *homily* may follow. Servers sit.

692. The book bearer attends with the *Book of Blessings* or folder for the *Prayer of Blessing*, the holy-water bearer waiting nearby. The *sprinkling with holy water* of the object or place requires the assistance of the holy-water bearer. Assisting clergy or servers may hold back the celebrant's cope during the sprinkling, especially if he walks around. If a place is being blessed, the cross bearer and candle bearers, with candles, should lead the celebrant around the place or building as he sprinkles it. The bishop wears his miter during the sprinkling, and the crozier bearer may carry the crozier, walking ahead of the bishop, if desired.

693. At the chair, the book bearer attends for the introduction of the *Prayer of the Faithful*, usually read by a lector from the ambo or lectern. The book bearer attends for the introduction of the *Lord's Prayer* by the celebrant. If the bishop is celebrant, he wears his miter for the final blessing, taking the crozier from the bearer for the blessing formula, after the short prayers of blessing or a prayer over the people. If the deacon assists, he gives the dismissal.

694. All make the customary reverence, if the blessing is in a church, and return in procession to the sacristy or the room set apart for preparations. Speeches may follow the ceremony, according to situation and local custom or the occasion. Servers assist the celebrant to remove vestments before any speeches begin.

The Blessing of Candles (February 2nd)

695. The Roman Missal provides for an ancient custom on the Feast of the Presentation of the Lord. Because this day commemorates the ritual presentation of the Infant Jesus in the Temple, candles are blessed and carried in procession to signify Jesus Christ, "a light for revelation to the Gentiles", in the words of Simeon (Lk 2:32). There are two forms for this blessing at the beginning of the Mass. (1) the *Procession* or (2) The *Solemn Entrance*. Either form replaces the Penitential Rite, and the Mass then continues as usual with the Gloria. Traditionally, this day is known as "Candlemas Day". The full number of servers for a Solemn Mass should assist, if possible, whatever form is chosen for the blessing of candles.

696. *Preparations.* Having vested, servers check that everything is ready for the blessing of candles and Mass. The usual preparations are made for Mass, depending on the degree of solemnity chosen. Incense may be used for the procession as well as for the Mass.

697. *The altar*: candles lit (white antependium).

698. *The ambo*: lectionary open for the readings, white fall.

699. *The chair*: the missal or book of the chair, marked for Mass and the blessing of candles, other chairs for deacon, concelebrants, and/or assisting clergy.

700. *The credence table*: the usual requirements for Mass.

701. *In the narthex, chapel, or place chosen for the blessing*: The candles are distributed before the procession or entrance, and/or the people may bring their own candles. It is customary for the sacristan to set out the supply of candles for use during the liturgy during the year, usually on a table. These are blessed along with the lighted candles for the procession or solemn entrance.

702. *The sacristy*: usual vestments as required for Mass, white; for the servers, holy-water bucket and sprinkler, processional cross, candles, incense, depending on the degree of solem-

nity chosen. In place of the chasuble, the celebrant may wear a white cope for the procession or solemn entrance; the chasuble is prepared at the chair. The missal marked for the blessing is to be carried by the book bearer,

703. *The Procession.* Having bowed to the sacristy cross, servers and celebrant proceed to the place chosen for the blessing of the candles and the beginning of the procession. The people's candles are lit while a hymn is sung. Servers not already carrying an object carry a lighted candle and should assist the people to light their candles.

704. The celebrant greets the people and invites them to take an active part in the celebration, which he explains. The book bearer attends as required, with the missal. The celebrant reads the prayer of blessing. The holy-water bearer approaches, and the celebrant sprinkles the candles as the people hold them. The deacon, M.C., acolyte, or servers may hold back his cope during the sprinkling, especially if he walks around. He returns the sprinkler to the holy-water bearer. The thurifer approaches, and incense is prepared and blessed as usual, the deacon, M.C., acolyte, or a server assisting.

705. The deacon, or M.C., acolyte, or server hands the celebrant a lighted candle. The procession forms up: thurifer, cross bearer, candle bearers, servers with hand candles, holy-water and book bearers, M.C. or acolyte, assisting deacon, celebrant, people with candles. The deacon or celebrant announces the beginning of the procession by singing or saying, "Let us go in peace to meet the Lord" or "Let us go forth in peace", and all respond "In the name of Christ. Amen." The canticle or another chant is sung as the procession goes forward by the chosen route, ultimately entering the church, when the entrance chant or hymn is sung.

706. On arrival at the sanctuary, all form up as usual, make the customary reverence, and proceed to their places. The M.C. or a server takes the celebrant's candle, extinguishes it, and places it on the credence table. Other hand candles are extinguished and laid aside. The celebrant kisses the altar and incenses it as usual. He goes to the chair, removes the cope, and puts on the chasuble, servers assisting. The book bearer attends at the chair as he intones the Gloria, and Mass proceeds as usual for the feast.

707. *The Solemn Entrance*: Where the procession cannot be arranged conveniently, the Solemn Entrance takes place within the church building. Having bowed to the sacristy cross, servers and celebrant proceed to the front porch or narthex of the church or even to a convenient place just outside the main door. A representative group of the faithful join them at this place with unlighted candles. The rest of the congregation are already in their seats with unlighted candles. The people's candles are lit while a hymn is sung, servers assisting as required.

708. All proceeds as set out above, but the procession is only to the altar, and there is only one processional hymn, the entrance hymn of the Mass. Mass proceeds as set out above.

The Blessing of Ashes (Ash Wednesday)

709. The season of Lent is an important time of prayer and penance, a deepening of faith, and good deeds as we approach the greatest Christian celebration, Easter. Following ancient Jewish custom as an outward sign of conversion and penance for sins, we receive blessed ashes on the first day of Lent, Ash Wednesday. The ashes are made from the branches blessed on the Passion (Palm) Sunday of the preceding year. The *Blessing and Distribution* of *Ashes* follows the homily of the Mass of Ash Wednesday or the homily of the Liturgy of the Word for that day, if it is not possible to celebrate Mass.

710. *Preparations.* Having vested, servers check that everything is ready for the Mass and the blessing and distribution of ashes.

711. Apart from the usual preparations for Mass, the following should be noted.

712. *The altar*: candles lit (violet antependium).

713. *The ambo*: lectionary open for the readings, violet fall.

714. *The chair*: the missal or book of the chair, marked for Mass and the blessing of ashes, other chairs as required for deacon, concelebrants, and/or assisting clergy.

715. *Before the chair*: a table, suitably covered, on which are vessels of powdered ash, perhaps moistened for easier use, which may be covered with a violet veil until the time of blessing.

716. *The credence table*: in addition to usual requirements, bowls of water, liquid soap, and towels for cleansing the fingers of those who give ashes, holy water and sprinkler. (If servers hold the ashes during blessing, the ashes are on the credence.)

717. *The sacristy*: usual vestments as required for Mass, violet; for the servers, processional cross, candles, incense, depending on the degree of solemnity chosen.

718. *Entrance procession*: Having bowed to the sacristy cross, servers and celebrant proceed to the sanctuary, and Mass follows as for the day.

719. *The Blessing of Ashes* follows the homily. The celebrant goes to the chair, the book bearer attending on his left. Two servers may bring the table before the chair, if not already in position. The holy-water bearer brings the bucket and sprinkler from the credence, standing to the left of the celebrant, facing across. The deacon, M.C., acolyte, or a server removes the veil from the ashes. The celebrant introduces the blessing, pauses for silent prayer, and says the prayer of blessing. The holy-water bearer approaches the celebrant (or deacon, if assisting), and the celebrant sprinkles the ashes. He receives back the holy water and bows.

720. *The Distribution of Ashes* is accompanied by the singing of the proper antiphons or other suitable Lenten hymns. A concelebrant, assisting priest, deacon, or a lay minister approved by the local bishop takes a vessel of blessed ashes from the table (or from a server holding the vessel) and imposes ashes on the celebrant, who bows forward. (If no other priest or deacon is present, the celebrant imposes ashes on himself.) He takes the vessel from the priest or deacon and then imposes ashes on him and then on any other clergy assisting. If they are to distribute ashes, they take vessels from the table (or from the servers who held them for blessing) and proceed to the places chosen for the giving of ashes. Servers come before the celebrant, either at the chair or before the altar, and he imposes ashes on them before proceeding to give ashes to the people.

721. It is customary for the ashes to be imposed by making the sign of the cross with blessed ash on the forehead, saying either, "Repent, and believe in the gospel" (Mk 1:15) or "Remember that you are dust and to dust you will return" (Gen 3:19). However, it is customary to sprinkle ashes on the heads of those in Sacred Orders. During the giving of ashes, the servers wait until all have received ashes in their group, then they bow to the altar together and go to their seats to sit quietly until the distribution is complete. As soon as the celebrant has finished giving ashes, he returns to the chair. The M.C. or a server takes the vessel of ashes from him, replacing it on the table (or taking it to the credence table, if the table for blessing is not used). The candle bearers approach from the credence with the ewer, bowl, towel, and soap and wash his hands at the chair, bowing to him before and after the procedure. They take the ewer, etc., back to the credence, where servers assist other clergy in cleansing their hands. The small table should be moved from its place in front of the chair. Mass continues as usual with the *General Intercessions* or *Prayer of the Faithful*.

722. After Mass, servers follow directions as to the blessed ashes whether they are to be taken to the sacristy or left in the church for use after Mass—for example, in a busy city church where ashes have to be given at various times. When permitted, they may be given by an authorized minister to those confined to home. After the final Mass of the day, the sacristan disposes of remaining ashes by pouring them down the sacrarium.

The Way of the Cross

723. On the walls of the church, we see fourteen crosses with pictures or images representing the "Way of the Cross", our Lord's journey from the judgment hall of Pontius Pilate to the Cross of Calvary. Sometimes a fifteenth image is added, the Resurrection, to remind us that this way of suffering was a journey of victory and triumph.

724. Commonly known as the *Stations of the Cross*, the Way of the Cross is a popular Catholic devotion. At each "station"

(stopping place), we pause to meditate on a particular event in the saving work of Jesus Christ. You may choose to make this devotion privately, making up your own prayers, meditating with your own thoughts, or use a booklet to help you to pray. The Church also encourages the public celebration of the Way of the Cross, in almost a liturgical form. Each year, in Rome, the Holy Father leads vast crowds in this devotion. In Jerusalem, many pilgrims constantly retrace the steps of the suffering Christ and his blessed Mother along the "Via Dolorosa", way of sorrows, the origin of the devotion. In our churches, especially during Lent or a mission, servers assist in the dignified public celebration of the Way of the Cross.

725. Because this is a flexible popular devotion, there are many ways of making a public devotion out of the Stations. What is described below is for the help of servers and would need to be adapted for local customs or pastoral needs. There should be three servers assisting: the cross bearer and two candle bearers. A book bearer is only required if the celebrant wishes to keep his hands free or if the Stations are part of a formal paraliturgy.

726. *Preparations.* Having vested, servers check that everything is ready for the Way of the Cross.

727. *The altar*: two candles lit, violet antependium (if used), or red for Passion (Palm) Sunday or if the celebrant wears a red stole. On Good Friday, the altar is bare, no cloths or candles.

728. *Before the altar*: unless worn by the celebrant, a microphone for the opening and closing prayers, if required. The ambo may be needed if a reader assists in the devotions.

729. *In the church*: booklets, hymnals, or programs for the people.

730. *The sacristy*: for the celebrant: soutane, surplice, or amice, alb, cincture, with a violet stole or a red stole for Passion Sunday, Good Friday, or if the devotion is seen as a celebration of the Passion. A violet or red cope may be used for extra solemnity or if the devotion is part of a longer paraliturgy. For the servers: the processional cross or a large plain black wooden cross (the Roman custom), processional candles prepared.

731. Having bowed to the sacristy cross, servers and celebrant proceed to the sanctuary, moving to one side or separating to allow the celebrant to come to the center, coming together behind him, the cross at the center, and all making the customary reverence (except the cross bearer).

732. The celebrant may introduce the Way of the Cross according to custom or the order chosen. If he kneels, the candle bearers and the cross bearer remain standing. Usually during the singing of the first verse of the chosen hymn, "Stabat Mater" or some other suitable hymn, the celebrant and candle bearers make the customary reverence and, led by the cross bearer, proceed to a position near the first station. If the celebrant recites the prayer, "We adore you, O Christ, and we bless you . . .", the candle bearers may genuflect with the people, but the cross bearer remains standing. The best position for them to take at each station is to form a line, candles flanking the cross, their backs to the station, facing outward, throughout all the prayers, and remaining standing, even if the celebrant and people kneel for particular prayers or meditations.

733. They lead the way to each succeeding station, where they act as above. After the last station, they come again before the altar, divide or move to one side, let the celebrant pass through, and come together again. The candle bearers make the customary reverence with the celebrant and remain standing together facing the altar for the final prayers. Unless a sermon or paraliturgy or Eucharistic devotions follow, all make the customary reverence and return to the sacristy.

734. Starting before first Vespers of the fifth Sunday of Lent, *"The practice of covering crosses and images throughout the church from this Sunday may be observed* [if the Conference of Bishops so decides]. *Crosses remain covered until the end of the Celebration of the Lord's Passion on Good Friday, but images remain covered until the beginning of the Easter Vigil"* (Introduction to the Fifth Sunday of Lent, *Roman Missal*).

10.

Holy Week

735. The summit of the liturgical year is Holy Week, when we celebrate the Paschal Mystery of the saving death and Resurrection of the Lord Jesus in richly symbolic ceremonies. Four major ceremonies require the assistance of *carefully trained* servers directed by an M.C.: (1) *Passion Sunday* (Palm Sunday), the solemn commemoration of our Lord's entrance into Jerusalem; (2) *Holy Thursday* (Maundy Thursday), the Evening Mass of the Lord's Supper with the Washing of the Feet and Transfer of the Holy Eucharist; (3) *Good Friday*, the Celebration of the Lord's Passion; (4) The *Easter Vigil in the Holy Night*, with the first Mass of Easter Sunday. On a suitable day in Holy Week, on Holy Thursday if possible, the bishop of the diocese celebrates the *Chrism Mass*, when he blesses the Holy Oils to be used during the year. This is described in the next chapter, on serving the bishop.

Passion Sunday (Palm Sunday)

736. On the first day of Holy Week, the Church celebrates the entry of our Lord into Jerusalem, as King and Redeemer, greeted by the people waving palm and olive branches. This entry into the holy city was his final decisive step toward his saving death and Resurrection.

737. The liturgy of Palm Sunday may take one of three different forms: (1) The *Procession*, (2) The *Solemn Entrance*, (3) The *Simple Entrance*. The Procession or Solemn Entrance is celebrated before the principal Mass of the day, with the Simple Entrance before the other Masses. The Solemn Entrance may be repeated, without the Procession, before other Masses that are usually well attended.

738. A full team of trained and *rehearsed* servers is required for (1) and (2). Any number of servers may assist at (3), which is an entrance procession to the altar, accompanied by the entrance antiphon, "Six days . . .", and Psalm 23:9–10, or a suitable chant or hymn.

739. *Preparations.* Having vested, servers check that everything is ready for (1) The *Procession*, or (2) The *Solemn Entrance*.

740. A. *At a suitable place outside the church*, e.g., school, hall, open area, garden: the missal or Holy Week book and the Book of the Gospels, unless these are brought in procession; a lectern for the Gospel, perhaps with a red fall, and a supply of "palms" for those who do not bring their own branches.

741. B. *At a suitable place inside the church*, e.g., porch, narthex, side chapel, the same requirements as for A.

742. *In the church*, for (1) and (2).

743. *The altar*: prepared for Mass, four or six candles, lit (red antependium).

744. *The ambo*: the lectionary, prepared for Mass, with the book(s) for the reading of the Passion and, if required, three lecterns with the books for the reading of the Passion, microphone(s). The fixed lectern may have a red fall.

745. *The chair*: prepared for Mass, red chasuble spread over it or near it, if the celebrant wears the cope for (A) or (B), chairs for deacon(s), concelebrants.

746. *The credence table*: prepared for Solemn Mass.

747. *The sacristy*: red vestments for the celebrant deacon, con-celebrants, if possible a red cope for the celebrant for (A) or (B); for the servers: the processional cross suitably decorated with "palm", etc., processional candles, prepared thurible and boat, holy water and sprinkler, candles for torch bearers, if used for the Mass. Three *readers of the Passion* (if not the deacon and/or celebrant), wear amice, alb, cincture. They may either take part in the ceremonies of (A) or (B) with the servers or vest during the first reading and enter the sanctuary before the Passion. Palms may be prepared for the servers who do not carry another object.

1. The Procession

748. When the people have gathered in the chosen place, hav-ing bowed to the sacristy cross, celebrant (concelebrants, deacon[s]), M.C., and servers proceed in procession to that place, in order: thurifer (thurible kindled, but no incense in it), cross, candles, other servers carrying palms and holy water, book bearer, M.C., concelebrants, deacon, celebrant. The antiphon "Hosanna to the Son of David" or a suitable hymn is sung as servers and clergy approach.

749. *The Blessing of Palms.* At the place of blessing, the cross bearer and candle bearers stand in line behind the celebrant, the deacon on his right, concelebrants ranged on each side, the book bearer holding the missal open and the M.C. on his left. The thurifer and holy-water bearer stand near the dea-con. Other servers bearing palms may form two lines at each side, ready for the procession. The priest greets the people, as for Mass, and introduces the celebration with words of explanation. He says the prayer of blessing, the book bearer attending. The holy-water bearer approaches the celebrant (or deacon), and the celebrant proceeds to sprinkle the palms that the people, clergy, and servers hold. As he moves about sprinkling, the deacon(s), M.C., or two concelebrants or servers may hold back his cope.

750. *The Gospel.* The thurifer approaches the celebrant, who places incense in the thurible, assisted by the deacon and M.C. or acolyte. If the deacon assists, he asks the celebrant for his blessing. If the celebrant or concelebrant reads, he bows and says the prayer before the Gospel. Meanwhile, candle bearers come and stand to each side of the Gospel reader. The celebrant receives a palm to hold during the Gospel, if read by another. If the deacon or concelebrant reads, he faces the celebrant, with the M.C., thurifer, and candle bearers. All bow and go to the lectern for the Gospel reading. If the celebrant has to read the Gospel, he joins the M.C., thurifer, and candle bearers. After he has said the private prayer, they bow to the cross and go to the lectern. The Gospel is read as at Solemn Mass. At the end of the reading, all return to their previous positions. A brief homily may be given.

751. *The Procession to the Church.* The thurifer comes to the celebrant, and incense is prepared as usual. The cross bearer and candle bearers move around to the front of the celebrant and stand facing him, candles flanking the cross. The thurifer stands *behind* them, so as to lead the procession when they turn around as it begins. The celebrant or deacon proclaims the beginning of the procession, attended by the book bearer, if he reads the formula in the missal. The choir begins to sing "The children of the Hebrews", and the responsory or another suitable hymn heralds the "Lord's entrance" into the holy city.

752. The thurifer, cross, and candles turn and begin to move forward in the direction chosen for the procession. If there is a robed choir, the singers follow the candles, then clergy

in choir dress, servers, book bearer, M.C., concelebrants, deacon(s), and celebrant, followed by the people. As soon as the procession begins, the M.C. gives the celebrant and deacon palms. Servers not carrying an object should carry a blessed palm. The book bearer carries the missal or Holy Week book.

753. *Solemn Mass.* When he arrives at the sanctuary, the celebrant gives up his palm. All make the customary reverence. A server takes the palms from the clergy in the sanctuary and places them on the credence table. The celebrant kisses the altar and incenses it as usual. More incense will be required, the thurifer attending. The celebrant goes to the chair. If he has been wearing the cope, he removes it and puts on the chasuble, assisted by a deacon, M.C., or server. The cope is put to one side or taken to the sacristy. The book bearer attends at the chair, with the missal, for the *Collect*, which concludes the procession and begins the Mass. The *Liturgy of the Word* is described below, after (2) and (3).

2. The Solemn Entrance

754. If the procession outdoors is not possible, the people gather inside the church. They bring their own palms or take them at the door. The servers and celebrant go to a place inside the church, in the same order of procession as for (1), where the Solemn Entrance will begin—narthex, porch, or chapel. A representative group of the people should join them there, to take part, carrying palms in the Entrance. The antiphon "Hosanna to the Son of David", or another suitable hymn, is sung as servers and clergy go to this prepared area. The congregation should turn to face the area.

755. *The Blessing of Palms.* As for (1) above, but the celebrant may walk around the church sprinkling the people's palms, accompanied by the deacon, M.C., or a server.

756. *The Gospel.* As for (1) above.

757. *The Entrance.* As above, but there is no proclamation of a procession, and only the entrance responsory or a hymn is sung. During the singing, servers, clergy, and a group of the people move through the church to the sanctuary.

758. *Solemn Mass.* As above, modified according to circumstances.

3. The Simple Entrance

759. Where the more solemn forms (1) or (2) are not possible, and at other Masses on the day, the entrance antiphon "Six days . . ." should be sung as servers and clergy go to the altar for Mass.

760. *The Passion Reading.* For options (1), (2), and perhaps (3), in place of the Gospel of the Liturgy of the Word, an account of the Passion of our Lord is sung or read. Servers do not assist with incense or candles. The Passion is read by the deacon of the Mass, or the celebrant, if there is no deacon, or by deacons or concelebrants, or even by skilled lay readers. If possible, the part of Christ should be reserved for the priest. In some places, it is sung with the choir and/or people taking various parts.

761. Lay readers wear albs, as noted above. If they are not already in the sanctuary, they come from the sacristy during the verse before the Passion. They make the customary reverence at the center, bow to the celebrant, and go to the lectern(s), where the texts should be open at the reading. Only a deacon asks for the blessing before reading the Passion. The greeting and sign of the cross are omitted before the reading. At the moment when the death of our Lord is recounted, all kneel in silent prayer, standing again for the last verses of the reading.

762. After the Passion, the readers come to the center, make the customary reverence, bow to the celebrant, and either return to the sacristy or take their places in the sanctuary. A brief homily may follow. Mass continues as usual according to the texts in the missal.

Holy Thursday of the Lord's Supper
(Maundy Thursday)

763. The three major liturgical days of Holy Week, known as the *Easter Triduum*, begin on Holy Thursday evening. The Church celebrates the evening of the Last Supper, when Jesus Christ gave us the sacrifice and Sacrament of the Holy Eucharist, when he ordained his apostles to the priesthood of the New Covenant and knelt to wash their feet as an example of service. After the Last Supper, he led his apostles to the garden of Gethsemane, where he prayed and suffered before Judas came to betray him, handing him over to arrest and trial.

764. As this is the day of the institution of the Holy Eucharist, the major celebration of the liturgy is the *Evening Mass of the Lord's Supper*. Masses without a congregation are forbidden on this day. In addition to the Chrism Mass, celebrated by the bishop with his priests, the bishop of the diocese may allow another public Mass for the pastoral needs of the people, but the focus of worship is the evening liturgy.

765. During the Mass of the Lord's Supper, the *Washing of Feet* is carried out, if possible, after the homily, a reenactment of our Lord's humble service. At the conclusion of the Mass, the *Blessed Sacrament is carried in procession* to a "place of reposition", altar of repose, a reenactment of the journey to Gethsemane. After the procession, adoration continues at

this Eucharistic shrine, a reenactment of the apostles watching and praying with our Lord in Gethsemane. A full team of trained and rehearsed servers is required for the Mass and procession.

766. *Preparations.* Having vested, servers check that everything is ready for the Mass of the Lord's Supper, the washing of feet, and the procession to the altar of repose.

767. *The altar*: prepared for Mass, four or six candles lit (white antependium); by custom the altar crucifix is veiled in white.

768. *The ambo*: the lectionary marked for the readings.

769. *The chair*: prepared for Mass, also chairs for deacon(s), concelebrants, the missal or book of the chair or Holy Week book, marked for Mass.

770. *The credence table*: prepared for Solemn Mass, with a white humeral veil folded, for the procession, bells for the Gloria. For the washing of feet, a large ewer of water and a bowl, twelve towels folded on a tray, if necessary on a second table.

771. *The table of the gifts*: prepared for the Procession of the Gifts, with as many ciboria/patens as may be needed for Holy Communion on Good Friday. Gifts for the poor may be prepared at this table, to be brought to the altar in the Procession of the Gifts. Monies collected for Lenten appeals or relief projects may be included in the procession.

772. *The tabernacle*: empty, no veil, the Blessed Sacrament having been removed to some secure place. (Holy Communion on this night and on Good Friday is from Hosts consecrated at this Mass).

773. *In or near the sanctuary*: benches or twelve chairs for the washing of feet, which should be carried out in full view of the congregation.

774. *In the church*: booklets or programs for the people.

775. *The altar of repose*: In a chapel or distinct area away from the sanctuary, the place of reposition is prepared. It is to be "suitably decorated" according to custom, with flowers, lamps, and dignified hangings. On the altar of repose, a white cloth and a corporal are spread in front of the open tabernacle, with the key next to the corporal. Candles should be arranged on or near the altar, four or six at least, more according to custom, to burn during the procession and solemn adoration until midnight, as for exposition of the Blessed Sacrament. Any image or picture above or behind the tabernacle of reposition should be removed or veiled. Convenient chairs and kneeling desks should be provided, if necessary, for the faithful who come to adore our Lord.

776. *The sacristy*: white vestments for the celebrant, deacon(s), concelebrants; for the procession; four or six torches (and a second thurible prepared, if possible); processional cross, processional candles, thurible as for Solemn Mass. If a safe is used in the sacristy for reserving the Blessed Sacrament, a corporal should be spread inside it and a lamp prepared near it.

1. Mass of the Lord's Supper

777. *Entrance Procession.* Having bowed to the sacristy cross, servers and celebrants proceed to the sanctuary: thurifer, cross bearer, candle bearers, servers acting as torch bearers, book bearer, M.C., concelebrants, deacon(s), celebrant. Because the Blessed Sacrament is not present, on arrival all bow to the altar. Solemn Mass proceeds as usual.

778. According to local custom, the church bells are rung joyously during the Gloria. A signal should be given to the bell ringer(s) to coordinate the bells with the Gloria. Servers may ring the Sanctus bells, usually at the credence table, but in a way planned to blend with the singing. The bell is not used later in the Mass for the elevations.

2. The Washing of Feet

779. In the homily, the priest sheds light on *"the principal mysteries that are commemorated in this Mass, namely, the institution of the Holy Eucharist and of the priestly Order, and the commandment of the Lord concerning fraternal charity"* (*Roman Missal*). At the conclusion of the homily, the celebrant goes to the chair. He removes the chasuble, which is draped over the chair. If the benches or chairs for those whose feet are to be washed are not already in position, servers arrange them now. Those whose feet will be washed (twelve or fewer) come forward, make the customary reverence together, and go to the seats. They remove footwear at least of the right foot, assisted by servers if necessary. The M.C. or servers should lead them to their seats and supervise these practical arrangements as conveniently as possible. The choir begins to sing the proper antiphons or other appropriate hymns.

780. The first candle bearer (first server) brings the large ewer of water; the second, the basin and towels. They join the celebrant, deacon, M.C., and/or another server, if required. Facing the altar, all make the customary reverence together and go to the first seat.

781. There are various ways of carrying out the washing of feet. This procedure seems to be the most convenient. The celebrant kneels, the deacon kneels on his right, the first candle bearer gives him the ewer and then kneels to his right. The second candle bearer and the M.C. kneel on the celebrant's

left. The second candle bearer gives the bowl to the M.C. or a server, who holds it under the foot. The deacon gives the ewer to the celebrant, who pours water over the foot. He gives the ewer back to the deacon. The second candle bearer gives the celebrant a towel, and he dries the foot, then gives the towel back to the second candle bearer, who hands used towels to a third server near him.

782. All stand after the washing of the feet at the first seat and go to the second, and so on, repeating the procedure, without haste. The choir should continue singing until the whole action is complete. If there is no deacon or concelebrant to assist with the ewer, the first candle bearer hands it to the celebrant at each washing of feet. If necessary, the second candle bearer could hold the bowl and the M.C. would supervise the towels, assisted by a third server.

783. After the washing of feet, the first candle bearer takes the ewer (unless already holding it); the second candle bearer takes the bowl and used towels. With the celebrant, deacon, and M.C., they make the customary reverence at the center and take the ewer, bowl, and towels back to the credence or to the sacristy. The celebrant goes to the chair. The candle bearers, or other servers, at once bring the smaller ewer, bowl, and towel to the celebrant, who washes his hands. The servers assist as usual, bowing together and taking the vessels back to the credence. Assisted by the deacon or M.C., the celebrant puts on the chasuble. The Prayer of the Faithful follows, the book bearer attending as usual.

784. During the *Procession of the Gifts*, the people may bring forward gifts for the poor, while the choir sings the antiphon "Where true charity is dwelling . . ." or a suitable hymn. Servers assist in taking these gifts and placing them in some convenient place near the altar.

785. Torch bearers should assist during the Eucharistic Prayer, remaining until the end of Mass because they will be required for the procession. The bell is not rung at the elevations, but in some places it is customary to use a wooden clapper.

3. The Procession to the Altar of Repose

786. *Preparations* for the procession must begin *during* the distribution of Holy Communion. The thurifer (with a second server who will act as second thurifer) form up at the center of the sanctuary, bow, and go to the sacristy. The second thurible is prepared. Thurifers wait in the sacristy until the Prayer after Communion. The M.C. directs a server or servers to take a taper and light the candles at the altar of repose.

787. After Holy Communion, the chalice and any other empty vessels are cleansed as usual and the missal is removed from the altar. A concelebrant, the deacon, or the celebrant, if necessary, takes all the ciboria, except the one chosen for the procession, to the sacristy or some other convenient place, escorted by a server. The ciborium for the procession remains on the corporal, veiled according to local custom.

788. At the chair, after customary silence or a psalm or song of thanksgiving, the celebrant sings or says the *Prayer after Communion*, attended by the book bearer. The Blessing and Dismissal are omitted. The celebrant goes to the center of the sanctuary with the deacon and M.C. and any concelebrants. The thurifer(s) come from the sacristy and join them immediately, as also the cross bearer, candle bearers (with their lighted candles), and the book bearer. All genuflect. Torch bearers should stand well back to each side, cross and candle bearers to one side.

789. The thurifers come to the celebrant, who places incense in the thuribles assisted as usual by the deacon and/or M.C. The celebrant kneels at the center, and all kneel at the same time, except the cross bearer and candle bearers. He takes the first thurible, from the deacon, M.C., or a concelebrant, and incenses the Blessed Sacrament with three double swings. He hands back the thurible, which the deacon, M.C., or a concelebrant gives to the thurifer. Still kneeling, he receives the humeral veil, brought from the step by the book bearer, who places it around his shoulders, as at Benediction. The celebrant (and the deacon or a concelebrant) stands and goes to the altar, he genuflects (with the deacon or a concelebrant) and takes the ciborium, enfolding it in the humeral veil (assisted by the deacon or a concelebrant, who hands him the ciborium). He comes to the center of the sanctuary. Torch bearers and any concelebrants stand. He turns and faces the people, the deacon standing on his right.

790. The cross bearer comes to the center with the candle bearers, ready to lead the procession, while the choir begins the hymn "Pange lingua" or another Eucharistic chant. The order of the procession is: cross bearer, candle bearers, robed choir, servers not carrying out specific duties, clergy in choir dress, M.C., concelebrants, thurifers, the celebrant carrying the Blessed Sacrament with a deacon on his right and torch bearers carrying lighted torches, flanking him, two or three in line on each side. If there is insufficient room for the torch bearers to walk beside the Blessed Sacrament, they may precede the celebrant. The procession should move at a slow and reverent pace, in perfect formation, according to the longest route to the place of reposition. The people should kneel during the procession and reposition, joining in the Eucharistic hymn.

791. *Reposition.* On arrival at the place of reposition, the cross and candle bearers move to one side and remain standing, facing across. The servers and clergy divide and form two lines (or more if necessary), allowing ample room for the celebrant, deacon, and torch bearers to pass through. They face inward and kneel as the celebrant arrives. Thurifers move to each side. Torch bearers stand in the same positions as for the procession, while the celebrant moves forward and places the ciborium on the corporal on the altar assisted by the deacon or a concelebrant. Servers not already kneeling kneel as soon as he places the ciborium on the altar, all facing the altar.

792. Having genuflected (with the assisting deacon or concelebrant), the celebrant comes down to the lowest step, or to whatever area is available in front of the altar. He kneels at the center, the deacon kneeling on his right. The book bearer or another server comes behind him, genuflects, and takes the humeral veil away, placing it in some convenient position to the side. The choir begins the hymn "Tantum ergo".

793. As at Benediction, at the end of the first verse, the celebrant stands and turns to the right. The first thurifer approaches at once, and, assisted by the deacon, M.C., or another server, the celebrant prepares incense as usual. The thurifer closes the thurible, hands it to the deacon, M.C., or assisting concelebrant, who hands it to the celebrant when all are kneeling once more. The celebrant incenses the Blessed Sacrament with three double swings. All bow before and after the incensation. The deacon may hold back his chasuble, if necessary, to free his right arm. The celebrant returns the thurible to the minister on his right, who hands it to the thurifer, who goes back to the chosen position and kneels.

794. While all remain kneeling, the deacon or an assisting concelebrant or celebrant stands, goes to the altar, places the ciborium in the tabernacle, genuflects, and locks it. After a

period of silent adoration, on a signal from the M.C., all stand, genuflect together and return to the sacristy, thurifer(s) leading the way, then the cross bearer, candle bearers, other servers and torch bearers, clergy in choir dress, M.C., deacons, concelebrants, deacon, and celebrant. By custom, all make the double genuflection.

795. Silence must be observed strictly in the sacristy and church, out of consideration for the faithful who are praying in adoration at the altar of repose. This adoration continues according to the local custom or local conditions. However, at midnight it ceases to be "solemn", that is, the candles are extinguished at that time or at any earlier time when the church is closed to the public.

796. After the liturgy, under the direction of the M.C., servers extinguish the candles at the main altar (*not* the altar of repose) and bring to the sacristy all that was used for the ceremonies. They carefully strip the altar of all candlesticks, cloths, and antependium. The fall is also removed from the ambo. Any other decorations, flowers, etc., are removed from the church (*not* from the altar of repose), and those crosses that cannot be removed from the church ought to be veiled, in preparation for the Good Friday ceremonies. Having completed all duties, servers remove their robes, but before leaving the church they should each spend some time in private prayer before our Lord at the place of reposition.

Friday of the Passion of the Lord (Good Friday)

797. We call this day "good" because we celebrate the saving death of Jesus Christ on the Cross, when he redeemed us and gained for us mercy and salvation. The liturgy of the

day reflects sorrow for the sufferings of our Savior and yet triumph, because his suffering was an eternal victory over sin, evil, and death.

798. According to the Church's ancient tradition, the sacraments are not celebrated on Good Friday or Holy Saturday. The altar remains completely bare, without cloths, candles, or cross. The *Celebration of the Lord's Passion* should take place in the afternoon, at about three o'clock, unless this time is not convenient for the people. Only during the celebration of the Lord's Passion may Holy Communion be given to the faithful, except for the sick who cannot take part in the liturgy and to whom Communion may be brought at any time.

799. The *Celebration of the Lord's Passion* consists of three parts. (a) *Liturgy of the Word*, (b) *Adoration of the Holy Cross*, (c) *Holy Communion*. There should be at least six servers. Incense is not used. The cross is not carried in procession, and the processional candles are only used at the adoration of the cross and the transfer of the Blessed Sacrament. A team of trained and rehearsed servers is required for Good Friday.

800. *Preparations*. Having vested, servers check that everything is ready for the Celebration of the Lord's Passion.

801. *The altar*: completely stripped.

802. *The ambo*: the lectionary marked for the Liturgy of the Word, with the books for the reading of the Passion and, if required, three lecterns with the books for the reading of the Passion, microphone(s). The ambo is bare.

803. *The chair*: prepared for Mass, also chairs for the deacon(s), other priests, the missal or Holy Week book marked for Good Friday.

804. *The credence table*: one folded or rolled-up altar cloth, a corporal folded (in a red burse), patens or ciboria into which Hosts may be transferred if necessary, missal stand or cushion, vessel of water and purifier for cleansing fingers, cruet of water (if vessels need to be purified after Communion), Communion plates, if used, towels to wipe the crucifix after it has been venerated.

805. *The tabernacle*: empty, no veil, doors open, lamp extinguished.

806. *The altar of repose*: Flowers, lamps, and other decorations from the Holy Thursday liturgy are removed. On or near the altar, two candles lit before the liturgy, suitable as processional candles. The cloth, corporal, and tabernacle key are set out as for Holy Thursday.

807. *In the church*: booklets or programs for the people.

808. *The sacristy*: red Mass vestments for the celebrant and deacon(s); amice, alb, cincture and red stole and chasuble or dalmatic for other priests and deacons assisting. Three readers of the Passion (if not the deacon[s] and/or celebrant) wear amice, alb, cincture. They may either take part in the celebration with the servers or vest during the first reading and enter the sanctuary before the Passion. The crucifix for veneration is prepared with a red or purple veil, pinned in such a way as to be easily removed, for the first form of the showing of the cross, or prepared without a veil, for the second form of the showing of the cross. Its stand or socket is near the altar, if used. Two processional candles are prepared in the sacristy, if possible matching those at the altar of repose.

The Celebration of the Passion of the Lord

809. *Entrance Procession.* Having bowed to the sacristy cross, servers and celebrant proceed to the sanctuary without processional cross or candles. All form up before the altar and bow. In silence, the priest and deacon and any assisting clergy either prostrate themselves (i.e., lie flat on the floor) or kneel. When they prostrate themselves or kneel, all servers kneel facing the altar, bowing their heads in silent prayer. At a signal from the M.C., clergy and servers stand. The celebrant goes directly to the chair, without kissing the altar. Servers go to their places.

A. LITURGY OF THE WORD

810. All remain standing while the celebrant sings or says the opening prayer, the book bearer attending with the missal. All sit for the readings. The reading from Isaiah with its responsorial psalm and the reading from Hebrews follow, the M.C. directing lectors if customary. During the sung verse before the Passion, all stand. The ritual of the Passion proceeds as described for Palm Sunday. All kneel in silence at the moment in Saint John's narrative when the death of our Lord is recounted, standing again as the last part of the reading continues.

811. The *General Intercessions* follow the Passion and short homily. All stand. The celebrant may lead the intercessions at the chair or at the altar. The book bearer either attends him at the chair with the missal or places the missal on the altar, on the book stand, brought to him from the credence table and placed at the center of the altar by a server. The server takes the book stand back to the credence at the end of the intercessions; the book bearer takes the missal.

812. During the intercessions, at the ambo, the deacon or a lay minister sings or says the introduction to each prayer, giving the particular intention. Then all kneel and pray silently for a time, standing again on a signal from the M.C. The celebrant then sings or says the prayer. The deacon may give the traditional invitations, "Let us kneel" and "Let us stand", with all kneeling for a short time in silent prayer. In some places, the people and servers either kneel or stand during the whole of the intercessions.

813. While awaiting the arrival of the cross for veneration, the annual collection may be made for the Holy Places in Israel.

B. THE ADORATION OF THE HOLY CROSS

814. At the conclusion of the intercessions, the celebrant (goes to the chair and) sits, if the deacon assists or if another priest is to bring the crucifix to the sanctuary. Otherwise, he goes to the sacristy or the entrance of the church with the servers, as described below.

815. Two servers carry candles on each side of the crucifix as it is brought to the sanctuary and venerated. If the celebrant wishes to read the music of "Behold the wood of the cross", the book bearer attends with the missal or a Holy Week manual. There are two procedures for the showing of the cross, according to custom and situation.

816. *First Form of the Showing the Holy Cross.* The deacon, assisting priest, or celebrant comes to the center, to be met by the two candle bearers and the M.C. All bow to the altar and go to the sacristy. Assisted by the M.C., the deacon (or assisting priest or celebrant) takes the veiled crucifix. Candle bearers light the candles and hold them on each side of the deacon or priest carrying the crucifix. In this formation, they return to the sanctuary, the M.C. behind them. Depending on the location of the sacristy or local custom, they should come down the main aisle. All stand as the crucifix is brought into the church.

817. The deacon, assisting priest, or celebrant carrying the crucifix ascends to the top step of the altar steps, in front of the altar, if possible, and turns to face the people. If the celebrant did not bring the crucifix from the sacristy, he comes from the chair accompanied by the book bearer, bows with him to the altar, and receives the veiled crucifix from the deacon or assisting priest, who steps aside to his right. The candle bearers face inward on the top step, flanking the celebrant as he holds the crucifix. Assisted if necessary by the deacon or M.C., the celebrant unveils the top of the crucifix and, raising it moderately, he intones, "Behold the wood of the cross . . .", the book bearer attending on his left, down a step, if convenient. The deacon and/or choir may assist in the singing. All respond with "Come let us adore", and *then* all kneel and venerate the cross in silence. The celebrant remains standing and holds the crucifix high.

818. Then the celebrant uncovers the right arm of the crucifix, lifting it up again, and repeats "Behold the wood of the cross . . .", according to custom, singing on a higher note. All respond and kneel again, as above. Finally, the celebrant uncovers the entire crucifix, lifts it up again, and repeats the invitation, all responding and kneeling as before. The M.C. takes the veil and gives it to a server, who takes it to the credence table.

819. The candle bearers face the people and move with the celebrant as he brings the crucifix down to the center of the sanctuary or some other convenient place chosen for the veneration. (Alternatively, the deacon or an assisting priest may take the crucifix from the celebrant and bring it to this position.) Two other servers immediately come to this place, standing behind the crucifix, each taking hold of it in the way chosen for the veneration. The candle bearers turn in again, flanking the crucifix. In some places the crucifix is placed on a large cushion or sloping frame or placed into a prepared socket, rather than being held by the two servers. The veneration may proceed as described below, after the alternative.

820. *Second Form of the Showing the Holy Cross.* The deacon, assisting priest, or celebrant comes to the center, to be met by the two candle bearers and the M.C. All bow to the altar and go to the sacristy if the crucifix is prepared there. Then the deacon, assisting priest, or celebrant, with candle bearers and M.C. (and book bearer, if required, with the book), go to the entrance of the church. It would be better if they did not go through the church but went some other way, so as to heighten the drama of the entrance. In the porch or narthex, processional candles are lit, and the deacon (or assisting priest or celebrant) takes the unveiled crucifix, entering the church in procession, in the same formation as for the first form. All stand as they enter.

821. This procession pauses three times: (a) near the entrance, (b) in the middle of the church, (c) at the entrance to the sanctuary. Each time the procession stops, the one carrying the crucifix lifts it up and sings "Behold the wood of the cross . . .", all responding and then kneeling briefly as above. If he turns to face the people and the book bearer, the candle bearers turn and face inward, flanking him, depending on the space available. On arrival at the sanctuary, the crucifix is placed in position, as for the first form.

822. The *Adoration of the Holy Cross* begins once the crucifix is in position, either in its socket, resting on a stand or cushion, or held by two servers. The candle bearers stand on each side, facing inward, during the veneration, unless the candlesticks are large enough to be placed on the ground on each side, but back slightly to avoid accidents.

823. There are various ways of venerating the cross. The first form suggested is the procession. The celebrant comes from the chair or from a position near the crucifix. Facing the crucifix, he genuflects once or makes some other customary reverence, according to local custom; for example, in place of the genuflection, he may kiss the feet of the figure on the cross. The deacon, assisting priests, and other clergy follow him in a single file, spaced neatly apart, making the same customary reverence. The servers follow the clergy, but it would be best for those holding the crucifix and candles to venerate the cross last, after the people. Other servers relieve them of these duties to make this possible.

824. The people approach to venerate the cross. If they kiss the feet of the figure, the servers holding the cross, or servers standing near it, wipe the feet with a towel after each kiss. Towels are brought from the credence as soon as the veneration begins and taken back to the credence after the veneration.

825. Only one cross should be used for the veneration. If the numbers are such that not everyone can venerate the cross personally, a representative group of the people may venerate it first. The celebrant then takes the crucifix from the servers or out of its socket, goes to the top step of the altar, faces the people, and invites them to venerate the cross. He holds it up briefly for them to venerate in silence as a community. The candle bearers accompany him and face inward on each side of the crucifix during this form of the veneration.

826. The choir sings the customary chant, the *Reproaches*, and other appropriate chants or hymns during the veneration.

After the veneration, two servers carry the crucifix to the position chosen for it, on, in front of, or near the altar, bringing the socket or stand for this purpose, unless a server has brought this from the credence already during the veneration. The candle bearers place their candles on or near the altar or on each side of the crucifix. If they place them on the altar, they may have to wait while other servers spread the cloth, as below. If a large crucifix is placed at the center of the altar, it would be appropriate for the Communion Rite to be celebrated facing east.

C. HOLY COMMUNION

827. The celebrant goes to the chair and sits. The people and those not engaged in duties sit. Two servers bring the altar cloth from the credence table and spread it neatly on the altar. (If not already in position, the candles are placed on the altar.) The corporal (in a red burse) is brought to the altar and spread at the center. The book stand is brought to the altar, and the book bearer brings the missal, placing it opened on the stand. (A server takes a taper and lights it from the candles on or near the altar and goes to the altar of repose to light the two candles there, if they are not already burning.) The M.C. supervises all these preparations.

828. The candle bearers, without candles, come to the center of the sanctuary, to be joined by the deacon, assisting priest, or celebrant. They genuflect to the cross and go by the shortest way to the altar of repose. On arrival at the place of reposition, they genuflect together. The candle bearers kneel while the deacon or priest takes the ciborium out of the tabernacle. (If there are several ciboria and many are to receive Holy Communion, other clergy, acolytes, or extraordinary ministers may assist in bringing the ciboria from the altar of repose, from the place of private reservation in

the sacristy, or elsewhere.) The candle bearers stand, take their candles from the altar, or from a place near it, and lead the deacon(s) or priest, etc., back to the sanctuary by the shortest way. All stand in reverent silence as the Blessed Sacrament is brought to the main altar.

829. When the Blessed Sacrament is placed on the corporal, the candle bearers place their candles on or near the altar. Then they come together at the center, genuflect, and go to their places near the credence table. If not already at the altar, the celebrant comes from the chair, genuflects, and takes his place at the center of the altar, the deacon on his right. Whoever brings the Blessed Sacrament to the altar uncovers the ciboria as soon as they are placed on the corporal.

830. The celebrant introduces the *Lord's Prayer*, which is sung or said by all. He continues with the "Deliver us . . .", all making the acclamation as usual. All kneel while he prays quietly. He shows the Host, saying "Behold the Lamb of God . . ."; all respond as usual. He receives Holy Communion. Then he gives Holy Communion to the deacon(s) and other clergy present, and the distribution of Communion proceeds as for Mass, according to local practice. Appropriate hymns may be sung during Communion.

831. After Communion, the ciboria are covered and the deacon, an assisting priest, acolyte, or lay minister takes the Blessed Sacrament to the place of reservation in the sacristy or elsewhere. (If the celebrant has no assistants authorized to repose the Eucharist, he should place the ciboria in the tabernacle of the altar of repose or the main tabernacle —temporarily, so as not to delay the Good Friday liturgy. He will later take the Blessed Sacrament to the place of reservation in the sacristy or elsewhere.) A server folds the corporal and takes it to the credence table.

832. Servers may assist the celebrant and other ministers of Holy Communion in cleansing their hands and, if necessary, in cleansing any empty ciboria or patens at the credence. The celebrant either remains at the altar for the final prayers or he goes to the chair, the book bearer attending with the missal or Holy Week book, a server having taken the book stand back to the credence. Before the final prayers, there may be a time of silence in thanksgiving for Holy Communion. After the *Prayer after Communion* and *Prayer over the People* (in place of the Blessing and Dismissal), the celebrant, deacon(s), other clergy, M.C., and servers form up as usual, *genuflect* to the crucifix, and return *in silence* to the sacristy. Candle bearers do not carry the candles in this procession.

833. Servers return to the sanctuary and remove the candles and cloth from the altar, leaving it completely bare. All other cloths, vessels, etc., are taken to the sacristy, so that the sanctuary is as it was before the liturgy, except that the crucifix is left in position. In some places, the crucifix and four candles, burning, are left on or near the altar, or the crucifix is placed at the entrance of the sanctuary, with candles burning on each side, for the private devotions of the people. It is customary to salute the crucifix with a genuflection. The Way of the Cross may be celebrated as an evening devotion on Good Friday.

Holy Saturday

834. The Church waits at the tomb of the Lord, meditating on his suffering and death. The altar is left bare, the Sacrifice of the Mass is not celebrated, but confessions are heard. On this day, Holy Communion may be given only as viaticum. *"Nevertheless, the paschal fast must be kept sacred. Let it be celebrated everywhere on Good Friday and, where possible, prolonged throughout Holy Saturday so that the joys of the Sunday* *of the resurrection may be attained with uplifted and clear mind"* (Vatican II, *Constitution on the Sacred Liturgy,* 110). The Roman Missal tells us when Easter begins: ". . . *after the solemn Vigil, that is, the anticipation by night of the Resurrection, when the time comes for paschal joys, the abundance of which overflows to occupy fifty days."*

Easter Sunday of the Resurrection of the Lord

835. On Easter Sunday, the Church celebrates the glorious Resurrection of our Lord and Savior. This is the central fact of our Catholic faith, which the Church has proclaimed as "good news" ever since the Lord left his tomb and rose in our human flesh, glorious and immortal. Through the sacraments, in the community of the Church, we already share in his victorious Resurrection. Freed from sin and death, we can look forward in joyful hope to that final day when he will raise us up.

836. Easter is both the most important day and the most important season in the Church year. The liturgy expresses the meaning of this time with special symbolism and the use of the very "best" vessels, vestments, and signs of "exterior solemnity" to mark the great celebration.

1. The Easter Vigil in the Holy Night

837. The rites of the Easter Vigil are very ancient and take us to the heart of the Paschal Mystery of the death and Resurrection of the Lord. The Easter Vigil consists of four parts: (1) the *Solemn Beginning of the Vigil or Lucernarium,* (2) the *Liturgy of the Word,* (3) *Baptismal Liturgy,* and (4) the *Liturgy of the Eucharist.* A full team of servers is required, carefully trained and rehearsed to assist the clergy and people.

838.   The central symbol of the Vigil is the *Paschal candle*, repre-
       senting the risen Christ, light of the world, light of faith.
       In the *Solemn Beginning of the Vigil or Lucernarium* (candle-
       lighting ceremony), the Easter fire is blessed and the can-
       dle is prepared and lit and carried into the church in pro-
       cession. The light of Christ is given to all present, as they
       light their candles from the Easter flame. The deacon or
       celebrant sings the *Easter Proclamation* or *Exsultet* in praise
       of the victory of the Lord.

839.   The readings of the *Liturgy of the Word* take us back to
       the Old Testament and lead into the New Testament. Nine
       readings are provided, but these may be reduced for pas-
       toral reasons. The readings and prayers remind us of what
       God has done for his people, how he gave them hope, and
       how he offers us new life today in Jesus Christ.

840.   The *Baptismal Liturgy* should be centered around a real cele-
       bration of Christian Initiation, if possible. This was the
       night of Baptism in the early Church, for, by our Baptism,
       we die and rise with Christ and are united to him. The
       litany is sung, invoking the great baptized Christians, the
       saints. The water is solemnly blessed, and the Easter candle
       may be lowered into it as a symbol of the dying and rising
       Christ. After the Baptism and Confirmation, we renew all
       our own baptismal promises and are sprinkled with the wa-
       ter of Baptism.

841.   The *Liturgy of the Eucharist* is the first Mass of Easter and
       should be celebrated with the greatest splendor and solem-
       nity. The bells silent since Holy Thursday, the repeated He-
       brew praise "Alleluia!", and the themes of joy and victory in
       the texts remind us vividly that this is the night that made
       us Christians, the night of our deliverance, and the dawn
       of our eternal hope.

842. *Preparations*. Well before the time chosen for the Vigil, servers vest and check that everything is ready for the Easter Vigil.

843. *The altar*: prepared for Mass, six or four candles (not lit), (best antependium), etc. The Book of the Gospels should be on the altar. The processional cross should be near the altar, if used as the altar cross, or at the side of the sanctuary.

844. *The ambo*: a book containing the text and music of the *Exsultet*, nearby, the lectionary for the readings, marked (the best white fall). Next to the ambo or in some prominent position is the large candlestick prepared for the Easter candle, suitably decorated, according to custom.

845. *The chair*: prepared for Mass, also chairs for the deacon(s) and/or concelebrants.

846. *The credence table*: vessels prepared for Solemn Mass. The two processional candles on it (but not lit), tapers for lighting the altar candles, etc., a tray for the servers' hand candles.

847. *For the blessing of the fire*: in the place chosen outside the church, or near or in the porch, the five "grains of incense", the stylus or sharp instrument, a taper for lighting the candle, a suitable torch to help the celebrant read the text of the rite, charcoal to be placed in the fire for the thurible, tongs for the charcoal. These objects are prepared on a convenient table or brought from the sacristy on a tray in the procession to the place chosen for the fire. According to local practice, the fire is kindled some time before the rites begin. Candles are distributed among the people as they wait at the gathering place outside the church.

848. *For the blessing of water*: a large vessel containing pure water, suitably decorated according to local custom, set on a secure table or stand, in a convenient place in the sanctuary or on or in the font, if this is near the sanctuary and the blessing is at the font; an empty holy water bucket and sprinkler and a pitcher to pour water.

849. *For rites of Christian Initiation* (if celebrated): near the font, on a table, a vessel for pouring water, towels, Sacred Chrism, baptismal candles, and baptismal robes or white garments for adults. (The Oil of Catechumens is also required, unless this has been used already for the adult catechumens or used already for babies to be baptized, privately just before the Vigil, as part of the rites preceding the celebration of the sacrament.) The appropriate volume of the ritual should be near the font.

850. *The table of the gifts*: prepared for Mass.

851. *The tabernacle*: prepared for reservation, the door slightly open, best white or gold veil, key, the lamp ready to be lit.

852. *Shrines, side altars etc.*: lamps and candles prepared to be lit, including the twelve candles near the anointing crosses in a dedicated church; statues and pictures unveiled, if the custom of veiling them has been observed during Passiontide. Floral decorations are to be in place before the Vigil.

853. *In the church*: booklets or programs for the people, supplies of hand candles at each door (if the people do not gather outside). The lights of the church are put out at some time before the Vigil so that the celebration begins in the darkness. A responsible person is in charge of the lights.

854. *The sacristy*: the best white Mass vestments for the celebrant, deacon, concelebrants, the missal or Holy Week book, boat with incense and an empty thurible, the Paschal candle, which is already decorated by the painting of the cross, alpha, omega, and the numerals of the year. As noted, the other requirements may be prepared on a tray to be carried to the fire if it is not convenient to have them ready on a table.

A. THE SOLEMN BEGINNING OF THE VIGIL OR LUCERNARIUM

855. Having bowed to the sacristy cross, celebrant and servers go to the place where the fire is prepared, preferably not passing through the church. The order of procession is: thurifer (with boat and empty thurible), cross and candle bearers (without candles and cross) and a server carrying the Paschal candle, other servers who will act as torch bearers, book bearer, M.C., concelebrants, deacon, celebrant. The book bearer brings the missal or Holy Week book, and servers may carry the implements for the preparation of the Paschal candle if these are to be brought from the sacristy. Servers not holding an object carry a hand candle and/or tapers to help spread the light at the procession of the Paschal candle. Hand candles should also be provided for clergy, other than the deacon or celebrant who carries the Paschal candle in the procession.

856. On arrival at the place where the people have assembled around the fire, the celebrant, clergy, and servers should take up positions between the fire and the church entrance, so that they will lead the people into the church after the blessing of the fire and preparation of the Paschal candle. The thurifer should stand looking from the church door behind the celebrant, who faces the fire. The deacon stands on the right of the celebrant, the M.C. on his left, the book bearer slightly in front of him to his left, with the missal or Holy Week book open at the rite and a server assisting with the torch, if necessary. Concelebrants may be ranged on each side of the celebrant and deacon, back a few paces. The candle bearers stand near the table, ready to bring objects to the celebrant. Other servers may best be grouped to each side of the fire, well back to avoid accidents.

857. *The Blessing of the Fire and Preparation of the Candle* begins as the celebrant greets the people, using a formula of the greeting from the rite of Mass, and then briefly instructs them about the Vigil. He blesses the fire with the prayer in the missal. The thurifer comes round to the fire where the M.C. assists in placing hot coals in the thurible, using the tongs (self-lighting charcoal should be used).

858. The bearer of the Paschal candle brings the candle to the celebrant. Before lighting it, he may prepare it with the metal stylus or instrument, and the "five grains of incense", brought to him by the second candle bearer. The bearer of the Paschal candle, assisted by another server if necessary, holds the candle firmly at an angle. The celebrant cuts a cross in the wax, then the Greek letter *Alpha*, above the cross (Christ, the beginning of all creation), and the letter *Omega*, below the cross (Christ the completion of all creation), and the numbers of the current year within the four angles of the cross. Meanwhile, he recites the text of the missal. He may insert the five "grains of incense" (the five wounds of our Lord), placing them at the five points of the cross, the vertical line, 1, 2, and 3, the horizontal line, 4, and 5, reciting the text of the missal at the same time.

859. *Lighting the Candle.* The bearer of the Paschal candle holds the candle upright. The deacon or M.C. lights a taper from the fire, gives it to the celebrant, who lights the candle, singing or saying, "May the light of Christ. . . ." (Here we see the meaning of "Lucernarium", ceremony of light.)

860. *The Procession.* The book bearer steps aside and closes the missal or Holy Week book. The thurifer comes to the celebrant with the thurible and boat, and incense is prepared as usual. The thurifer returns to a position behind the celebrant, so as to lead the way into the church. If a deacon assists, he takes the Paschal candle; if not, another suitable minister takes it. At the door of the church, the deacon or minister raises the candle high and sings "The Light of Christ", all responding, "Thanks be to God." The M.C. or a server assists the celebrant in taking light from the candle as the deacon holds it.

861. Preceded only by the thurifer, he leads all into the church and, at the middle of the church, again sings "The Light of Christ". Immediately behind him in the procession are the celebrant, the M.C., two servers with tapers ready, concelebrants, other servers, and the people. Immediately after the response to "The Light of Christ", the servers take Easter fire from the candle and pass it along to other servers, clergy, and the people.

862. The deacon goes farther into the darkened church. At the entrance to the sanctuary, facing the people, he sings "The Light of Christ", all responding. The thurifer moves to the ambo or a lectern where the candlestick is ready. The (celebrant), concelebrants, and servers form up at the center of the sanctuary while the deacon places the candle in the socket of the candlestick. The lights of the church are now switched on, although in some places this is not customary until after the *Exsultet*. The celebrant, concelebrants, and servers go to their seats.

863. (*Alternative Procedure.* If it is not possible to light the fire outside, the people gather in the church. A small fire is prepared inside the porch or narthex in a suitable brazier.

The celebrant and servers come to this area for the blessing of the fire and preparation of the candle, as set out above. If possible, the people turn to face the priest. The procession takes place, through the darkened church, and servers pass the light to the people at the end of each seat, and so through the whole church.)

864. *The Easter Proclamation (Exsultet).* The thurifer comes to the celebrant seated in the chair. Incense is prepared as usual. If the deacon sings the *Exsultet*, he comes to the celebrant and receives the blessing. The blessing is omitted if the celebrant or another priest sings the *Exsultet*. The Easter Proclamation may be sung by a lay cantor, and in this case a blessing is not sought and there are modifications in the text. The thurifer joins the deacon or celebrant, if he sings the *Exsultet*, at the center of the sanctuary. They bow to the altar. The deacon or celebrant takes the thurible and incenses the Paschal candle and then the book at the ambo or a lectern. He returns the thurible to the thurifer, who takes it back to the sacristy. It will be needed again for the Gospel, after the Mass readings. The thurifer returns to the sanctuary without the thurible and stands with the two candle bearers at the credence table or their seats.

865. During the singing of the *Exsultet*, the M.C. or a server may be required to shine a torch on the text if the lights of the church have not yet been switched on. During the singing of the *Exsultet*, all stand holding their lighted candles. If the deacon sings it, the M.C. supervises the celebrant's candle, taking it from him for the preparation of incense and the blessing of the deacon, returning it to him for the *Exsultet*. At the end of the *Exsultet*, all hand candles are extinguished and servers place the candles of clergy and other servers on a tray on a credence table. The deacon or celebrant returns to the center, bows to the altar, and goes to his chair and sits. The book bearer goes to the ambo, with the lectionary, and puts it there in place of the missal or Holy Week book. He takes the missal or Holy Week book to the chair, to attend the celebrant.

B. LITURGY OF THE WORD

866. All sit for the beginning of the Liturgy of the Word. The celebrant stands at the chair and introduces the readings, the book bearer attending him if he chooses to read the introduction in the missal. He sits for the first reading. According to local custom, the M.C. or another server conducts the readers to the ambo for the chosen lessons. A responsorial psalm may be sung by cantor, choir, and people after each reading. All stand for the prayer that follows the psalm, the book bearer attending the celebrant at the chair, the M.C. indicating the place in the missal. Instead of the responsorial psalm, a period of silence may be observed.

867. This procedure is repeated according to the number of readings chosen. After the prayer after the last reading, two (or more) servers take tapers from the credence table, light them from the Easter candle, bow to the altar, and wait until the celebrant intones the *Gloria*, which is taken up by all present. The servers now light the altar candles. According to local custom, they go to other altars and shrines to light lamps and candles (and the twelve dedication cross candles). They return to the credence, light the two processional candles, and extinguish the tapers. According to local custom, the church bells are rung joyously during the Gloria. Servers may ring the Sanctus bells at the credence table, but in a way planned to blend with the singing. At the end of the Gloria, the thurifer goes to the sacristy and the book bearer attends the celebrant at the chair for the Collect.

868. All sit for the reading of the Epistle. At the conclusion of this reading, all stand. If the celebrant himself intones the Easter *Alleluia*, the book bearer attends at the chair, otherwise a cantor intones the *Alleluia*. The thurifer comes from the sacristy with the thurible, goes to the celebrant, and incense is prepared as usual. If the deacon reads the Gospel, he comes to the celebrant to be blessed. He takes the Gospel Book from the altar. The Gospel procession forms up as usual: deacon (or the celebrant or a concelebrant), M.C., thurifer, and the two candle bearers *without* their candles (because the Paschal candle represents the light of Christ on this night). They bow and go to the ambo, where the Gospel is read as usual. A homily follows the Gospel.

C. BAPTISMAL LITURGY

869. Every parish church has a baptismal font, and the water blessed at the Vigil is used for celebrating Baptisms throughout the whole Easter season to signify more clearly the relationship between the sacrament and the Paschal Mystery. Outside the Easter season, the water is blessed during the Rite of Baptism. Therefore, if no one is to be baptized at the Vigil but the church has a baptismal font, the litany is still sung and sufficient baptismal water is blessed to last until Pentecost. Only when the Vigil is celebrated in chapels that do not have a font are the litany and blessing of baptismal water omitted to be replaced by the simple blessing of Easter water.

870. There are three different procedures for the *Baptismal Liturgy*, each concluding with the *Renewal of Baptismal Promises*: (1) Christian Initiation and the Blessing of the Font, (2) Blessing of the Font without Initiation, (3) Blessing of Water.

D. CHRISTIAN INITIATION AND
THE BLESSING OF THE FONT

871. When Christian Initiation is celebrated, a procession forms up to go either to the font, if this can be seen by the congregation, or to that part of the sanctuary where the large vessel of water has been prepared. The procession is led by the deacon or a server, who has taken the Paschal candle from its stand and who leads the procession carrying the candle carefully. The deacon or senior server is followed by the candle bearers, without their candles, the book bearer with the missal or Holy Week book, the M.C., deacon, and celebrant. At the font or vessel of water, the celebrant may stand directly behind the font or table for the water, the deacon on his right, the book bearer on his left, with the M.C. nearby. The candle bearers stand near the table prepared with objects to be used for Christian Initiation. If the deacon has brought the Easter candle, he either hands it to a server to hold or, more conveniently, places it in a stand near the font or vessel of water. If a server has brought the candle, he may place it on a stand.

872. The deacon or celebrant calls the candidates for Baptism to come forward, and they are presented by their sponsors. If they are infants or children, they are brought forward by their parents and godparents. They stand at the font or vessel of water in such a way that they do not block the view of the people. The book bearer attends the celebrant, with the missal or Holy Week book or the ritual, as he instructs the people and asks for their prayers. All remain standing, as is customary in the Easter season, for the singing of the litany, to which may be added the names of local saints and the saints of those to be baptized.

873. *However*, if Christian Initiation is to be celebrated in a suitable baptistery, located at some distance from the sanctuary, the candidates for Baptism are called forward, then the procession forms up and goes to the baptistery slowly, while the litany is sung. The deacon or a server leads this solemn procession, carrying the Paschal candle, followed by the candidates and sponsors, or children, parents, and godparents. In the baptistery, all form up around the font as in (a). The people should be directed to turn toward the baptistery for the rites that follow.

874. The book bearer attends the celebrant at the font as he sings or says the *Blessing of Water*. The Paschal candle is lowered into the water at "May the power of the Holy Spirit . . .", the deacon, a server, or a concelebrant holds it during the prayer, ready to hand it to him. After the "Amen", it is taken out of the water as the people, led by the choir, sing "Springs of water, bless the Lord." The deacon or server receives the candle.

875. The book bearer lays aside the missal or Holy Week book and receives the ritual from one of the candle bearers at the table. Christian Initiation follows, beginning with the renunciation of the devil. In the infants' Baptism, the concluding rites are omitted. The Sacrament of Confirmation is given to adults after Baptism, in the sanctuary or baptistery. The *Renewal of Baptismal Promises* follows as below.

876. *If the Blessing of the Font is celebrated without Initiation*, the procession forms up, as above, and goes to the font or vessel of water. The Paschal candle is carried, but requirements for Christian Initiation are omitted. The litany is sung without changes to the text that relate to Baptism, but the names of local saints, patrons, etc., may be added. After the Blessing of Baptismal Water, the *Renewal of Baptismal Promises* follows as below.

877. *If the Blessing of Water takes place in the simple form*, the procession forms up, as above, and goes to the place in the sanctuary where a vessel of water has been prepared. The Paschal candle is not carried. Alternatively, servers could bring a vessel of water to the celebrant at his chair, and there would be no procession. All proceeds as above, using a different instruction, but the litany is omitted. The simpler Prayer of Blessing follows without the use of the Paschal candle. The *Renewal of Baptismal Promises* follows as below.

878. *The Renewal of Baptismal Promises* is led by the celebrant, either from the sanctuary, at the font or vessel of blessed water, or from the baptistery. Servers go to the credence table and take tapers to the Paschal candle to light the hand candles of the people, servers, and clergy. The M.C. supervises the distribution of candles to clergy and servers and the lighting of these candles. (If the baptismal promises are renewed in the baptistery, a supply of candles should be prepared on the table.) If Christian Initiation has been celebrated, those baptized and confirmed or the parents of baptized children will already be holding their baptismal candles.

879. The book bearer attends the celebrant with the missal or Holy Week book as he addresses the people and asks the questions. The M.C. or a server fills the empty holy-water bucket from the blessed water in the font or vessel. At the end of the questions, having said a short prayer, the celebrant takes the sprinkler from the deacon or M.C., and, accompanied by the deacon or M.C. with the holy-water bucket, he goes through the church sprinkling the servers and people. Everyone makes the sign of the cross when sprinkled. The choir sings a suitable chant or baptismal hymn. The singing should continue to accompany all movements up to the *Prayer of the Faithful*.

880. Having returned to the sanctuary or baptistery, the celebrant gives the sprinkler to the deacon or M.C., who hands the bucket and sprinkler to a server, to place on the small table near the font or vessel of water or on the credence table. If the rites have been celebrated in the baptistery, the procession forms up in the same order as before, and, led by the Paschal candle, clergy, servers, and the newly baptized return to the sanctuary. If the rites have been celebrated in or near the sanctuary, all move to the center, bow to the altar, and go to their places. The celebrant goes to the chair. The newly baptized are shown to their seats among the people.

881. Hand candles are extinguished, and servers collect those of the clergy and servers and place them on a credence table. The Paschal candle is placed on its stand. If the baptismal water was blessed in the sanctuary, in a place apart from the font or baptistery, two servers reverently carry the vessel of water to the font or baptistery. If the simple procedure was followed, they may take the vessel of water directly to the sacristy or some other convenient place. At the chair, the celebrant leads the *Prayer of the Faithful*, attended by the book bearer with the book or folder. The newly baptized take part in the prayer. The Creed is omitted, because the baptismal promises take its place on this night. The thurifer goes to the sacristy for the thurible.

E. THE LITURGY OF THE EUCHARIST

882. Because the Easter Vigil is the climax of the Church year, the whole liturgy should be celebrated in its most solemn form. The Procession of the Gifts and Preparation of the Gifts follow as usual. It is fitting that the bread and wine be brought forward by the newly baptized. After Holy Communion, the Blessed Sacrament is placed in the tabernacle. A server takes a taper and lights the lamp. If the veil is not already in place, a server reverently veils the tabernacle and genuflects. At the end of Mass, two "alleluias" are added to the Dismissal and its response.

883. For the final procession, the processional cross and candles are used. After Mass, a priest or deacon brings the Blessed Sacrament from the place of reservation in the sacristy or elsewhere and adds these Hosts to those already in the tabernacle. While putting everything away after the ceremonies, servers should check that the Paschal candle has been extinguished. Easter water should be available for the faithful to take to their homes.

2. *Easter Sunday*

884. In the Easter Sunday Masses, the rite of the Renewal of Baptismal Promises is repeated after the homily and the Creed is omitted. The book bearer attends the celebrant at the chair with the missal. Another server brings the holy-water bucket and sprinkler from the credence and stands to the right of the celebrant. At a Solemn Mass, the deacon or M.C. holds the bucket and sprinkler. After the questions and responses, the celebrant takes the sprinkler from the deacon, M.C., or server, who accompanies him as he goes through the church sprinkling the servers and people, as at the Vigil. The choir sings a suitable baptismal chant or hymn. Having returned to the chair, the celebrant gives the sprinkler to the deacon, M.C., or server and leads the Prayer of the Faithful. Mass continues as usual. At the end of Mass, two "alleluias" are added to the Dismissal and its response.

885. *The Easter Octave* is unique in the Church's calendar. As the Solemnity of Easter is too great for one day, the Church extends its celebration for a week. On every day during the

octave, the Church proclaims: "This is the day the Lord has made, let us rejoice and be glad in it."

886. *The Easter season* continues until Pentecost. Its Sundays are designated quite deliberately as "Sundays of Easter" rather than Sundays "after" Easter. There are special Mass texts for each weekday. The Church invites us who have risen with Christ and had our sins forgiven to rejoice in the company of our risen Lord, to let him shine through our everyday lives. The Second Sunday of Easter is also Divine Mercy Sunday, celebrating the mercy of God revealed in the Lord Jesus. The Fourth Sunday of Easter is Good Shepherd Sunday, when we pray for vocations to the priesthood.

11.

Serving the Bishop

887. It is a privilege to be asked to serve the bishop when he celebrates the liturgy and sacraments. You are assisting the man God has called and ordained to be a true and direct successor of the apostles. He has received "the fullness of the priesthood", so that he may be the leader, teacher, sanctifier, and shepherd of God's People.

888. When the bishop celebrates the liturgy and sacraments, we see a complete "picture" of the Church. Here is the apostolic community, gathered around the successor of the apostles. Here is the complete hierarchy of service, clergy, and laity, in communion with Jesus Christ and with one another. Each bishop, in turn, is in communion with his brother bishops, members of the worldwide "Apostolic College". This community of bishops is held together in unity "with and under Peter", that is, by communion with the pope, successor of Saint Peter.

889. We show respect for our bishops. When you meet a bishop, you should know the correct way to address him. Depending on local custom, which varies between countries, when you speak to a bishop, you say "Your Excellency", "My Lord", or "Bishop". When you speak to an archbishop, you say "Your Excellency", "Your Grace", or "Archbishop". When you speak to a cardinal, you say "Your Eminence" or "Cardinal". If you have the honor of speaking to the pope, you say "Your Holiness" or "Holy Father".

890. To describe ceremonies over which the bishop presides, we use the word "pontifical", which comes from the Latin word for a high priest, *pontifex*, the bridge builder. The bishop continues the saving work of Christ in building a bridge between heaven and earth. In this chapter, the following ceremonies have been selected: (1) *Pontifical Mass*, (2) *Confirmation*, (3) *Holy Orders*, (4) *Religious Profession*, (5) The *Chrism Mass*, and (6) *Institution of Readers and Acolytes*. These are described to assist servers, hence the details have been selected so as to make serving the bishop an easy procedure.

Pontifical Mass

891. *Capitular Mass*. In the cathedral on certain major solemnities and for "capitular Mass", the canons or cathedral clergy formally receive their bishop, usually at the main door. The bishop wears choir dress, unless he chooses to vest first in the sacristy. Unless vested to concelebrate with the bishop, canons wear choir dress (and copes on solemn occasions). Clergy and servers escort the bishop to the sacristy or a designated chapel, where he vests for Pontifical Mass.

892. *The Bishop's Visitation*. When the bishop makes a formal parish visitation, the parish priest (in cope or concelebrant's vestments), clergy, and the servers for Pontifical Mass or a ceremony receive the bishop at the entrance to the Church. The bishop wears choir dress. The parish priest offers him a crucifix to kiss, then holy water, with which he sprinkles himself and those standing near him. He is then led in procession to where he vests for Mass, or, if Mass is not to follow, he is led to the Blessed Sacrament, where he makes a brief visit, followed by a customary ceremonial welcome and prayers in the sanctuary.

The Bishop's Attendants

893. On solemn occasions or whenever deacons are available, the bishop is assisted by a deacon or two deacons. Two "deacons of honor" may also attend him on important occasions, such as a Solemn Pontifical Mass. Priests also take part as concelebrants, assistants, or as M.C.s. On important occasions, there may be two or more M.C.s. A full team of trained servers is required, working under the direction of the M.C.: a cross bearer, candle bearers, book bearer, thurifer (boat bearer), torch bearers. However, three other servers are directly associated with the bishop: the *miter bearer*, the *crozier bearer*, and the *book bearer*. In procession, these episcopal servers walk immediately behind the bishop, usually coming last in the procession.

894. The *miter bearer* holds the miter when the bishop is not wearing it. The two tails of the miter (lappets or infulae) are held toward him. To protect the miter, hands are covered with the *vimpa*, a silk scarf worn around the neck like a stole. The miter bearer should know the times in a ceremony when a bishop wears his miter: (a) in procession, (b) when moving from place to place (if the distance is not too short), (c) when seated, (d) when he stands to speak to the people—for example, the homily, (e) when he receives the gifts at the Procession of the Gifts, (f) while he baptizes, confirms, witnesses a marriage, during the laying on of hands at ordination and when anointing the sick in a public celebration, (g) when giving a liturgical blessing. The bishop does not wear a miter when he stands to pray, e.g., in the prayers of the Mass. The deacon or M.C. puts on and removes the miter unless the bishop prefers to do this himself.

895. The *crozier bearer* holds the crozier or pastoral staff when the bishop is not using it, hands wrapped in a vimpa. The bearer holds the crozier with the curved portion, or "crook", turned in and hands the crozier to the bishop so that the crook points away from the bishop. The bearer never leaves the crozier leaning against a wall, as it may be damaged or fall down. The crozier bearer should know the times in the ceremony when the bishop requires it: (a) carried in his left hand in procession, (b) likewise when moving from place to place (if the distance is not too short), (c) held in both hands during the Gospel at Mass, (d) while giving the homily, (e) during the final blessing at Mass and other liturgical celebrations, (f) when he confirms, if he wishes to use it.

896. The *book bearer* attends the bishop in the same way as he assists a priest during the liturgy and sacraments. The crozier, miter, and book bearers should be seated close to the bishop, near or behind the cathedra or chair. They should not sit beside him, facing the people, as if they were concelebrants. If the miter and crozier bearers have to carry the miter and crozier for a long period of time—for example, during a homily or during the prayers of the Liturgy of the Eucharist—the M.C. may direct them to place the miter on a credence table and the crozier in a stand.

897. In procession, the bearers of the crozier, miter, and book walk last of all behind the bishop, the miter bearer at the right, the crozier bearer on his left (because he holds the crozier in his left hand), and the book bearer behind these two. When not carrying miter and crozier, they join their hands outside the vimpa.

898. The other servers assist at pontifical ceremonies in the same way as they would serve a priest, noting some different details mentioned below. Because the celebrating bishop represents our Lord, servers bow to him whenever approaching, leaving, or passing in front of him.

A. SERVING PONTIFICAL MASS

899. The sanctuary is prepared as for other forms of Mass, depending on the solemnity of the occasion. The following variations should be noted.

900. *The altar*: if the diocesan bishop celebrates, a seventh candle is added to the six, especially on solemn occasions.

901. *The bishop's cathedra or chair*, beside it, seats for the deacon(s) and concelebrant(s); behind it or to one side, seats for miter, crozier, and book bearers.

902. *The credence table*: a ewer with a basin, both preferably of noble metal, such as silver, two towels on a tray.

903. *The sacristy (vesting room or chapel)*: vestments set out for the bishop: chasuble, dalmatic (if used), stole, pectoral cross on the cord, cincture (if used), alb, amice (if used); the miter, ornate or plain according to the occasion, zucchetto (skull cap) perhaps on a small metal tray (salver), the pallium with pins, for archbishops with the right to wear it on major occasions. Another ewer, bowl, and towel are prepared in the sacristy to wash his hands before Mass.

904. On solemn occasions, indicated as the *Stational Mass*, a full team of trained servers is required as indicated above. *On less solemn occasions*, such as a weekday Mass, the bishop may only require the ring, pectoral cross, and zucchetto as signs of his office. On some occasions, he may wear a miter but not use the crozier. Details are given below when the deacon or M.C. puts the miter on the bishop, but this is not

an easy procedure, and the bishop may choose to put it on and take it off himself, as noted above.

905. *Before the bishop vests for Mass*, he washes his hands, attended by two servers. The deacon, M.C., or servers assist him as he vests at the vesting bench, table, or sacristy altar. The crozier and miter bearers attend with crozier and miter. (The first deacon puts the pallium on an archbishop just before the miter is received.) Having received the miter, he prepares and blesses incense, and then he receives the crozier. On a signal from the M.C., all bow to the sacristy cross and proceed to the sanctuary according to local custom.

1. Introductory Rites

906. On arrival at the sanctuary, the crozier is given away and the bishop's miter is removed by the deacon or M.C. On a signal from the M.C., all make the customary reverence. The bishop kisses the altar, incenses it (fresh incense may first be added to the thurible), and goes to the cathedra or chair, where he begins the Mass with the greeting "Peace be with you."

2. The Liturgy of the Word

907. The miter bearer brings the miter to the deacon or M.C., who places it on the bishop when he sits. The bishop remains seated to put incense into the thurible and bless it before the Gospel. After he has blessed the deacon, his miter is removed and he stands for the alleluia or verse before the Gospel.

908. The crozier bearer gives him the crozier, which he holds during the Gospel even though he does not wear the miter. If the bishop preaches the homily, he may give up the crozier, receive the miter, and then receive the crozier again

for the homily, if he wishes to use it. He may preach either from the throne seated, as a sign of his apostolic teaching authority, or from the ambo. (He blesses a guest preacher, seated, wearing the miter.) After the homily, the crozier is given away and the miter removed for the Creed and the Prayer of the Faithful.

3. The Liturgy of the Eucharist

909. Wearing the miter, the bishop is escorted to the place where the Procession of Gifts is received. Clergy and servers take the gifts from him and bring them to the altar. At the altar, the bishop gives up the miter, the miter bearer attending. From this point until after Communion, the miter bearer and crozier bearer are not required, except that the miter bearer receives the zucchetto after the Prayer over the Offerings. They remain at their seats. The miter may be placed on the credence table. The crozier may be placed in a suitable stand, but securely so that it does not fall to the ground.

910. After the bishop has incensed the gifts and altar, and after he has been incensed himself, the candle bearers bring the ewer, basin, and the first towel and wash his hands. As soon as the bishop has said the Prayer over the Offerings, the M.C. removes the zucchetto from his head. He gives it to the miter bearer, who places it on the credence or on top of the miter. At a Solemn Pontifical Mass, as many as eight torch bearers may assist at the Eucharistic Prayer, escorted by the thurifer.

911. Mass proceeds as usual according to the occasion. After Holy Communion, the deacons or concelebrants attend to the cleansing of vessels. The bishop goes to his cathedra or chair. The candle bearers come to the chair with the ewer and basin and a towel. They wash the bishop's hands, bowing before and after washing, and take the ewer and basin

back to the credence table. If they are assisting with the cleansing of the vessels, other servers may bring the ewer, basin, and second towel to the bishop. When the vessels have been cleansed or once the tabernacle has been closed, the M.C. gives the bishop his zucchetto.

912. The bishop stands to say or sing the Prayer after Communion, attended by the book bearer. (Alternatively, he may choose to return to the altar for this prayer and the final blessing. The missal would remain on the altar, moved to the center.)

913. After any notices, the bishop receives the miter, *before* singing or saying "The Lord be with you. . . ." If a solemn blessing is used, the deacon invites the people to receive the blessing. The bishop sings or says the prayers of the blessing, his hands extended over the people. If a simpler blessing is used, the pontifical versicles and responses are sung or said. Just before the blessing formula, the crozier bearer comes forward and gives the bishop the crozier, which he holds as he blesses the assembly. The deacon sings the dismissal.

914. If he is already at the altar, the bishop lays aside the crozier briefly and kisses the altar. He receives the crozier and comes to the center for the final customary reverence. If he has given the blessing from the cathedra or chair, as is more usual, he may go to the altar, lay aside the crozier, and kiss the altar with the deacon(s) but *not* concelebrating priests, and then come to the center with the crozier for the final reverence. If thought more convenient, he may go directly from the cathedra to the center, omitting the kissing of the altar.

915. Meanwhile, the bearers of book, miter, and crozier take suitable positions in the sanctuary, usually in front of the altar

or to one side, so as to come last in the procession to the sacristy. When the bishop is ready, on a signal from the M.C., all bow to the altar. In the procession, servers should take care not to move too far ahead of the bishop because he will be giving personal blessings to the faithful as he walks along. On arrival in the sacristy, all bow to the cross. The bishop may bless the clergy and servers, and it is customary to kneel for the blessing. Then the bearers of book, miter, and crozier attend the bishop as he gives up the miter and crozier and removes his vestments. If the procession has gone through the church to the main door, the bishop may wish to wait there to meet the people. Servers usually return to the sacristy, and the bearer may take the crozier back to the sacristy.

B. THE BISHOP PRESIDING AT MASS

916. On certain occasions, the bishop may preside at the Liturgy of the Word and concluding rite, but not celebrate the Mass itself. The priest celebrant would precede the bishop in procession and may sit next to the cathedra or chair. Instead of the chasuble, the bishop wears a cope over amice, alb, pectoral cross, and stole. He wears the miter and may use the crozier. He does everything normally done by the celebrant until after the Prayer of the Faithful.

917. When the priest celebrant goes to the altar for the Liturgy of the Eucharist, the bishop remains at the chair. He is incensed after the celebrant. He kneels at the *epiklesis* in the Eucharistic Prayer, on a kneeling desk, prepared either at the cathedra or chair (if this faces the altar) or at the center of the sanctuary in front of the altar. He stands (and returns to the cathedra) after the elevation of the chalice. If he receives Communion, he remains at the cathedra until the celebrant comes to him there. The celebrant says the Prayer after Communion at the chair or altar and then

returns to his place next to the bishop. The bishop blesses the assembly as for Pontifical Mass. The book, miter, and crozier bearers assist as for Pontifical Mass.

918.   When the bishop assists without presiding at the Liturgy of the Word, he wears choir dress. The episcopal servers are not required, but two priests or deacons in choir dress may accompany him. He walks after the celebrant in procession and sits at the side in a seat of honor with a kneeling desk or in the "first place in choir", if there are choir stalls. In his own cathedral, he sits on the cathedra, and he should be flanked by two clergy in choir dress. He is incensed after the celebrant and concelebrants. If he receives Communion, he receives under both kinds from the celebrant. In the procession to the sacristy, he walks after the celebrant. The same principles apply when a group of bishops assist in choir at a Mass.

Confirmation

919.   You have been confirmed. You received the Holy Spirit to perfect your initiation as a Christian, to strengthen you to be an adult Catholic. With a permanent effect or *character*, you have been "sealed" with the gift of the Holy Spirit so as to be "more like Christ", using the seven gifts of the Spirit to live and work as a mature Christian in this world. Confirmation is the second *Sacrament of Christian Initiation*.

920.   The *matter* of Confirmation is Sacred Chrism, perfumed oil consecrated by a bishop. The *form* of Confirmation is, "N, be sealed with the gift of the Holy Spirit", said as the forehead is anointed with Chrism. The ordinary *minister* of

Confirmation is a bishop, who may delegate the celebration of the sacrament to a priest, under certain circumstances.

The Rite of Confirmation

921. Confirmation is the second part of Christian Initiation, which begins with Baptism and is completed by the Eucharist. This sacrament is usually celebrated during Mass, immediately after the Gospel, or at the same point during a Liturgy of the Word.

922. There are six steps in the rite of Confirmation: (1) *Presentation of the Candidates*, (2) *Homily*, (3) *Renewal of Baptismal Promises*, (4) *Laying on of Hands*, (5) *Anointing with Chrism*, and (6) *General Intercessions*. At Mass, the Procession and Preparation of the Gifts follows. A full team of trained and rehearsed servers is required for Confirmation.

923. *Presentation of the Candidates*. The parish priest, a priest, deacon, or catechist responsible for the candidates presents them to the bishop. If the numbers are few, they may be called individually by name. This is a sign of their wish to be confirmed and the welcome of the Church as they approach the sacrament. Each candidate has a sponsor.

924. *Homily*. The bishop gives a brief homily, addressed mainly to the candidates, explaining the sacrament and their responsibilities in the light of the readings.

925. *Renewal of Baptismal Promises*. Underlining the direct link with Baptism, the candidates renew the promises made for them in the celebration of that sacrament. The Holy Spirit comes to strengthen the faith they received in Baptism, the faith they now profess in public.

926. *Laying on the Hands.* The bishop and assisting priests extend their hands over the candidates to call the Holy Spirit to come to them with his seven gifts: wisdom, understanding, right judgment, courage, knowledge, reverence, and wonder and awe in the presence of God.

927. *Anointing with Chrism.* The bishop gives the sacrament to each candidate, signing the forehead with Chrism and saying the form, as set out above. The Holy Spirit makes each confirmed Christian his own temple forever. The bishop may gently strike each confirmed Christian on the cheek as he says, "Peace be with you", a sign of peace that also reminds them of the need to be strong in bearing any suffering for the sake of Jesus Christ.

928. *General Intercessions.* The Prayer of the Faithful is offered especially for those who have been confirmed, their families, and sponsors.

A. SERVING CONFIRMATION DURING MASS

929. *Preparations.* Everything is prepared for a Pontifical Mass, as set out above. The bishop uses the miter and crozier, so book, miter, and crozier bearers are required in addition to the usual servers of the Mass: cross bearer, candle bearers, thurifer, boat bearer (if incense is used), torch bearers (if desired). Additional requirements are as follows:

930. *Credence table*: Sacred Chrism in a chrismatory, a gremial veil or large amice (if used during anointing to protect the vestments), ewer (warm water), basin and towels, sliced lemons on a suitable dish (soap, if desired). (Cotton balls are not needed as it is no longer customary to wipe the foreheads of those confirmed after anointing.)

931. *On the table with the missal*: the Roman Pontifical, marked for the rite or a folder prepared with the texts.

932. If there are only a few candidates, they may enter the church in the procession to take the seats reserved for them. But it is preferable for the candidates and sponsors to enter in procession and be seated before the bishop enters in the entrance procession. They are arranged, with their sponsors or in family groups, according to local custom and the practice of the school or CCD. Parish clergy normally concelebrate with the bishop unless they wish to assist in surplice and stole. When the Ritual Mass of Confirmation is celebrated, the color is red or white. On those days when that Mass is not permitted, the color of the day is used.

933. The procession enters as for Pontifical Mass, and the bishop celebrates Mass as usual. After the Gospel, the bishop gives up the crozier, sits, and receives the miter.

934. *Presentation of the Candidates.* The parish priest goes to the ambo (unless he is already there, having read the Gospel) and asks the candidates to stand while he presents them. If the numbers are few, he may call them to stand or come forward, one by one, by name. As is more usual, he reads a customary formula of presentation for the whole group. The bishop directs the candidates to sit after presentation.

935. *Homily.* The bishop may give his homily seated or standing at the chair, at the ambo, or at the center of the church. He may take the crozier for the homily, or he may prefer not to use the crozier. If he reads the homily provided in the Pontifical, the book bearer attends him with this book.

936. *Renewal of Baptismal Promises.* The candidates stand. At the chair, the bishop sits, receives the miter and crozier, and proceeds to ask the questions. The book bearer attends with the Pontifical, the M.C. turning the page. The bishop may prefer to stand for the promises, either at the chair or in front of the altar. All stand after the promises.

937. *Laying on of Hands.* The bishop gives up the crozier and miter, and, standing at the chair or in front of the altar, he introduces the prayer, attended by the book bearer. Other priests may stand near him, facing the candidates. During the prayer, sung or said by the bishop alone, they also extend their hands over the candidates if they assist in the anointing. After the prayer, the people and candidates may sit as the anointing begins.

938. *Anointing with Chrism.* Unless the candidates are to come to the chair where the bishop has presided over the Mass, a suitable chair or faldstool is brought forward by two servers and placed in front of the altar or at some other convenient place. (This chair may have been arranged before the rite began.) A cushion may be placed in front of the chair, on which candidates kneel. The bishop goes to the chair, sits, and receives the miter. (If the gremial veil is used, the M.C. or a server brings it from the credence and arranges it on his knees, tying it securely to the chair if necessary.) The deacon or the parish priest opens the chrismatory and brings the Chrism to the bishop. (If the numbers are large and the bishop delegates priests to assist in the anointing, the deacon brings all the vessels of Chrism to the bishop, who then gives one to each priest.) If convenient, the bishop may receive the crozier, while he sits to confirm, holding the Chrism with it in his left hand. In a better arrangement, the deacon or a priest may hold the open chrismatory near him on his right so he can conveniently dip his thumb in the holy oil.

939. Candidates come to the bishop at the chair and kneel to be confirmed, more conveniently on the same step or on the cushion. Each sponsor places his or her right hand on the right shoulder of the candidate during the anointing. The miter and crozier bearers may stand behind the chair, back several paces. If the bishop does not hold the crozier during the anointing, the crozier bearer stands holding it on his left near him. Priests take the cards from the sponsors to inform the bishop of the candidates' Confirmation names. Servers may take these cards from the priests and place them on the credence table.

940. *A different procedure* is followed when the bishop goes to the candidates to confirm them. The candidates may stand in line across or around the sanctuary area or kneel at an altar rail while he walks along anointing them. Alternatively, if the candidates are already seated with their sponsors in places along the aisle of the church, they step out into the aisle with their sponsors while the bishop walks along anointing them. Whatever procedure is chosen, he wears the miter, may use the crozier, and is assisted by a deacon or priest as above.

941. While the last candidates are being confirmed, the candle bearers prepare to cleanse the bishop's hands. One brings the lemons, (soap), and towel. The other brings the ewer of warm water and the bowl. A soon as the bishop has finished anointing, the deacon or parish priest takes the chrismatory back to the credence table and replaces its cover. The bishop gives up the crozier, if he has used it. The servers come before him at the chair, bow, and offer him lemon, (soap), which removes the oil, and then pour water over his fingers, finally offering him the towel. They bow and take the lemon and ewer, etc., back to the credence table. (The M.C. removes the gremial veil if used, and a server takes it back to the credence table and folds it neatly.)

942. The bishop stands and returns to the chair where he presided, if he did not confirm at that place. Servers remove the other chair from the front of the altar, with the cushion, if used. (If priests have also anointed candidates, they take their vessels

of Chrism to the credence table and cleanse their fingers there, assisted by servers.)

943. *General Intercessions.* The bishop gives up the miter, stands, and introduces the Prayer of the Faithful, attended by the book bearer with the Pontifical or folder. The Mass continues as usual with the Procession and Preparation of the Gifts. The final blessing may be taken from the rite of Confirmation, the book bearer attending with the Pontifical or missal, as directed by the M.C.

B. SERVING CONFIRMATION DURING A LITURGY OF THE WORD

944. When Confirmation is celebrated during a Liturgy of the Word, the rite is served as above. The bishop wears a red or white cope in place of the chasuble, and he wears the miter and uses the crozier. The final blessing follows the General Intercessions and the Lord's Prayer, which replace the Liturgy of the Eucharist.

945. After any celebration of the Sacrament of Confirmation, water and lemon juice used for the cleansing of the bishop's hands is poured into the sacrarium in the sacristy. The M.C. or a teacher or catechist will ensure that the cards bearing the candidates' names are given to the parish priest so that the register may be in order.

Holy Orders

946. God calls certain men in his Church to the Sacrament of Holy Orders. Ordained as bishops, priests, or deacons, these chosen ones serve God's People as true representatives of Jesus Christ, Priest, Teacher, and Servant. The bishop has the fullness of priesthood and is a direct successor of the

apostles, ordained to sanctify, teach, and govern the Church. The priest, in the "order of presbyters", shares in the priesthood and is empowered to offer Mass, celebrate the sacraments, and to teach with authority in union with his bishop. The deacon has been ordained to serve the Church associated with the bishop and his priests. Together, the three orders build up the Church, the People of God. Holy Orders is therefore, with Matrimony, a *Sacrament at the Service of Communion*.

947.   As with Baptism and Confirmation, Holy Orders has a permanent effect on those who receive it, the *indelible character*, the seal of the Spirit. Young men should reflect in prayer as to whether God calls them to receive this gift of special service in the Church. The *matter* of Holy Orders is the laying on of hands. The *form* of Holy Orders is the prayer of consecration, which expresses the intention to confer a specific Order. The *minister* of Holy Orders is a bishop.

1. The Rites of Ordination

948.   Ordination is always celebrated during Mass, immediately after the Gospel. The Creed and Prayer of the Faithful are omitted. There are four major steps in the rite of ordination, with details that differ according to the Order conferred: (1) The *Calling of the Candidate* to be ordained a deacon or priest, which includes the *Consent of the People* or the *Presentation of the Bishop-elect*; (2) the *Homily and Examination of the Candidate*, with a *Promise of Obedience* for those to be ordained deacon or priest; (3) the *Litany of the Saints*, the *Laying on of Hands*, and *Prayer of Consecration*, which ordains the candidates to the appropriate Order; (4) the *Investiture* with vestments for the deacons and priests, *Presentation of the Book of the Gospels* to the deacons, *Anointing of Hands* and *Presentation of the Gifts* to the priests, or, the *Anointing of the*

Bishop's Head, the Presentation of the Book of the Gospels, Investiture with Ring, Miter, and Pastoral Staff, Seating of the Bishop in his cathedra or chair. A *Kiss of Peace* completes the rite of ordination. Mass continues as usual with the Preparation of the Gifts. Newly ordained deacons assist at the Mass. Newly ordained priests and bishops concelebrate the Mass with the ordaining prelate.

949. In the four steps, we see how the rite expresses the meaning of Holy Orders. (1) The *call of God* comes through his Church, with the recognition that the candidate is worthy and ready to be ordained. (2) The candidate is instructed to remind himself of the responsibilities of Holy Orders. He *promises obedience*, unity with the Church, and his willingness to serve God and his People. (3) All pray for the candidate in the Litany of the Saints as he lies prostrate before the altar, a sign of total self-surrender. As the successor of the apostles, the bishop *lays his hands* on the candidate and offers *the prayer of consecration*, thus raising the candidate to the specific sacramental Order. (4) The symbolic rites of putting on vestments, anointing, and the giving of vessels, books, and regalia express the meaning of the powers and ministries that have just been received in the sacrament. The Kiss of Peace is the welcome given to the ordained man by his brothers in the sacred ministry. As the Mass continues, he carries out his proper role in the celebration of the Lord's Sacrifice, for which he was ordained.

2. Serving an Ordination

950. *Preparations.* Everything is prepared for a Solemn Pontifical Mass, as set out above. The bishop uses the ornate miter and crozier. Book, miter, and crozier bearers are required, in addition to the usual servers of a Solemn Mass. Additional requirements are as follows:

951. *Credence table*: (a) *Ordination of Deacons*: no extra requirements. (b) *Ordination of Priests*: Sacred Chrism, gremial veil, lemons, soap, with the episcopal ewer, basin, and *three* towels, a principal chalice with a paten and celebrant's host. (c) *Ordination of a Bishop*: Sacred Chrism, gremial veil, lemons, soap, etc., as for the ordination of priests.

952. *Second credence table*: (a) *Ordination of Deacons*: stoles and dalmatics unless candidates carry these over the left arm. (b) *Ordination of Priests*: chasubles, unless candidates carry these over the left arm; lemons, soap, warm water, and towels for washing Chrism from the new priests' hands. (c) *Ordination of a Bishop*: clearly printed texts of the prayer of consecration for the bishops who act as co-consecrators; for the new bishop, a ring, crozier, and ornate miter, blessed before the ceremony, two vimpae for his attendants.

953. *The cathedra*: If the ordination takes place at the cathedra, the Roman Pontifical, marked for the rite, otherwise the portable throne, *faldstool*, is placed in front of the altar, immediately after the Gospel, and the book is on the second credence. (At the cathedra or faldstool, the linen gremial veil, or an amice, is spread over the bishop's lap during the anointing.) Other seats are prepared at the cathedra for deacons, concelebrants, etc. At the ordination of a bishop, seats are prepared on each side of the cathedra for the two principal co-consecrators and portable seats to flank the faldstool, if used.

954. *Sacristy*: For the ordaining bishop, complete pontifical Mass vestments including dalmatic (pallium). At the ordination of a bishop, co-consecrators vest for Mass, simple miters, or wear cope and miter if not concelebrating. For those to be ordained; deacons—amice, alb, cincture; priests—amice, alb, cincture, stole (worn as a deacon); a bishop—amice, alb, cincture, stole, pectoral cross, dalmatic, chasuble, zucchetto. Full vestments for assisting deacons and concelebrants. If the proper Mass of Ordination is allowed, the color is white. If the Mass of the day takes precedence, the color of the day is used for all vestments.

955. Ordinations should always be celebrated with full solemnity, usually as a concelebration with incense, torch bearers, etc., so a full team of trained and rehearsed servers is essential. The candle bearers of the Mass are required to assist in bringing objects to the ordaining prelate. Other servers must be trained and rehearsed as well under the guidance of two M.C.s. The first M.C. attends the bishop and directs the rites of ordination and the Mass. The second M.C. directs the servers, readers, and concelebrants.

956. *Entrance Procession.* Solemn Pontifical Mass begins as usual. Candidates for the diaconate walk in procession after the deacon of the Mass (who carries the Book of the Gospels). Candidates for the priesthood come in the same position, followed by any concelebrants. A bishop-elect comes after concelebrants, immediately before the consecrating bishops and the principal consecrator and his deacons. He is escorted on either side by two priests. If they are not concelebrants, they wear copes over albs or choir dress. A bishop-elect must always be seated inside the sanctuary.

957. After the Gospel of the Mass, the deacon places the Book of the Gospels on the altar if deacons or a bishop are being ordained, as it is required in the rites. If the ordination does not take place at the cathedra, because the people would not be able to see the rites easily, two servers bring the faldstool to the front of the altar.

A. ORDINATION OF DEACONS

958. *The Calling of the Candidates.* After the Gospel, the crozier bearer takes the crozier, and the bishop sits and receives the miter. He either remains at the cathedra or stands (and he may take the crozier again) and goes to faldstool, where he sits with miter and crozier. Miter, crozier, and book bearers attend him. The book bearer kneels with the Pontifical open, on the bishop's left. The deacon of the Mass calls the candidates by name. They respond, come before the bishop, bow to him, and stand in the chosen positions. The appointed priest, usually the rector of the seminary, presents them to the bishop, who accepts them for ordination and asks the people to show their consent, according to local custom.

959. *The Homily and Examination.* All sit. The candidates kneel or sit during the homily. If the bishop reads it from the Pontifical, the book bearer remains kneeling next to him; otherwise, he stands, bows, and steps to the side, facing across. He returns to the bishop and kneels again with the book open for the *Commitment to Celibacy* (which is made if the deacons are to proceed to priesthood or if permanent deacons have chosen celibacy) and for the *Examination of the Candidates.* The candidates stand during these rites. After this, the bishop gives away the crozier. Then, each candidate comes to the bishop, kneels before him, places his joined hands between those of the bishop, and makes the *Promise of Obedience*, the book bearer attending as before.

960. *The Litany of the Saints.* All stand. The bishop gives up his miter and stands. He invites the people to pray, the book bearer attending, standing. The deacon asks all to kneel for the litany (except during the Easter season and on Sundays, when all remain standing according to ancient custom). All kneel for the litany. The bishop kneels, facing the throne or faldstool. The book bearer kneels, facing the same way. Candidates prostrate themselves during the litany and the prayer. At the end of the litany, only the bishop and the book bearer stand, and the bishop sings or says the prayer for those to be ordained. All respond "Amen", and the deacon asks all to stand. The miter bearer comes forward, and the bishop receives the miter.

961. One by one the candidates go to the bishop and kneel before him. Standing in front of the cathedra or faldstool, he lays his hands on the head of each in silence. During the *Laying on of Hands*, the book bearer steps away, back to one side. The candidates then kneel at appointed places before the bishop. He gives up his miter. The book bearer approaches with the Pontifical. The bishop extends his hands over the candidates and sings or says the *Prayer of Consecration*, thereby conferring the sacrament.

962. *The Investiture.* The bishop sits and receives the miter. The new deacons stand. Servers go to the second credence and give deacons or priests the stoles and dalmatics, which they put on the new deacons. Meanwhile, an appropriate antiphon and psalm or another hymn is sung. Having been vested, one by one, the deacons go to the bishop, who has received the Book of the Gospels from the deacon of the Mass, taken from the altar. The new deacons kneel before the bishop for the *Presentation of the Book of the Gospels*, the book bearer attending, kneeling as before. The deacons return to the bishop, one by one, for the Kiss of Peace. The bishop and book bearer may stand for the greeting. Other deacons present go to the new deacons to give them the Kiss of Peace, as a sign of welcome into the Order of Deacons. Singing or music accompanies the Kiss of Peace.

963. The Mass continues with the Preparation of the Gifts. Assisted by the candle bearers at the credence, some of the new deacons bring the gifts to the bishop at the cathedra or faldstool. When the bishop leaves it, two servers remove the faldstool. (If it can be arranged conveniently, the gifts may be brought from the table of the gifts. The candle bearers [without candles] escort the lay faithful to and from the table.) Servers take the gifts from the bishop and his assistants to the altar. One of the new deacons should replace the deacon of the Mass. He prepares the vessels and assists as deacon from the Preparation of the Gifts through the whole celebration of Mass. The bishop goes to the altar, removes his miter, and proceeds with the Preparation of the Gifts as usual. The new deacons receive Communion under both kinds. The deacon assisting the bishop ministers the Chalice. Some of the new deacons assist in giving Communion to the servers and people. A solemn blessing concludes the rites, the book bearer attending as usual.

B. ORDINATION OF PRIESTS

964. *The Calling of the Candidates.* As for the ordination of deacons above.

965. *The Homily and Examination.* As for the ordination of deacons above.

966. *The Litany of the Saints.* As for the ordination of deacons above.

967. After the bishop, wearing his miter, has laid his hands on each candidate for the priesthood, the candidates kneel at their places and other priests present lay hands on them in silence, as directed by the second M.C. Those who are not concelebrants wear choir dress and a stole. Singing or music may accompany this action. The bishop then removes his miter and sings or says the *Prayer of Consecration* for the priesthood, thereby conferring the sacrament.

968. *The Investiture.* As for the ordination of deacons above, the servers assist the priests who rearrange the stoles and place the chasuble on the new priests. The bishop is seated, wearing the miter, as servers prepare for the *Anointing of Hands*. The deacon of the Mass brings the open chrismatory with Chrism, and the candle bearers bring the gremial veil, which they arrange on the lap of the bishop. Taking the Chrism, the bishop anoints the palms of the hands of each priest, the book bearer kneeling with the book open. During the vesting and anointing, "Veni Creator" or an antiphon or hymn is sung. After being anointed, each priest goes to the second credence table, where two servers assist him in removing the Chrism with the lemon, soap, and warm water. At the end of the anointing, the candle bearers bring the lemons, ewer and basin, and towel from the first credence. The deacon takes the Chrism back to the credence and covers the chrismatory. The M.C. removes the gremial veil. The candle bearers assist the bishop in removing Chrism from his hands; one takes the gremial veil from the M.C.; they bow and take the lemons, ewer, etc., and veil back to the first credence table.

969. *The Presentation of the Gifts.* The faithful, especially relatives of the new priests, may bring the gifts to the bishop, seated at the cathedra or faldstool. The candle bearers, and other servers if necessary, assist the deacon of the Mass in taking the gifts to the altar. A candle bearer brings the chalice with the paten and bread to the altar, with the corporal, purifier, and pall. The corporal is spread while the other candle bearer assists the deacon, who pours wine and water into the main chalice. The deacon takes the prepared chalice with the paten and bread to the bishop. One by one, the new priests come to the bishop, who presents them with the gifts to be offered, saying the words in the Pontifical. The book bearer kneels with the book open. Having touched the chalice and paten, the new priests return to their places and the deacon takes the chalice and paten back to the altar.

970. The bishop and book bearer may stand as the new priests return, one by one, for the *Kiss of Peace*. They return to their places, and other priests present go to them to give the Kiss of Peace, as a sign of welcome to the Order of Presbyters. Singing or music accompanies the Kiss of Peace.

971. The Mass continues with the Preparation of the Gifts already brought to the altar. (Candle bearers may have to bring more chalices to the altar from the first credence table, to be prepared in addition to the main chalice already prepared.) As soon as the bishop leaves it, two servers remove the fald-stool. The bishop goes to the altar, removes his miter, and begins the prayers of the Preparation of the Gifts.

2. The new priests concelebrate with the bishop, taking first place among the concelebrants. After the Kiss of Peace, they may move to chosen positions at the sides of the sanctuary. After the Prayer over the Offerings, they take positions at, near, or behind the altar, according to local custom. The second M.C. distributes booklets or cards with the text of the chosen Eucharistic Prayer. The new priests assist the bishop in distributing Holy Communion. A solemn blessing concludes the rites, the book bearer attending as usual. After the final procession, the new priests may give their blessing to the bishop, clergy, and servers in the sacristy and then return to the sanctuary or some other suitable place to give their first blessings to family and friends.

C. ORDINATION OF A BISHOP

973. *Hymn and Presentation of the Bishop-elect.* During or after the Gospel, the faldstool and two chairs for the co-consecrators are set up, unless the cathedra is used. The hymn "Veni Creator", or a similar hymn, is sung. The principal consecrator and the co-consecrators, wearing their miters, go to the faldstool and chairs and sit. The principal consecrator holds the crozier. Miter, crozier, and book bearers attend. All remain standing during the hymn, as the bishop-elect is led before the consecrators by his assisting priests. They bow to the consecrators. The book bearer kneels as the bishop-elect is presented and the *Apostolic Letter* is read. All sit during the reading of the letter from the pope, authorizing the ordination. The people show their consent, according to local custom, usually by applause.

974. *The Homily and Examination.* As for the ordination of deacons and priests above. At the end of the examination, the principal consecrator returns the crozier to the server.

975. *The Litany of the Saints.* As for the ordination of deacons and priests above.

976. After the principal consecrator has laid his hands on the bishop-elect, the two co-consecrators and all the other bishops present do the same, wearing their miters. The deacon of the Mass takes the Book of the Gospels from the altar and presents it to the principal consecrator, who places i open upon the head of the kneeling bishop-elect as two dea cons take hold of the book on each side and hold it raise above his head. The principal consecrator and bishops re move their miters. The principal consecrator sings or sa the *Prayer of Consecration* for the episcopate, accompani for the words of the essential form by co-consecrators.

they do not have booklets, the bishops receive printed texts of the prayer and essential form from the second M.C. The deacons remove the Book of the Gospels, and one of them holds it, closed, until it is needed. The bishops sit and put on their miters.

977. *Anointing of the Bishop's Head.* A deacon brings the Chrism, and the candle bearers bring the gremial veil, which they arrange on the lap of the principal consecrator. Taking the Chrism, he anoints the head of the bishop, who kneels before him. The book bearer attends, kneeling. During the anointing, the candle bearers bring the lemon, ewer, basin, and towel from the first credence. They wait while the new bishop stands and steps back a few paces, the deacon takes the Chrism back to the credence, and the M.C. removes the gremial veil. They step forward and assist the consecrator in removing Chrism from his thumb. One takes the gremial veil from the M.C. They bow and take the lemons, ewer, etc., and veil back to the first credence table.

978. *Presentation of the Book of the Gospels.* The new bishop kneels before the principal consecrator, who receives the Book of the Gospels from the deacon and then presents it to the new bishop. The book bearer attends, kneeling. The deacon takes the Book of the Gospels. He may give it to a candle bearer, who places it on the credence table.

979. *Investiture with Ring, Miter, and Pastoral Staff.* Meanwhile, supervised by the second M.C., three servers bring the ring, miter, and crozier from the second credence. The second two servers use vimpae and later act as miter and crozier bearers for the new bishop, as required. They give the regalia to a deacon, who hands each object to the principal consecrator, as he invests the new bishop with the signs of his office. The book bearer attends, kneeling. Fully vested, the new bishop stands.

980. *Seating of the Bishop.* All stand. Depending on circumstances, the new bishop is escorted by the consecrators to the cathedra in his own cathedral or to a similar chair if not in his cathedral. He is seated as a sign of his office or jurisdiction. The second crozier bearer receives his crozier, and the consecrators and any other bishops present give him the *Kiss of Peace*. Singing or music may accompany the seating and Kiss of Peace.

981. For Mass, the new bishop should be the principal celebrant if he has been ordained in his own cathedral. Otherwise, the principal consecrator is principal celebrant, and the new bishop is the first concelebrant. Immediately after the Prayer after Communion, the new bishop receives the miter and crozier; the two co-consecrators, their miters. While "Te Deum" or a similar hymn is sung, they lead the new bishop through the church as he blesses the people. His miter and crozier bearers may follow him as he is escorted through the church by the consecrators. He may then stand at the cathedra or ambo with miter and crozier and address the people briefly. A solemn blessing concludes the rites, depending on who the principal celebrant is, the book bearer attending as usual.

982. In the final procession to the sacristy, the new bishop comes last, if he is principal celebrant of the Mass, followed by the miter, crozier, and book bearers. Otherwise, the principal consecrator comes last, followed by the miter, crozier, and book bearers, and the new bishop walks in front of him; followed by his miter and crozier bearers. Alternatively, the principal consecrator may choose to walk with the new bishop, and the five attendants would come behind both prelates.

Religious Profession

983. God calls certain members of his Church to the religious life, as monks, regular clergy, brothers, or as nuns or sisters. There are various forms of religious life, various degrees of commitment and consecration, and a series of steps by which the Church recognizes the call of God. Incorporating customs and traditions proper to the Order or Congregation, three liturgical rites embody the major steps.

984. *The Rite of Initiation* into religious life, or "entering", is a simple ceremony, in the presence of the religious community alone outside of Mass.

985. *The Rite of First Profession* takes place at the end of the novitiate, during Mass, but without special solemnity. The religious habit is given as the visible sign of dedication to God.

986. *The Rite of Final Profession* is made after a period prescribed by law. By it, the religious binds himself or herself permanently to the service of God and his Church, in a public ceremony, during a Solemn Mass.

987. First Profession and Final Profession rites come immediately after the Gospel. The Creed is omitted. A faldstool or chair is set up in front of the altar for the bishop or priest celebrant, who is attended by the book bearer, with the Pontifical or another authorized text.

1. First Profession

988. All is prepared for Mass, with four or five servers, but not great solemnity. A bishop or priest presides. The formula of profession and the habit or some other sign are prepared on a second credence, depending on customs of the Order or congregation. Holy water may be required for the blessing of the habit, etc. A chair is also prepared in a suitable part of the sanctuary if the religious superior to receive the vows is not celebrant of the Mass.

989. After the Gospel, those to be professed are received by the celebrant at the chair, the book bearer attending. A homily follows. Those to be professed are questioned. Prayer is offered for them. Before their religious superior, they read the formula of profession. The habit or some other sign of commitment is received. Mass continues with the Prayer of the Faithful. The newly professed may take part in the Procession of the Gifts, and they receive Communion under both kinds. At the conclusion of Mass, they may go in procession from the sanctuary.

2. *Final Profession*

990. All is prepared for Solemn Mass, with the full number of servers and bishop's attendants if it is a Pontifical Mass. The rites and customs vary, depending on the nature of the Order or congregation, whether the religious work in the world or are contemplatives, or whether the vows are made solemnly with consecration. (The rites of solemn consecration of women religious, nuns, are in the Pontifical.) Preparations are adapted to the customs and rules of the congregation or Order, with respect, for example, to whether hand candles are used or whether the ring, veil, and Office book are to be given. Solemn Mass begins as usual.

991. After the Gospel, those making Final Profession are received, as above, with the homily and questions. The Litany of the Saints follows, as at an ordination, the candidates lying prostrate, if customary. Before their religious superior, one by one, the religious come forward and recite the formula

of perpetual profession. (For consecration, they come one by one to the bishop and, kneeling before him, each makes a renewal of intention, with joined hands placed between his hands.) The book bearer attends, kneeling. Those making Final Profession sign the formula. The celebrant then stands and says the prayer of consecration of the professed (or consecrated religious), the book bearer attending. He sits and presents to each the customary signs of Final Profession (or consecration). The other members of the community may then give the newly professed a sign of peace or, according to custom, some other sign of acceptance. Mass continues as for First Profession above.

The Chrism Mass

992. Only a bishop may consecrate Sacred Chrism. It is prepared and blessed, together with the Oil of the Catechumens and the Oil of the Sick, on Holy Thursday or some other suitable day in Holy Week before Holy Thursday. To underline the sacramental meaning of the oils, they are blessed during Solemn Pontifical Mass, concelebrated by the bishop and the priests of his diocese. He is attended by his deacons, who act as custodians of the oils. His priests offer the one sacrifice with him as an expression of the unity of the priesthood. With the bishop, they will use the oils that have been blessed and consecrated at this Mass. In the presence of the bishop and the people, they also renew their commitment to the ministerial priesthood.

993. *The Rites.* The Creed and Prayer of the Faithful are omitted. The oils to be blessed or consecrated are brought to the bishop after the homily and renewal of priestly commitment. After the Procession of the Oils and the Gifts, the Mass continues up to the end of the Eucharistic Prayer. Just

before the doxology, the bishop blesses the Oil of the Sick. After the Prayer after Communion, he blesses the Oil of the Catechumens and prepares and consecrates the Sacred Chrism. After the final blessing of the Mass, the oils are taken from the sanctuary in solemn procession. But an *alternative procedure* is allowed when the three oils are blessed or consecrated, one after the other, before the Preparation of the Gifts. This is also described below.

1. The Traditional Procedure

994. *Preparations.* All is prepared for the solemn concelebration of Pontifical Mass, white vestments. The full number of trained and rehearsed servers is required. Those acting as torch bearers assist in arranging the table(s) on which the oils are blessed or consecrated. Extra M.C.'s are required if there are many concelebrants. Additional requirements are as follow:

995. *The altar*: the seventh candle, if the diocesan bishop celebrates Mass; by custom, the altar crucifix is veiled in white (white antependium).

996. *The cathedra*: seats for concelebrants, deacons assisting and deacons attending to the oils, a faldstool, if oils are to be blessed in front of the altar and not at the cathedra.

997. *Credence table*: the *Roman Pontifical* containing the prayers for the blessing.

998. *A table or tables*: for the oils after they have been brought to the sanctuary and during the blessing of the Oil of Catechumens and consecration of the Chrism. The table may be suitably covered with a noble cloth or frontal.

999. *The sacristy or a chapel*: enough large vessels to contain the three oils according to the quantities required. Each vessel must be clearly and securely marked according to its contents. It is also customary for the deacon carrying a vessel of oil to wear a colored vimpa: violet for the Oil of the Sick, green for the Oil of the Catechumens, white for the Sacred Chrism. A vessel contains balsam or perfume essence for the making of Chrism, with a suitable spoon or implement to mingle it with the oil, unless the oil for Chrism has been prepared beforehand. Pontifical vestments for the bishop, including dalmatic (pallium), ornate miter, and crozier. Full Mass vestments for concelebrants and deacons and dalmatics for deacons attending to the oils. The color is white. If there are not enough deacons for the oils, priests may take their place. The bread and wine for the Mass is also prepared in the sacristy or chapel, as the faithful will bring it forward in the Procession of the Oils.

1000. *Entrance Procession.* The deacons attending to the oils walk ahead of the concelebrants. Solemn Pontifical Mass proceeds as usual according to the texts and readings for the Chrism Mass. After the homily, the bishop sits in the cathedra and receives the miter and crozier. The book bearer attends, kneeling, as the priests present stand and renew their priestly commitment, as set out in the missal. The bishop and book bearer stand, and the bishop asks the people to pray for their priests and for himself.

1001. *Procession of the Oils and Gifts.* The bishop gives up his crozier and sits, wearing the miter. The candle bearers (without candles) lead the deacons, other clergy, servers, and members of the faithful to the sacristy or chapel. They return in this order: (1) a candle bearer carrying the vessel of balsam or perfume, unless this has already been placed in the oil for the Chrism, (2) deacon(s) or priest(s) carrying the vessel(s) for the Oil of the Catechumens, by custom wearing a green vimpa, (3) deacon(s) or priest(s) carrying the vessel(s) for the Oil of the Sick, wearing a violet vimpa, (4) deacon(s) or priest(s) carrying the vessel(s) for the Sacred Chrism, wearing a white vimpa, (5) the faithful with the gifts of bread and wine for Mass.

1002.   As the procession slowly moves to the sanctuary, the hymn "O Redeemer" or some other hymn is sung. All stand. Having arrived at the sanctuary, the procession group makes the customary reverence. The oils and gifts may be presented to the bishop at the cathedra, or the bishop may choose to come in front of the altar, according to custom. The deacons of the Mass flank the bishop. The oil for Chrism is presented first and named aloud. The bishop takes it, or lays his hands on it, and it is given immediately to a deacon of the Mass, who takes it to the table prepared, assisted by servers, as required. Likewise, the oils to be blessed for catechumens and the sick are presented and named aloud. The balsam or perfume is then presented in silence. Finally the Eucharistic gifts are presented by the lay faithful and taken as usual by deacons and servers to the altar, and the Mass proceeds with the Preparation of the Gifts. Those in procession bow to the altar and return to their places. The oils remain on the table until required for blessing or consecration. The colored vimpae are left folded on the table or draped over the appropriate vessels.

1003.   *Blessing of the Oil of the Sick. After the acclamation after the Consecration* in the Eucharistic Prayer, the deacon(s) or priest(s) who brought the vessel of oil for the sick quietly goes to the table of oils. Wearing the vimpa, he brings the vessel of oil to the altar toward the end of the Eucharistic Prayer. He holds it in front of the bishop, who may either bless it turning away from the altar (the book bearer taking the Pontifical or missal and holding it open at the place marked by the M.C.), or he may bless it across the altar, the deacon(s) standing with the vessel(s) on the people's side of the altar (and the book bearer would not be required, as the M.C. would indicate the text in the missal or Pontifical on the altar). After the blessing, the deacon(s) takes the Oil of the Sick back to the table and the Mass continues.

1004. *Blessing of the Oil of Catechumens. After the prayer after Communion*, the bishop sits and receives the miter. Servers and the deacons or priests attending to the oils go to the table. Wearing the vimpae, the deacons or priests take the vessels of oil in their hands, while the servers carefully bring the table and the balsam to the cathedra or to the faldstool, which another server arranges at this time. The deacons or priests follow them and place the vessels of oil on the table. The lids of the vessels for the Oil of the Catechumens and Chrism are removed. Concelebrants come forward to stand near the cathedra, or they follow the bishop when he takes the crozier and goes to the faldstool. They form a neat semicircle around the bishop, facing the people and the table of oils, or they group on both sides of the table as directed by the M.C. The bishop gives up the crozier and miter and sings or says the prayer of blessing, attended by the book bearer.

1005. *Consecration of the Chrism.* The M.C. presents the balsam or perfume essence to the bishop, who sits and receives the miter. He pours the balsam into the vessel of oil for Chrism, which may be brought to him by the deacon, or he may stand and pour it into the vessel. This is permitted if the balsam has already been mingled with the oil for Chrism. He gives up the miter. Standing, the bishop sings or says the invitation to prayer. He then breathes over the open vessel of Chrism, as a sign of the Creator Spirit. Attended by the book bearer, he sings or says the prayer of consecration of Chrism. Concelebrants extend their hands during the second part of the prayer but do not recite the words with the bishop.

1006. *Concluding Rite.* The thurifer brings the thurible and boat from the sacristy and waits at the side. The bishop gives the final blessing, either at the cathedra or at the faldstool. If it impedes the area of the sanctuary, servers and deacons come forward, and the table is removed to the side, and the holy oils are taken up for the final procession. As soon as the bishop has given the final blessing, the thurifer (and boat bearer) comes to the cathedra or faldstool. The bishop gives up the crozier and prepares and blesses incense. He takes the crozier. The thurifer goes to a position at the front of the sanctuary to lead the procession. The deacon of the Mass sings the dismissal.

1007. *Procession of the Oils.* During the hymn "O Redeemer" or another hymn, the oils are solemnly taken to the sacristy. The order of procession is: thurifer (boat bearer), cross, candles, deacons or priests carrying the holy oils, servers, clergy, concelebrants, the bishop and his deacons, the bishop's servers. In the sacristy, the bishop may instruct the priests about the reverent use and safe keeping of the oils, which are then bottled and distributed to clergy, under the strict supervision of the sacristans.

2. *The Alternative Procedure*

1008. For pastoral reasons, the three oils may be blessed or consecrated one after the other *immediately after* the renewal of priestly service, that is, *before* the Preparation of the Gifts. After the renewal of priestly commitment, the oils are brought in procession, as described above. Servers arrange the table for the oils as above before the cathedra or the altar, the deacons attending to the vessels, removing the lids as appropriate for each blessing. The book bearer attends, at the cathedra or faldstool. After the consecration of Chrism, the table and blessed oils are moved to the side of the sanctuary or to some convenient place. The Preparation of the Gifts and the rest of the Liturgy of the Eucharist follow as usual. The final blessing and Procession of the Oils proceed as described above.

Institution of Lectors and Acolytes

1009. The ministries of lector (reader) and acolyte have been restored as distinct roles of service in the Church. Because they are "ministries", formerly called "minor orders", and do not require the Sacrament of Orders, men are "instituted" to these ministries by the bishop or the major superior of a clerical religious institute. These ministries are open (a) to laymen and (b) those proceeding to the diaconate or priesthood.

1010. *Institution of Lectors.* The institution takes place during Mass or a Liturgy of the Word. The rite of institution comes after the Gospel.

1011. *Preparations.* Everything is prepared for a Pontifical Mass, according to the solemnity desired. A faldstool or chair is to be placed in front of the altar, unless the bishop presides at the cathedra. A Bible and the Pontifical are required. The Bible may be on the credence table.

1012. *The Rite.* After the Gospel, the faldstool is prepared, if used. The bishop sits and receives the miter and, if he wishes, the crozier. The deacon or a priest calls the candidates forward. Each comes to the bishop and bows. All sit for the homily, which relates to the ministry of the lector. The candidates return to their seats or kneel before the bishop during this homily. The bishop concludes the homily with words in the Pontifical or similar words, the book bearer attending.

1013. The bishop gives up the miter and crozier and stands. All stand as the candidates come before him and kneel in chosen places. He invites all present to pray, and after a time of silence he says the prayer of blessing. All sit, as the bishop sits and receives the miter. A server brings the Bible from the credence and gives it to the deacon or M.C., who then gives it to the bishop. One by one, the candidates come to the bishop, who gives each the Bible, saying the words of institution, the book bearer kneeling. A psalm or hymn may be sung during the institution. After the institution, the deacon takes the Bible and gives it to a server, who takes it to the credence. The bishop gives up the miter and returns to the cathedra or chair. Mass continues with the Creed (if prescribed) and the Prayer of the Faithful, which includes petitions for those instituted to the ministry.

1014. *Institution of Acolytes.* The rite of institution takes place during Mass after the Gospel.

1015. *Preparations.* As for the institution of lectors, except that a paten or ciborium with bread for Mass or a cruet of wine is prepared on the credence table, to be given as a sign of institution, just as the Bible was given to the lectors. Those to be instituted as acolyte wear amice, alb, and cincture or soutane and surplice, or other vesture prescribed by the local bishop.

1016. *The Rite.* After the Gospel, all proceeds as for the institution of lectors: the calling, homily, invitation to prayer, and prayer of blessing. After the bishop has said the prayer of blessing, the paten or ciborium with bread, or the cruet of wine, is brought to him, and he presents this to each candidate, attended by the book bearer, kneeling at the cathedra, chair, or faldstool. After the institution, the vessel is taken back to the credence and Mass proceeds as for the institution of lectors.

1017. The new acolytes assist in the Preparation of the Gifts, or, if many are instituted, several are chosen to assist. They all receive Communion immediately after the deacon(s). The bishop may direct the new acolyte(s) to act as an extraordinary minister in giving Communion at this Mass.

Appendices

I.

LIGHTING CANDLES

1018. A taper is used to light candles. It may be held in a metal tube, which may also be attached to a rod, to make it easy to light tall candles, such as the Paschal candle. To provide a convenient angle for the taper to meet the candle wick, the taper may be bent or curved slightly, but never broken. New servers must practice before attempting to light candles with a taper.

1019. An order of lighting candles on an altar is as follows: (a) Bring the lighted taper from the sacristy. Make the customary reverence in front of the altar. (b) Light the candles from whatever side of the altar is more convenient for you to reach them, but do not stretch out across the altar. (c) Start on the right-hand end, then go to the left-hand end, making the customary reverence at the center. (d) If there are four or six candles to light, start by lighting the inside candles on the right hand end first, moving out to the next candle. (e) If these candles are arranged along each side of the altar, light the candle at the back first, moving forward. (f) Make the customary reverence, return to the sacristy, and *then* extinguish the taper.

1020. To extinguish candles, take the snuffer and proceed exactly as for the lighting of candles, except (a) you extinguish them beginning on the left-hand end of the altar, and, (b) if there are four or six candles, extinguish the outside candle first, moving in to the next candle. Never force the snuffer down onto the wax. It works best when it is lowered steadily over the flame, which burns up the air inside it and then the flame goes out. Never leave a wick smoldering, as it may burn away to powder.

1021. The number of candles visibly expresses the different degrees of "exterior solemnity". These are customary: two candles for a weekday Mass, six or four candles for a solemn or sung Mass on Sundays and solemnities, and seven candles when the bishop of the diocese celebrates the liturgy —for example, when he confirms or ordains.

2.

SETTING OUT VESTMENTS

1022. If in doubt as to what vestment to put out next, always remember that you put out a set of vestments in the *reverse
order* to that followed by a priest when he puts them on,
i.e., the last one he puts on is the first vestment spread on
the vesting table.

1023. Spread the *chasuble* or *dalmatic* with the back of the vestment uppermost. You may fold it back neatly, so that the
priest or deacon can put it on easily.

1024. Arrange the *stole* on the chasuble or dalmatic in such a way
that the neck of the stole can be taken up and placed around
the priest or deacon's neck without having to turn it around.

1025. The *maniple* is always worn at the traditional Latin Mass.
Place it vertically at the center, above the stole.

1026. If the *cincture* is used, arrange it neatly above the stole. If
it is long, double it over, so that the tassels are arranged
together.

1027. Spread the *alb* over the other vestments, with the back uppermost. You may bring up the hem and fold it back neatly,
so that the priest or deacon can put it on easily.

1028. If the *amice* is used, spread it out flat over all the vestments,
with the side to which the tapes are attached farthest from
you. Fold back the tapes in a neat arrangement so that the
priest or deacon can take them into his hands when he begins to vest.

1029. If you have to put out many sets of vestments for concelebrants, it may be helpful to place cards on each set, bearing
either the names of the clergy, if known, or the relative sizes
of albs: small, medium, large.

1030. In setting out a bishop's vestments, the *episcopal dalmatic* may
be required, spread over the chasuble. Unless the bishop is
already wearing it, the *pectoral cross* on its cord is arranged
to one side. The miter is set up beside the vestments, with
the *zucchetto* (skullcap). When worn by a metropolitan archbishop, the *pallium* and its pins are arranged beside the vestments.

1031. For the solemn forms of Pontifical Mass according to the
traditional Latin Mass, a *tunicle* is spread above the dalmatic
and the bishop's *gloves* and a ceremonial *ring* are arranged to
one side. The bishop puts on the *maniple* during the *Prayers
at the Foot of the Altar*. He wears a *precious miter* and a *gold
miter* at different moments during the liturgy.

3.

PRAYERS FOR SERVERS

Customary Sacristy Prayers

1032. Before leaving the sacristy in procession, the celebrant may say, "Let us go forth in peace", to which servers respond, "In the name of Christ. Amen."; in Latin: ℣.: "Procedamus in pace"; ℟.: "In nomine Christi. Amen." Or the celebrant may say, "Our help is in the Name of the Lord", to which the servers respond, "Who made heaven and earth."

1033. On returning to the sacristy, all bow to the cross. The celebrant may say "Prosit" or "Proficiat" (*May the Mass be of benefit*) to which the servers may respond "Pro omnibus et singulis" (*for every person and for each person*) or "tibi quoque" (*to you too*). In some churches it is customary for servers to kneel and receive the celebrant's blessing, which is customary when the bishop presides.

Servers' Prayer before Mass

1034. God our Father, we come to serve at the altar of Jesus Christ your Son. May your Holy Spirit help us to serve you well, with reverence and skill. We pray through Christ our Lord. Amen.

Servers' Prayer after Mass

1035. God our Father, we thank you for the privilege of serving at the altar of Jesus Christ your Son. May we go from this holy place to witness to him and to spread the good news of his Resurrection. We pray through Christ our Lord. Amen.

A Prayer of Saint Ignatius

1036. Lord, teach me to be generous,
To serve you as you deserve to be served,
To give and not to count the cost,
To fight and not to heed the wounds,
To work and not to seek for rest,
To toil and not to ask for any reward,
Save that of knowing that I do your holy will.

A Prayer to Our Lady

1037. Mary, Mother of God and Mother of the Church, you served the Lord by saying "Yes" to God's call. Help me to grow as a Christian, day by day, responding to the will of God by loving and helping other people, especially the poor and those in need of God's mercy.

Virgin Mother of Nazareth, pray for us who serve at the altar of your Son.

Saints appropriate to the ministry of serving may also be invoked, for example:

1038. Saint Stephen, deacon and martyr, pray for us.
Saint Agnes, virgin and martyr, pray for us.
Saint Laurence, deacon and martyr, pray for us.
Saint Tarcisius, server and martyr, pray for us.
Saint Vincent, deacon and martyr, pray for us.
Saint Gregory the Great, Pope and Doctor of
    the Church, pray for us.
Saint Clare, servant of the poor, pray for us.
Saint Joan of Arc, virgin and martyr, pray for us.
Saint Aloysius Gonzaga, patron of youth, pray for us.
Saint John Berchmans, patron of servers, pray for us.
Saint Pedro Calungsod, martyr of Guam, pray for us.

Saint Nunzio Sulprizio, a suffering youth, pray for us.

Saint Dominic Savio, patron of youth, pray for us.

Saint Thérèse of Lisieux, virgin and Doctor of the Church, pray for us.

Saint Gemma Galgani, virgin and mystic, pray for us.

Saint Maria Goretti, virgin and martyr, pray for us.

Saint Pius X, Pope of the Eucharist, pray for us.

Saint José Sanchez del Rio, server, soldier, and martyr, pray for us.

Saint Teresa of Kolkata, servant of the poor, pray for us.

Blessed Pier Giorgio Frassati, patron of youth, pray for us.

Blessed Rolando Rivi, server, seminarian, and martyr, pray for us.

Blessed Chiara Badano, virgin and apostle of suffering, pray for us.

Index

Ablutions, 319–22
Absolution, 257, 496–97, 502, 514, 583
Acclamation, 274
Acolyte/acolytes, 7–8, 61–63
  Institution of lectors and acolytes, 890, 1009–17
  Servers and, 8, 61–63
  See also Server; specific topics, ceremonies, and occasions
Actions, basic, 154–91
  Bows, 189–91
  Genuflections, 180–88
  Hands, 160–62, 296
  Kneeling, 178–79
  Sign of the Cross, 163–73
  Sitting, 174–75
  Walking, 176–77, 198
  See also Mass, procedures during; *specific topics, e.g.,* Candles: Carrying; Missal: Carrying; Silence
Actions, ceremonial, 111–252
  Availability, 251–52
  Emergencies, 247–50
  Movement in the sanctuary, 192–99
  Sacred objects, 112–30
  Server's robes, 60, 152–53, 176, 250

See also Actions, basic; Mass, procedures during; Vestments
Actions, visible, 2, 32
Adoration, 456
  of the Holy Cross, 799, 814–26
  See also Public adoration of the Blessed Sacrament
Advent, 87
Agnus Dei, 364
Alb, 133
Alleluia, 264, 841
Altar, 33–36, 94–95
  Reverencing, 661
  See also Sanctuary
Altar server. *See* Acolyte; Server
Altar vessels, 112–30
Altar of repose, 483, 765–66, 775, 806, 808, 827–28, 831
  Procession to, 786–96
Ambo, 96
Ambry, 567
Amice, 132, 152
  See also specific ceremonies and occasions, *e.g.,* Holy Week; Bishop, serving
Anamnesis, 275
Anointing of the Sick, 545–73
  Rite of Anointing, 547–51
  Serving Anointing during Mass, 552–67

The numbers in this index refer to the paragraph numbers in the text rather than to page numbers.

INDEX